While some authors talk down to readers and others pander to their audience, Aby Jacob treats his readers respectfully as those desiring to be wise. Weaving parts of his own personal search for wisdom together with arguments for God's existence from philosophy, science, and other disciplines, Jacob builds a strong case that the wise person will be a theist. But he is not done, as he goes on to ask what kind of theism the wise person should embrace. Comparing different religions, Jacob shows why Christianity, grounded on the historical fact of the resurrection of Jesus Christ, will lead the wise person to belief. Wide ranging and engaging, this book will surely be the standard apologetics text in India for years to come.

Garrett J. DeWeese, Ph.D., Professor of Philosophy, Talbot School of Theology. Author of several books, including *Philosophy Made Slightly Less Difficult: A Beginner's Guide to Life's Big Questions*, 2nd ed. (InterVarsity-Academic, 2021) (co-authored with Dr. J.P. Moreland).

Who is Wise Enough to Understand This? is a well-crafted piece of knowledge that walks any 21st-century reader through the popular quests that resonate through our minds about the existence, purpose, and connection of the true God and us. It can be considered as: ***an introductory book*** for those who want to jump into the philosophical path to seek God through rationality, ***a reference*** for preachers and teachers to get guidance to navigate through the knowledge base without being lost in the vast ocean of ever expanding debates over rationality and the Truth, ***a testimony and findings*** of a truth seeker for those who like to read about reality that meets our life, and ***a Gospel*** for those who do not know and want to know more about the True God. I thankfully acknowledge the author's commitment to stand for the Truth and greatly appreciate his hard work from its conception to the final presentation.

Maju Kuriakose (Ph.D. in Physics, France), Physicist and Senior Engineer.

What Aby Jacob has done is gift us with a much needed and succinct apologetics book. However, this is not just another book on apologetics, this book is an autobiographical journey of a man after God's own heart. Whether you are new to apologetics and philosophy or have been studying it for years, this book will tug at your heart, while stretching your mind.

Bill Scott, Assistant Director of *Ratio Christi International*.

How Christians of different generations have seen science, the great scientists who came out of the Judeo-Christian community, narration on different myths common people have, and views on how God's creation makes perfect sense are all well put together in this book. As a biochemist and a scientist, I am always amazed at how beautifully and wonderfully we are made. Without a master mind designing this, how can the Universe, the Earth, the humans, and all we see around us be so orderly formed, and functioning? *Who is Wise Enough to Understand This?* will enable the readers to discover the truth and know more about the omniscient God behind creation. I personally have known Aby since 2018 and have seen him as a hard-working student and a faithful servant of God. I appreciate him for the effort he has taken in writing this book that really broadens my understanding as well.

Rooban B. Nahomi (Ph.D. in Biochemistry), Scientist and former Research Instructor at the University of Colorado.

For those who want an introduction into how we can know Christianity is true, I can't think of a better beginning work than this one written by Aby Jacob. Every reader will be drawn into his personal story and discover an array of facts, arguments, and evidence for the truth of Christianity. Even those who don't believe in Christianity have to contend with the content of this book. If you want to grow in your Christian faith, read this work!

Bernard J. Mauser, Ph.D., Associate Professor of Philosophy and Dean of Southern Evangelical Seminary and Bible College.

A compelling worldview should address life's fundamental questions in a satisfying manner, and this book accomplishes just that. The author candidly acknowledges life's hardships, poses sincere inquiries, seeks whether there are hopeful answers, and invites readers to conduct their own thorough examination. Rather than resorting to shortcuts, the author patiently guides readers through complex concepts, offering clarity every step of the way.

"Who is Wise Enough to Understand This?" is a well-researched book, evidenced by the abundance of quotes and cited resources. Through arguments rooted in philosophy, science, history, and Scripture, the author presents a compelling case for Christian theism. Drawing from the insights of esteemed philosophers and experts in apologetics and natural theology, the book challenges readers to carefully consider the Christian faith and also empowers Christians to share their faith confidently.

Kaon Serjani, Founder and Director of the *Institute for Faith and Cultural Engagement,* Albania, and author of several books.

Aby Jacob is a testimony of God's transforming grace through Jesus Christ, as he mentions in this book. When I met him, he had little knowledge of apologetics, theology, or philosophy, and yet he would be studying all of these subjects in a language not his native tongue. Yet Mr. Jacob excelled as a student, received our Master's Degree in Apologetics and Ethics, got another Master's degree in Philosophy from Southern Seminary, and is working on yet another degree in biblical languages. In his book, *Who is*

Wise Enough to Understand This? Mr. Jacob has written a compelling case for the objective truth, rationality, and pertinence of the Christian worldview. He addresses the importance of truth and meaning, the arguments for God's existence, the supposed conflict between Christianity and science (there isn't any!), the evidence for the Bible, and the unique message of Jesus Christ, as Lord and Savior (John 14:6; Acts 4:12). Attentive readers of *Who is Wise Enough to Understand This?* will receive a rich and robust understanding of apologetics and be given deep reasons for the Christian hope (1 Peter 3:15).

Douglas Groothuis, Ph.D., Professor of Philosophy Denver Seminary and the author of twenty books, including *Christian Apologetics: A Comprehensive Case for Biblical Faith*, 2nd ed. (InterVarsity-Academic, 2022) and *Beyond the Wager: The Christian Brilliance of Blaise Pascal* (InterVarsity-Academic, 2024).

Who is Wise Enough to Understand This?

Who is Wise Enough to Understand This?

Aby Jacob

2024

Who is Wise Enough to Understand This? — published by the Indian Society for Promoting Christian Knowledge (ISPCK), Post Box 1585, 1654, Madarsa Road, Kashmere Gate, Delhi-110006.

© Author, 2024

ISBN: 978-81-19434-78-7

Cover Design: Jobin Jose

Cover page image: https://www.shutterstock.com/license
ostill/Shutterstock.com
Stock Photo Id: 87733534

Laser typeset by

ISPCK, Post Box 1585, 1654, Madarsa Road, Kashmere Gate, Delhi-110006
• *Tel:* 23866323/22

e-mail: mail@ispck.org.in • ella@ispck.org.in
website: www.ispck.org.in

Printed at Allianz Enterprises, Delhi.

Dedicated to

My intellectual mentor, professor, and friend

Dr. Douglas Groothuis

My family

Father, Kunjumon Jacob

Mother, Emily Jacob

Brother, Job K. Jacob, and Sister-in-Law, Dr. Pallavi Jacob

Contents

PART THREE: THE JOURNEY AS A JUDEO-CHRISTIAN APOLOGIST

Section 1: Preparing for an Apologetic Journey

Section 2: Biblical Apologetics

Section 3: Scientific Apologetics

Acknowledgments

Jesus Christ, My Lord and Savior, changed my life around.

My great-grandfather and late Fr. Jacob's life and mission in Sri Lanka.

My father, Kunjumon Jacob, is a lover of wisdom. He encouraged me to think critically, and his childhood training gave me great courage.

My only brother, Job K. Jacob, is my greatest supporter, advisor, and pillar. Words cannot describe what he is to me and what he has done to pursue my calling.

Dr. Douglas Groothuis is my intellectual mentor and professor. He treated me like a father to a son. I am incredibly grateful for his investment in me and his time on the manuscript. He also wrote the foreword for this book.

Dr. Garry DeWeese was my first professor of apologetics and ethics at Denver Seminary. He was genuinely encouraging and kind. Dr. DeWeese spent a lot of time reading and commenting on the manuscript to improve it.

Lillianna Drye was the first reader of my manuscript. Her comments and feedback helped me restructure the book and improve several things.

SBMC Colorado (My friend's group in Colorado). These friends became my strong ministry partners and supporters. My supporters are Abraham George, Abel Skariah, Dinosh Babu, Heman Vora, Jerison Joy, Jobin Jose, Dr. Jacob George, Lijo John Samuel, Dr. Maju Kuriakose, Dr. Rooban Nahomi, Ronsy Thomas, Roye Varghese, Stanley Samuel, and Sam C. Thomas.

Dr. Ganesh Desai had set a timeline at the book's initial stage and kept checking on my progress. Jerrin Joseph ensured I had a peaceful environment in which to complete this work.

I acknowledge some professors, including Dr. Bernard James Mauser, Dr. Andrew Ike Shepardon, Dr. Hugh Ross, Dr. J.T. Bridges, Dr. Jeffrey Zweerink, Dr. Philip Marshall, and Dr. Timothy Brookins.

Houston Church of God, Texas, and Pr. Mathew K. Philip. I am part of this church family in Texas. I am truly grateful for my pastor's initiative and the incredible support I received from this church members towards book publication.

Trinity Full Gospel Church, North Carolina, and Pr. David Livingston Jr. I was part of this church family during my time in North Carolina. I began writing this book with a prayer from this church. The whole church was loving and supportive of my mission in various ways.

Denver Salem Church of God, Colorado, and Pr. Benson Abraham. I was part of this church family during my time in Colorado. I appreciate the care I received from my fellow brethren.

International Assemblies of God, Arizona, and Pr. Dr. Roy Cherian. I was part of this church family in Arizona, and the church prayerfully sent me out to pursue my calling.

Jobin Jose used his amazing talents to design the cover page. I also acknowledge Sam C. Thomas, who not only took the initiative and brought ideas to create the cover but also labored for this book's mission in various ways.

I honor Mr. John Samuel & family (CO) for their incredible care during my deepest trial while pursuing my apologetics journey. I became part of this family as one of their children. Mrs. Mariyamma John treated me like a mother to a son, and I call her "mummy." Lijo and Leena John supported me tremendously as one of their siblings.

My family-like friends, Dhanesh Haridas and Dhanya Jagadev (VA) and Robins George and Remya Robins (MD) have always supported my work and life amazingly. In addition to these friends, my other family-like friends (called *Kinginni Arts & Sports Club*) in NC have been highly encouraging throughout the different stages of this work.

Many others contributed to this book in various ways. These include Pr. Finny Jacob (AZ), Mr. Simjan Jacob Cheeran (GA), The Drye Family (NC), Binoy & Gimi Babu (TX), Shibu & Shibi Varghese (TX), and Andy Bueno (TX).

I am grateful for the partnership of the mission organization *Ecclesia United International*.

I have greatly benefited from the works of *Discovery Institute's Centre for Science and Culture*.

Since 2018, a long list of people have supported me in various ways for my mission. Many became like my own family, and I am extremely grateful for their care and concern.

Finally, I acknowledge the ISPCK team for their excellent work and thank Dr. Ella of ISPCK for her abundant support and timely responses.

Foreword

The Christian movement flounders when it neglects its birthright and its long heritage of rigorous intellectual engagement in the defense of its central message (the gospel) and its overall worldview (Christian theism). Although Jesus himself was a philosopher and an apologist who had a coherent worldview and who used rational arguments against his interlocutors, many followers of Jesus foreswear using rational arguments and appeals to evidence in order to defend the Christian message of redemption through Jesus Christ.[1] Moreover, the preaching of the Apostles Peter and Paul in the Book of Acts reveals their intellectual savvy in addressing their audiences in rationally compelling ways. Paul's address at the Areopagus in Athens is particularly brilliant, given his zeal for God's truth, his understanding of Greek philosophy, his use of common ground, his critique of their worldview, and his commendation of Jesus Christ (Acts 17:16-34).[2]

The Apostle Peter gave us the *locus classicus* for apologetics when he wrote, "But in your hearts revere Christ as Lord. Always be prepared to give an answer to everyone who asks you to give the reason for the hope that you have. But do this with gentleness and respect" (1 Peter 3:15, NIV). Jude chimes in by writing, "Dear friends, although I was very eager to write to you about the salvation we share, I felt compelled to write and urge you to contend for the faith that was once for all entrusted to God's holy people" (Jude 1:3).

True to the Bible, great Christian intellects down through the centuries have explained and defended Christianity as objectively true, compellingly rational, and pertinent and meaningful to the whole of life. A short list includes St. Irenaeus, St. Augustine, St. Thomas Aquinas, Jonathan Edwards, William Paley, Blaise Pascal and, more recently, C. S. Lewis, J. Gresham Machen, Francis Schaeffer, Gordon R. Lewis, William Lane Craig, and J. P. Moreland. Apologetics has been vital in the conversion of non-Christians to Christian faith in the cases of St. Augustine,[3] C. S. Lewis[4], Lee Strobel,[5] and Nabeel Qureshi.[6] Propaganda to the contrary, modern Western science was developed by scientists and philosophers with an essentially Christian worldview. These men, such as Issac Newton, Johannes Kepler,[7] and Blaise Pascal, believed that the universe was created by a rational God who made it knowable through reasoning and investigation; that the world was created good and worth studying; and that by investigating nature, they could fulfill the creation mandate to develop nature for scientific benefit.[8] The modern claims that science opposes Christianity, that only science gives knowledge, and that Christianity is not a source of knowledge are all demonstrably false, as Aby Jacob argues in this book.

Much of my long ministry and academic career as a philosopher has been taken up with the apologetic task. After converting to Christianity in 1976 at age nineteen, I soon began to pursue a rational understanding and defense of my new faith and worldview, which began by listening to Josh McDowell's lectures and reading Francis Schaeffer's book, *The God Who is There*.[9] I developed a parallel curriculum of Christian knowledge to counteract and complement what I was learning at my secular university. Besides Schaeffer, whose books I devoured, my unpaid tutors included St. Augustine, C. S. Lewis, James Sire, Os Guinness, Blaise Pascal, and others.

Before receiving my doctorate in philosophy from the University of Oregon in 1993, I participated in twelve years of campus ministry at two schools. My focus was always on explaining the Christian worldview and practicing, apologetics, mostly in secular settings. From 1993 until 2024, I was a Professor of Philosophy at Denver Seminary in Denver, Colorado, where I taught various courses in apologetics, philosophy, and ethics. I relished the opportunity to teach young people about the truth, significance, and rationality of the Christian system of thought and to take this message to the unbelieving world. During this time, I met Aby Jacob, who enrolled in our master's program in Apologetics and Ethics. Although he had little background in philosophy or the humanities, and even though English was not his first language, Mr. Jacob diligently applied himself to rigorous study, did well in classes, and produced a thesis on how the Intelligent Design movement contributes to the philosophy of science and to apologetics.

Mr. Jacob then went on to receive another master's degree from Southern Evangelical Seminary in philosophy. We stayed in touch, and I was impressed by his study ethic and how well he was doing academically. He then enrolled in another master's degree program in biblical languages at Houston Baptist University and somehow found the time to write *Who is Wise Enough to Understand This?*, a total apologetic for the Christian faith. By "total apologetic" I don't mean that he covers every apologetic topic, but, rather, that he offers a system of defending Christianity that covers all the essential areas that need to be addressed.

It is not a book about one apologetic topic—such as the resurrection of Jesus or the relationship between science and Christianity—but a book about many topics that integrates all the required constitutive apologetic elements. Specifically, Mr. Jacob addresses the need to find the truth about what matters most, commends philosophy to this task, defends the discipline of apologetics biblically, explains his apologetic method, offers scientific and other arguments for God's existence, defends the reliability of the Bible, argues that Jesus Christ is the way of eternal salvation, and advocates for a Christian ethic. He writes with a clear, warm tone, drawing on his personal experience as a Christian as part of his apologetic. All these points are well documented in the book.

Soon after meeting Aby Jacob, I sensed that God was going to use him powerfully to bring apologetics to his native land of India for the sake of evangelism and for building up the Church. This book is evidence of God's hand on this young man's life. May God use *Who is Wise Enough to Understand This?* to bring the saving truth of Jesus Christ to many needy souls in India!

Douglas Groothuis, Ph.D.

Douglas Groothuis, Ph.D. is Distinguished University Research Professor of Apologetics and Christian Worldview at Cornerstone University. He is the author of *Christian Apologetics: A Comprehensive Case for Biblical Faith,* 2nd ed. (InterVarsity Academic, 2022), as well as nineteen other books, including *Truth Decay: Defending Christianity Against the Challenges of Postmodernism* (InterVarsity, 2000) *and Beyond the Wager: The Christian Brilliance of Blaise Pascal* (InterVarsity-Academic, 2024).

Endnotes

1   See Douglas Groothuis, *On Jesus* (Belmont, CA: Wadsworth, 2003) and in an article, "Jesus: Philosopher and Apologist," *Christian Research Journal,* Volume 25, No. 2 (2002), *https://www.equip.org/articles/jesus-philosopher-and-apologist.*

2   See Douglas Groothuis, *Christian Apologetics: A Comprehensive Case for Biblical Faith,* 2nd ed (Downers Grove, IL: InterVarsity-Academic, 2022), 23-26. 39. For a book-length treatment of Paul in Athens and its pertinence today, see Paul Copan and Kenneth Litwak, *The Gospel in the Marketplace of Ideas: Paul's Mars Hill Experience for Our Pluralistic World* (Downers Grove, IL: IVP Academic, 2014).

3   Augustine, *The Confessions.* Many editions.

4   C. S. Lewis, *Surprised by Joy: The Shape of My Early Life* (New York: HarperOne, 1917).

5   Lee Strobel, *The Case for Christ* (Grand Rapids, MI: Zondervan, 1998).

6   Nabeel Qureshi, *Seeking Allah, Finding Jesus*, 3rd ed. (Grand Rapids, MI: Zondervan, 2018).

7   See the excellent work of Melissa Cain Travis, *Thinking God's Thoughts: Johannes Kepler and the Miracle of Cosmic Comprehensibility* (Moscow, ID: Romans Roads Press, 2022).

8   See Stephen C. Meyer, "The Rise and Fall of Theistic Science," *Return of the God Hypothesis* (New York: HarperOne, 2021). For Pascal's contribution (omitted by Meyer), see Douglas Groothuis, "Scientist and Philosopher of Science" in *Beyond the Wager: The Christian Brilliance of Blaise Pascal* (Downers Grove, IL: InterVarsity-Academic, 2024).

9   Francis A. Schaeffer, *The God Who is There*, IVP Signature Collection (Downers Grove, IL: InterVarsity Press, 2020).

Preface

The pursuit of truth is worthwhile as it can enlighten our minds and hearts, enrich our lives, help us understand ourselves and the world around us better, and give us true hope for living. In the Western world, many books have been published by the finest thinkers. As an Indian who has been living in the Western world for more than 14 years, I recognized the need for philosophical and apologetic materials in Asian and African countries. Most people in those countries cannot afford to purchase books published in the Western world. My goal is to put all my effort into publishing and making such materials available in those countries where they have little to no access to such works. I wrote this book out of my deep love for Jesus Christ and his Great Commission. I hope that this book will impact the lives of many people in India and other Asian/African countries.

Aby Jacob

PART ONE
THE PURSUIT OF TRUTH

CHAPTER 1

My Personal Journey and Introduction

We all have stories to tell. Who doesn't like to hear good stories? The story I present here is a real-life one—a true story of a young hunter who lived in the Western world. He had a great passion for collecting and trading guns, knives, and taxidermies. He also enjoyed target sport shooting, participating in shooting competitions, and hunting wild animals. He spent most of his free time thinking about something related to guns. In his early 20s, he owned twelve guns. His dream was to collect as many guns (and hunting gear) as possible so that he could build a personal outdoor gallery someday. Whenever he traveled in the countryside, his eyes were always naturally inclined to spot wild animals because his mind was filled with thoughts about them. As soon as he spotted an animal, even if it was not during a hunting trip, he started imagining himself as a hunter, and the first thought that came to his mind was how to make a perfect shot. He enjoyed it thoroughly. His hunting trips were not due to a desire for wild game meats, or proper control of animal populations. Those were for mere pleasure. Every time he killed something, he celebrated it. He hunted many animals and birds as the country's law permitted.

Once, during a vacation, on a beautiful rainy day, he was relaxing under a canopy. He was enjoying the beauty of rain with a cup of black tea in hand. The trees and plants were dancing to the sound of rain and wind. The nature looked joyful and fresh. The smell of rain added a mesmerizing feel. Later, the rain became lighter and lighter and came to a stop. The sun began to shine. The sun's rays were hitting the ground through the gaps between the leaves and branches of the trees. After a while, he saw two little birds chirping and playing on the branches of a small tree. He enjoyed watching them. However, at some point, the spirit of the hunter awakened in him. His imagination went that route. He immediately thought about the rifle that was there and desired to target practice. He went to pick up the gun. Instead of setting up a shooting target box, he decided to consider one of the birds the target.

In his mind, he had two thoughts. One, if he cannot shoot the bird, he will be worried about his shooting skills. Two, if he can shoot it, he can be proud of his marksmanship and celebrate it. He loaded the rifle, placed it on his shoulder, and aimed at the head of a bird. He took a breath and pulled the trigger. Bang! The shot was perfect. The targeted bird was down. Suddenly, the chirping of the birds came to an end. The second bird didn't know what had happened. As always, he was supposed to be cheering about his marksmanship as he placed a precise shot. However, for the first time in his life, what he experienced was something opposite and unexpected. His heart began to feel pain. He never had such a hurting experience after shooting a bird or an animal any time before this event. He immediately leaned the gun by the wall, ran to the fallen bird, and picked it up in his hand. His heart was pounding faster. The pain became deeper. His mind was filled with some strange, piercing thoughts of conviction that he had done a cruel thing to a poor little bird for mere pleasure. What a brutal man! How can he do this?

The bird was not dead yet. When he looked at its face, it gazed at his eyes, looking helpless. This brought tears to his eyes. He also felt helpless at that point to save the life that he just attempted to take for no reason. For the first time in his life, he hated his passion for guns. He cursed his guns, himself, and that moment. He tried to offer some water to the little bird, but it could not take it. He noticed that the bird's life was coming to an end. With deep pain, he gently closed the poor bird's eyes. In a few seconds, it took the last breath while laying on his hand defenseless. A painful moment! The shooter fell down on his knees and cried in his heart with intense pain. Many thoughts overtook him.

After some time, he disposed of the dead bird and returned to his bedroom. He became deeply saddened about his unkindness. He began to imagine some thoughts. He not only thought about his cruelty to one of the birds but also began to worry about the other bird, which was alive. Surely, they were a couple. Many questions came to his mind about that living bird and the bird's thoughts in his imagination. The one that was shot no longer exists alive to feel any pain. But the other one may be in deep pain. Its love of life is no longer alive. It became alone all of a sudden. All the joy they were experiencing together came to an end abruptly. The shooter wished that if he could communicate with that bird, he would lay at its feet and beg for forgiveness. But it was impossible to do so. His heart continued to remain restless. He was desiring forgiveness and peace. What happened then?

Although the story up to this point is painful, it also resulted in a beautiful turnaround in his life. Before I reveal it, I encourage you to ponder on these questions: How did he have such a strange experience in this particular event? What caused the conviction and pain in him all of a sudden? Can we explain this mystery naturally? How does that work? A sense of guilt and pain cannot be explained by pointing to some sudden random chemical changes within him, but there must be a reason or cause behind those impulses in the first place. What happened to the shooter?

Interestingly, something happened (which I will explain later) that offered him peace. This real-life experience taught the young man valuable lessons as he continued to reflect on it. He sincerely felt regretful and moaned about what happened to the birds, but he no longer lived with guilt and pain. He also had a beautiful transformation inside and out. He not only became compassionate to birds and animals but also became a deep thinker about life and the world. He embarked on a philosophical journey, which was a huge change of direction from his adventurous life in the outdoors. His extreme passion for guns and hunting declined, and it was replaced with a passion for truth, knowledge, and wisdom. His love and desire were then to find out what was true, good, and beautiful. He began to purchase books instead of guns when he made such an unbelievable shift in his life.

Now, it's time to reveal the person in this story. He is the author of this book. Yes! It is my story! I have some good reasons for sharing this personal story before I enter into the major subject of this book. There are some personal insights that I want to connect to some things I will address later. Before we begin the philosophical journey of pursuit of truth, I think it is good that I also share my testimony and worldview.

My Testimony and Worldview

I was raised very well in a Christian family in Kerala, India. My great-grandfather (Fr. Jacob) was a priest of the Mar Thoma Syrian Church (a church named after Apostle Thomas) in south India. He later became a missionary in Sri Lanka along with several British missionaries in the 1900s. Since childhood, I have practiced the Christian faith along with my family. After higher secondary education in India, my family sent me to England for higher studies at the age of 19.

In my early 20s, I began to think critically about my life, God, and the world. I realized that I genuinely didn't know what I believed about God. I became secretly skeptical about my Christian faith with some honest questions in mind. I remember pondering these at different times – 'I don't know God truly,' 'I don't know how to talk about God,' 'I would love to know him,' 'I would love to know the truth.' I gradually started to backslide from practicing faith as I didn't find any interest in God. Although I was backslidden from pursuing God, I never became an atheist because I did not have sufficient reasons to disbelieve in God. I was never rebellious; I always had high regard for God. But I knew that if I pursued God, I had to be honest about matters related to God. I became an honest skeptic. I reached a point when I entirely stopped attending church on Sundays. Instead, I completely focused on fulfilling my dreams.

My life was going well, filled with material things of my passion during that time. As I mentioned earlier, my greatest passion was collecting and trading guns, knives, taxidermies, and hunting.[1] I also worked hard and always maintained a good work ethic. Though I walked away from God, I have always loved truth and honesty in my life. To me, truth has always been more valuable than anything else. Even though I was always chasing my dreams, my quest for the truth about God, life, and the world remained a secret. But I wasn't actively trying to find it; I didn't know where to search for it. At that time, I had no clue that God had already listened to the questions in my heart and would reveal the truth to me through a series of events.

---

[1]   Many Westerners are gun users and hunters. It is part of their life. Therefore, owning a gun is not a big deal in the West. In India, gun users are very rare. There are only very limited gun license holders. Moreover, hunting is illegal in India. For an Indian, having such a deep love for guns is very uncommon. My father is a licensed gun owner for self-protection. When I say I have a passion for guns, it is a rare passion among Indians, unlike Westerners. Since I lived in the Western world, I had the privilege to purchase guns.

Several years later, I had an unexpected reason to travel back to India abruptly. My plan was to return to England soon. However, after I arrived in India, I had a series of Christian experiences while staying with my family. One of them was my mother's life. She was a devout Christian. When I was staying with my parents, I noticed something unique in my mother. She used to wake up early in the morning for her daily devotions, Scripture reading, and prayer. I often noticed her on her knees praying. Whenever she finished her devotions or walked out of a prayer meeting, I noticed something reflecting on her face. I always wondered how it was possible. I knew my mother to be a person who only spoke the truth in her life, was transparent in all her conversations, and was bold to stand for the truth. She never forced my brother or me to spend time in prayer or Bible study. Indeed, she shared with us great wisdom from the Scripture. But that wasn't something that moved me. To me, she not only shared great wisdom but also lived a model life. In my heart, I had a lot of admiration for her nature. I recognized that my mother's unique life was the result of her devoted Christian life. I truly desired to be like her and experience what she was experiencing.

Since truth-seeking was secretly active within me, my mother's life additionally inspired me to find the truth about God intentionally. I decided to put serious effort into the pursuit of truth. I knew that if God existed, then knowing, listening, and obeying him mattered the most; everything else was secondary. If God created me, only he could tell me the true value, meaning, and purpose of my life. I did not want the answer to be probably true, nor did I want some delusion. I wanted to know the absolute truth so that I could follow and defend it without fear and shame. I knew that it takes courage to pursue truth. I was sure I would never be afraid to follow it. Since the question was about God, I decided to ask him directly.

I supposed that if God exists, he must be all-knowing. Therefore, he would be able to listen to my voice. And if God is all-loving, he would also respond to the honest question from the bottom of my heart. So I went into my room, knelt, and said a prayer, 'God, if you are true, please reveal the truth to me.' My prayer was sincere; it did not come from a rebellious heart but from a humble one. Indeed, God heard my voice. God led me to read the Bible. (I am thankful I had the privilege of easy access to the Bible, being raised in a Christian family). And what happened after was something I never expected. I encountered Jesus Christ. It was a mysterious event, an exercise of raw divine power. I had entered into the joy of God. I received love, grace, forgiveness, and eternal life through Christ.

It was the most significant turning point in my life at the age of 24. Words cannot express the immense joy, light, and wonder I have been experiencing since I began a relationship with the Triune God. It was also the starting point of my intellectual journey to gain more knowledge and wisdom about God. God redirected my path to the United States. I realized that my sudden trip to India was divinely scheduled to bring me to the perfect arena where God could reveal the truth and redirect my path.

Following my encounter with Christ, my heart always thirsted to attain a more profound knowledge and wisdom of God. The topics related to God became the most exciting as I dug deeper. I felt like I had begun a journey in a mysterious wonderland, and every turn I made overwhelmed my heart with great joy. Then, a more powerful spiritual explosion occurred within me at the age of 27. I eventually felt a higher calling from the Lord. God has a mysterious way of leading us to where we need to be. For me, that meant leaving my job in the US and giving up a billion-dollar business project plan that I developed that was accepted by a foreign direct investment company. Instead, I felt compelled to delve deeper into the rational side of faith and gain knowledge and wisdom. It wasn't about money, success, or fame anymore but about discovering God's truth intellectually. So, I decided to embark on a new adventure and pursue graduate studies to learn from the scholars in the field instead of relying on random internet resources.

When I set out on an intellectual journey in the academy, I received warnings from several people that I would lose my faith in God if I tried to reason it out, but I ignored those words. I knew that if what I was trying to understand was the truth, even after studies and investigations, the truth would remain the same because that is the nature of truth. So, I had confidence in that journey. I also thought that after my studies, if I came to the conclusion that it was not reasonable, I would not pursue my faith journey the way I desired. I gave up everything I could have gained and went to study the major world religions, philosophy, theology, science, apologetics, ethics, etc., and tried to understand the major worldviews.

I have looked into the reasons and evidence for the existence of God and found overwhelmingly convincing, undeniable philosophical and scientific reasons. I have studied the truth claims of the Judeo-Christian worldview and discovered abundant evidence for the biblical truth claims, including the resurrection of Jesus Christ. I compared the Judeo-Christian worldview with all other major worldviews. I concluded that only the Judeo-Christian worldview sufficiently and satisfactorily answers the big questions about life and the world. In every possible way, I tested to see if I could find reasons to doubt the Christian faith, but I didn't find one. So, there was no way I could run away from it for intellectual reasons because the Judeo-Christian truth claims are objectively evident knowledge and are verifiable. Anyone can test it. As a result, my faith in God became stronger as I found intellectual reasons for it.

I realized that if Christianity were not true, there would be no other hope in this world. If it were not true, I certainly would not have decided to spend the rest of my life defending it. Christianity is a system of objective truth. In history, on the cross of Calvary, God's perfect justice and perfect love were displayed in perfect unity. The resurrection of Christ gave the greatest assurance of eternal life. Knowing that truth and accepting God's grace through Christ brought me into an eternal relationship with the Triune God. He gave me the greatest freedom from the bondage of sin and freedom from an eternal separation from God. When my experiential journey of faith became intellectually charged, my life journey became extraordinarily thrilling, meaningful, purposeful, and filled with tears of joy. I dedicated my life to giving reasons to believe in Christ and answering people's honest questions about God, life, and the world. I have gone through a tremendous transformation.

From that moment of my encounter with Christ at 24, I was no longer alone, but the Holy Spirit resided in me. The Spirit of the living God continued to convict me of my sins and guided and corrected me. God also began to build a deeper compassionate heart in me. Recalling my story of shooting the bird, I reflected on the cause of such a mysterious experience in my life. I realized that my mysterious experience in that incident was purely a supernatural intervention. The event happened after I became a faithful follower of Christ.

In that incident, God convicted me of my cruelty in killing that bird for mere pleasure. As a result, I became restless and guilty. How did the storm of pain and guilt calm down? I had to ask forgiveness from the Creator of the heaven and the earth. Through Jesus Christ, the gracious God forgave me when I surrendered to him. He cleansed my heart and soul. He gave me a soft and compassionate heart. He gave me peace and love instead of letting me live with guilt and pain.

These are mysterious elements of life. The human condition cannot be reasonably explained without the supernatural element.

Many people are seeking peace and hope in life. God cannot only give peace and hope in life, but he can also transform a person in a way one can never imagine. My own life is a good example of a transformed person. God gave me a new passion and goal in a route I had never imagined. I will briefly tell that story, too, because it helps to realize the visible effect of the transforming power of Christ. This is called the story of the "Academic Refugee." You may be wondering what that means!

The Story of the Academic Refugee

When I began my school journey in India as a little one, I was forced to sit for two years at the first school level because I hadn't learned to write and read the alphabet by the end of the first academic year. I had a painful school journey in India while studying at five different schools. I can recall the spankings I received on my tiny palm with a long stick (which the teachers used back in those days) for not studying. I can also recollect the moments when I was forced to stand outside the classroom for study-related issues. I received mockery and insults in classrooms multiple times.

For my final higher secondary (12th grade or Plus 2) exam, which is the biggest public exam before starting college, I was the only one who failed out of 76 students in my batch. In India, it is a big shame in society. I brought shame not only to myself but also to the school. Every year, when the school achieves a 100% pass rate, they usually display the picture of the whole batch in a column of the major newspapers. That year, it didn't happen because I failed. The school lost its reputation. This was a painful time as a teenager because I had to face it alone. (Thankfully, my parents were very supportive).

I was able to retake the mathematics exam later. Although I passed in the second attempt, I was no longer interested in studying in India. It was also late to secure college admission for the same academic year. When an opportunity came up, my deeply supportive family decided to send me to England for college at the age of 19. To me, it was also an escape from shame at that age. Because of those experiences, throughout my life, I hated books, studies, reading, and teachers. I also hated the school system in India when I left the country. (Definitely, there were other areas in which I excelled, apart from the academic side)

Long story short, my later encounter with Christ at the age of 24 changed my whole life. Today, at the age of 33, while writing this book, I hold a bachelor's degree from the United Kingdom and three master's degrees from the United States of America, and I am currently working on my 4th master's degree with an aim to get into doctoral work. Today, I spend most of my time in the academy-- reading, writing, and studying. The one who was once forced to repeat another year to study the alphabet is now studying multiple languages at a time. This is not written to boast about my achievements but to boast in Christ-- the source of all wisdom-- who changed my life upside down. Isn't God's transformative power amazing? I no longer feel ashamed about my past academic journey. I treasure those painful experiences. Now I have a beautiful story to tell.

Several years ago, while having dinner with Dr. Douglas Groothuis (my very dear professor, amazing friend, and intellectual mentor) and his loving wife, Mrs. Groothuis, at their house, I amusingly shared with them my story of leaving India for academic reasons. After hearing my story, Dr. Groothuis, with his sense of humor, named me "Academic Refugee." I absolutely loved this term, and it made me laugh as it aptly describes my story.

When I continued the philosophical journey, my extreme passion for guns and hunting declined. They were replaced with a passion for truth, knowledge, and wisdom. I was never a natural book reader in my life. But now I collect books instead of guns when I made such a shift from my adventurous life in the outdoors. This doesn't mean I hate guns. I neither hate hunting for food nor controlling the animal population by following the country's laws. I love guns, but I do not worship guns anymore. I enjoy wisdom and knowledge more than guns. Everything in this world, including guns, will perish, but the truth will last forever. I want to spend more time on more meaningful and mightier things, that is, gaining treasures of wisdom and knowledge. This is my true story of transformation (from guns to books) after encountering Christ.

My family and close friends from other faiths testify about my transformation. One of them is my closest friend (his name is Dhanesh), who has known me for many years, recently commented that my change in life was similar to the change from night to daylight. My friends still find it amazing to see this change in me. However, at this point, I want to point out one thing very clearly! That is, sharing personal experiences can be powerful, but my transformation does not prove the truthfulness of the Christian belief system. Proving the truthfulness of something requires a lot of work. Now, I will move on to give an introduction to this book.

What is this Book all About?

My chief motive behind writing this book, "*Who is Wise Enough to Understand This?*" is to help people discover the truth, bring clarity to their understanding, and find true answers to the deepest questions of life and the world that have puzzled human beings. I intend to make people think critically about life and the world, build a foundation for truth, and provide the best explanation that may benefit their life journey. My goal is not to present a new ideology or a personal opinion. I aim to present a system of objective truth that is verifiable. (The objective truth is that which deals with facts, and it is independent of personal feelings, prejudices, or biases. I will address the nature of truth in more detail later in the book.)

In this book, I did not simply presuppose that the Christian faith is true. I wrote it from a skeptical standpoint as a truth-seeker analyzing life and the world around us. The natural world, history, and conscience are fundamental sources of information that have much to teach us about our lives and the world. Many thinkers in the past have used the metaphor "the Book of Nature" by considering nature as a book to be read rightly. It's fascinating to consider nature as a book with its own language that can be interpreted using appropriate tools. I think it's important to examine these sources to gain a better understanding of the truth, the existence of God, the concept of God, and the problem of evil. However, I also believe that while these sources are undeniably valuable, they are not sufficient for a comprehensive understanding. These general data undeniably point us to the supernatural. It's also important to evaluate various sources of data from different disciplines, such as philosophy, theology, science, religion, ethics, and history, to draw well-rounded conclusions.

In the first part, *The Pursuit of Truth*, I laid out several important questions to begin the intellectual journey to discover a system of objective truth. In the second part, *The Journey as a Philosopher*, I gave a general introduction to philosophy and introduced the right tools for critical thinking. Moving forward, I applied these tools to topics such as the nature of truth, the existence of God, and the knowledge of God. Until that point, the journey uses natural reason and evidence from various subjects that are accessible to all people to draw certain conclusions. Parts one and two lay the foundation for part three. Part three, *The Journey as a Judeo-Christian Apologist,* contains distinctly Christian content. It prepares the reader for an apologetics journey, which covers topics including the importance of apologetics, biblical apologetics, scientific apologetics, and the problem of evil.

Regarding the quest for truth, someone's opinion does not matter. Opinions can only give temporary relief, but objective truth provides permanent comfort once it is understood and persuaded properly. I am not expecting everyone to agree with me on everything, but I hope you will read this work completely. I also warn you that this book may challenge your preconceived notions or beliefs. But that is what critical thinking does to the minds! So, the critical thinking should do its job. To develop a life of the mind, we must be intellectually challenged by the right thoughts, unlearn falsehoods and preconceived false notions, and replace them with the truth perceived. You may evaluate the arguments, reasons, and evidence I presented in this book and draw a conclusion for yourself. You may then make a rational choice based on your evaluation as you have a desire to know the truth. Let's begin.

CHAPTER 2

The Quests of a Thinker

We live in a busy and overwhelmingly distracted world. People are constantly immersed in various entertaining activities such as parties, movies, games, music, outdoor adventures, and social media. Many individuals are drawn to their smart devices even from a young age. Some may feel depressed or lonely when faced with instances of lengthy solitude, as they are accustomed to constant stimulation. For many, engaging their minds with some form of entertainment is crucial to feeling fulfilled and avoiding boredom.

The advancement of technology has undoubtedly made life easier in many ways. However, there is a growing tendency in many people to replace their natural capabilities with artificial intelligence for many tasks. Many people suggest going with the flow without considering the potential consequences. While artificial intelligence is beneficial in many ways, most people often do not realize the damage it can cause to our natural cognitive ability to think when they allow it without wise boundaries in place. On the other hand, some people are thoughtful and reflective about life and the world around them. They are wise enough to establish limits and use their cognitive skills for critical thinking. I am glad you are among them; otherwise, you would not be interested in reading this book. Congratulations on being wise to embark on this journey!

When I was a little boy, our house was in the middle of a plantation in Kerala, India, where mosquitoes were plentiful. When I got mosquitoes bites as a kid, I asked, "Why does this world contain mosquitoes that drain blood from my body?" "Are they assigned to make my life uncomfortable?" These were some questions that came to my mind as a little man. Even if I did not find answers, it did not affect my life more than a little discomfort of itchy bumps that formed on the skin after mosquitoes fed on my blood. However, as I became a more mature thinker, I recognized that there are questions that are more significant than these. I realized it is crucial to find true answers to the questions related to our lives and the world around us. Incorrect answers and living in accordance with them may lead to disastrous consequences. Perhaps it is like playing a life-or-death game with a guaranteed outcome of death. In this life journey, have you ever paused for a moment and pondered on questions such as,

"Why am I here?"

"Where am I going?"

"What is the true meaning and purpose of life?"

"Did I come into existence for no reason?"

"Am I here to seek pleasure and happiness during my lifetime and completely vanish away when I die?"

"Why am I experiencing pain and suffering?"

"Why is there evil?"

"Why am I facing health issues?"

"Why is the world such a mess?"

"Why the world seems so cruel?"

"Am I just an accidental byproduct of blind natural processes?"

"Am I just an animal with a higher value?"

"Why does the universe exist?"

"How did the universe come into existence?"

"Why my heart cannot find rest?"

"Why do I feel a vacuum deep within me?"

"Why am I not fully satisfied even if I have everything I need?"

"Why am I worried?"

"What is the ultimate reality?"

"Does God exist?"

"Is physical death the end?"

"Is there life after death?"

"Is there truly a Heaven and Hell?"

"Is the idea of Heaven a wish fulfillment?"

"Why are there different religions and ideologies?"

"Is every religion just the opinions of people?"

"Can all religion be true?"

"Is there one true religion?"

"Is there hope for mankind?"

"How should I live?"

"What is the ultimate ethic?"

"Is there objective truth?"

"Can I know the truth?" "

"How do I know the truth?" and many more. There is no end to the number of questions people can frame.

Even little kids ask all kinds of questions when they are grown enough to speak. By looking at the night sky, kids may ask, "Daddy, what is that light in the sky?" "How many stars are there in the sky?" "Can I touch the moon?" As they grow older, they ask more complex questions. I recently had a conversation with a few children from seven to ten years of age, and the weight of the questions they asked amazed me. People raise deeper questions along the way when they become more mature.

Many people find temporarily satisfying answers and press on with life. Some keep a positive attitude toward life without overthinking these questions. Some drive into deep disappointment, despair, darkness, misery, and sleeplessness because life does not make sense to them. Many are seeking true answers. However, they often do not arrive at the true answers to the most important questions of life and the world. Many don't know where to find answers. Some people think there are no true answers to these questions. Some people need help to frame the right questions, where to begin the search, and whom to ask. All the above questions have great importance and deserve true answers. You are reading the right book if you have pondered any of the above questions or if you would love to think deeply.

Our Desire to Know the Truth

We have some knowledge about the real world. We know without a doubt that the universe exists, and that we exist. As rational beings, we all desire deeper knowledge about reality. As the ancient philosopher Aristotle wrote, "All men by nature desire to know."[1] This statement must be true; that is why we are asking questions to discover the truth. At his trial in Athens, philosopher Socrates famously said, "The unexamined life is not worth living."[2] In this statement, Socrates

---

[1]   Aristotle, *Metaphysics* 1.1.1, in *The Basic Works of Aristotle*, ed. Richard McKeon (New York: Random House, 1941), 689. Also see Douglas Groothuis, *Philosophy in Seven Sentences* (Downers Grove, IL: InterVarsity, 2017), 49-64.

[2]   Plato, *The Apology* 38a. Also see Groothuis, *Philosophy in Seven Sentences*, 35-48.

encourages individuals to think deeply about the challenging aspects of life, as doing so can bring purpose and significance to one's existence. If we consult a doctor or go to a medical lab, we want the true health report because it affects our lives if it is not true. If we go to the police department to file a case, we want the truth to be investigated. In all such matters, we want the objective truth to be revealed instead of personal feelings, prejudices, or biases. What about the truth about life?

French mathematician and philosopher Blaise Pascal wrote, "Truth is so obscure in these times, and falsehood so established, that, unless we love the truth, we cannot know it."[3] Most people are comfortable with their preconceived notions. They tend to align their lives with popular opinion. Some suggest following their hearts and feelings and prioritizing worshiping their own selves. Such people do not like to be challenged about their beliefs or ideologies that govern their lives. They do not like the idea of seeking the absolute truth. They do not allow their minds to think outside their comfort zones.

American professor of philosophy Douglas Groothuis writes, "It is revealing that so many people today express approval by saying, 'I'm comfortable with that,' and disapproval by saying, 'I'm not comfortable with that.' Comfort is important when it comes to furniture and headphones, but it is irrelevant when it comes to truth."[4] Philosopher Stephen McAndrew states, "In order to discover truth it is necessary to coldly dissect and examine all of our prejudices and inherent biases to ensure we receive unbiased answers. This takes

---

[3]   Blaise Pascal, *Pensées* 864, *The Great Books of the Western World* 33, ed. Robert M. Hutchins and trans. W. F. Trotter (Chicago: Encyclopedia Britannica, 1952), 343.

[4]   Douglas R. Groothuis, *Christian Apologetics: A Comprehensive Case for Biblical Faith* (Downers Grove: IVP Academic, 2011), 141. The second edition of the book came out in 2022.

effort. It is always easier to simply accept the ideas presented to us than to question the status quo."[5]

Before we continue this journey, let us pause for a moment and ask these questions to ourselves: "Am I a truth seeker?" "Am I honest in my truth search?" "Do I really love to find the truth?" "Am I ready to be intellectually challenged?" We should be honest with ourselves about the answers we give to these questions. If we are not genuine in our truth search, we will never arrive at it. Perhaps we are sincere individuals, but there is a possibility that we may be sincerely wrong about our current philosophy of life or beliefs. Truth is more important than sincerely holding a wrong philosophy of life and the world. We should not let other people rule our intellectual lives. We have to do the thinking ourselves; It is our responsibility. It may demand courage to pursue the truth; but it's worth pursuing. We should keep an open mind. Now, with a thirst to find the objective truth, let us shift the gear to move forward in our journey of critical thinking. Let's dive into reality.

---

[5] Stephen McAndrew. *Why It Doesn't Matter What You Believe If It's Not True: Is There Absolute Truth?* (Oregon: Deep River Books, 2012), 75.

CHAPTER 3

A Dive into the Human Problems

Have you experienced tears of joy? Can you think of some reasons that caused it? We can think of some general examples. When a child is born into the world, it fills the mother's heart with joy. When aged parents receive a visit from their loving children after a long time, it makes their hearts overflow with joy. When one receives love and forgiveness from someone, it fills the receiver's heart with joy. When a broken relationship gets restored, it can bring delight to the heart. When one meets a loved one after a very long time, it can bring tears of joy. Isn't it beautiful when our body reacts in the form of producing that beautiful substance called 'tears' and the immense pleasure that comes with it? No material possessions like wealth, power, or luxury can substitute for the joy of such moments. How frequently do we experience such moments? Don't we wish to experience such joyful tears more often?

People travel the world to experience the wonders of the natural world. How beautiful it is to watch the night sky, butterflies, waterfalls, sceneries, oceans, mountains, birds, animals, and the growth of a child. People enjoy art forms such as music, dance, painting, literature, photography, performance, film, sculpture, architecture, etc. Those are moments of glory. People desire such a life. Most people are not worried about spending a lot of money on experiencing those moments of joy. Because of that, planning holidays is probably one of the most exciting moments for many people. The reality of human life is that we all have moments of joy and glory along the way. When those moments come, we may think we are made to live a life like that. How beautiful would it be if life always gives such moments? Don't we desire to live a joyful life? Unfortunately, we cannot ignore the scary and depressing side of the reality of human life. We also deal with tears of pain. Perhaps we are dealing with pain more than joy. We can think of some examples.

When a mother loses her deeply loving child or a husband loses his loving wife, it can bring tears of pain. When a relationship breaks, it can bring heartbreaks and painful tears. When we see tragedies like sickness, deaths, cruelties, injustices, and poverty, it brings pain. When we experience tears of pain, we think this is not what we want to experience in this life. We ask a lot of "why?" questions when depressing moments hit us. How do we find answers? Before we deal with questions and answers, we must dive a little deeper into the problems of the reality of human life.

A dive into human problems may make you feel like you are sinking into a deep and cold ocean surrounded by darkness without hope. Trust me! I assure you that after a while, you will reach the bottom of the ocean, where you can firmly rest your feet and gain the strength to push upward to come to a tremendous, meaningful life with a joyful heart grounded in the truth. At this moment, I want to make you sink in deep water because I do not want to ignore the reality of human predicaments before I build a foundation for the system of objective truth. People may be seriously hurting and crying deep within them as they seek true answers to the questions of life. If you are not in such a life situation, somebody you know may be going through it. Some may not know how to get out of their miserable lives and which direction to go.

Perhaps there are people who feel like they are stuck in a boat in the middle of an ocean without a paddle and not knowing how to get out of the ocean. Can you imagine such a situation where you have no hope of a rescuer? Sadly, many people live in similar hopeless situations. So, I imagine myself in such situations so that my overall case makes more sense and the answers I give would pierce directly into people's minds and hearts. Through this, I aim to create a bridge between the mind and the heart for a great transformation and true hope for living. I want to help people by giving them the right tools for life and directing them in the right direction where they can meet the deepest needs of a whole person. At the end of your reading of this book, I want you to rejoice with all your heart and mind. What are some of the problems we can think of?

The Desire of the Human Heart

Everyone desires a happy and fulfilled life. Some people think wealth and success can bring them these. So, they work hard their entire lives to acquire wealth and success. In the end, they realize that wealth and success do not bring them happiness and fulfillment. Some of the wealthiest and most successful people on the planet are the unhappiest people. Their wealth and success can help them as a means to find some ways to distract themselves with some temporary pleasure. After a while, they have to face the misery of loneliness, darkness, or emptiness covering their lives. Many chase after power, fame, honor, and bodily goods. Some upgrade their lives with the most modern technologies, yet these don't satisfy them. Some buy the best mattresses they could ever find, yet they lack sleep. Many people try to impress others by showing off or living an extraordinary, luxurious life. In reality, these lifestyles only satisfy them for a short moment. Some people save all their money to enjoy retirement, but often, they end up in unhealthy situations that take away all the joy they were hoping for. This is reality.

People chase after all kinds of pleasure with the best resources and try to fulfill all their fleshly desires. All they can experience is a temporary pleasure or a little bit of passing of time. Even if they have more than what is needed, many people feel an emptiness and restlessness inside their hearts. They do not find a permanent cure for this situation of the heart. Pascal writes, "Being unable to cure death, wretchedness, and ignorance, men have decided, to be happy, not to think about such things."[1] To satisfy a vacuum or restlessness of the heart, many people consume a large amount of alcohol or use illicit drugs. They want to forget and escape their real conscience for some time. They want to somehow escape from the reality of emptiness. Unfortunately, they only find temporary satisfaction. What is it that human beings are seeking within them?

They are seeking something good, but a line separates them from enjoying the ultimate satisfaction in a fully conscious state of life. Russian writer Aleksandr Solzhenitsyn writes, "…the line separating good and evil passes not through states, nor between classes, nor between political parties-- but right through every human heart-- and through all human hearts."[2] The condition of the human heart proves that the heart hunger for something to satisfy its need. A great British thinker, C. S. Lewis, writes,

> Creatures are not born with desires unless satisfaction for those desires exists. A baby feels hunger; well, there is such a thing as food. A duckling wants to swim; well, there is such a thing as water. Men feel sexual desire; well, there is such a

---

[1]   Blaise Pascal, *Pensees*, ed. and trans. Alban Krailsheimer (New York: Penguin, 1966), 66.

[2]   Aleksandr Solzhenitsyn, *The Gulag Archipelago II*, quoted in Daniel J. Mahoney, *Aleksander Solzhenitsyn: The Ascent from Ideology*, (Maryland: Rowman & Littlefield Publishers, 2001), 50.

thing as sex. If I find in myself a desire which no experience in this world can satisfy, the most probable explanation is that I was made for another world. If none of my earthly pleasures satisfy it, that does not prove that the universe is a fraud. Probably earthly desires were never meant to satisfy it, but only to arouse it, to suggest the real thing.[3]

This is a real problem that human beings face in this life. They have an arousal of deep desire within their hearts. Is there a real thing that can permanently satisfy the heart's desire? We need sufficient and satisfactory answers for it.

Pain and Suffering

We all deal with pain and suffering in this world sometimes along the way. People may get physically ill unexpectedly. This produces a lot of trauma and tears. Those who always rely on their wealth, power, fame, and abilities when suddenly diagnosed with a life-threatening health issue lose hope. They often cry out loudly. It is painful to watch our loved ones suffer. We are often helpless in many situations. Money may help some people get the best medical treatments, but that patient still has to endure a lot of torment with these treatments. When people get sick, they alone have to suffer physically. One cannot transfer the pain to another person. If the disease has no potential cure, it leaves no hope of returning to a normal life.

I deal with migraine headaches. Those who struggle with it know the depth of the pain and suffering it brings. When the migraine gets triggered, I cannot do anything other than put my head into rest mode until the painkillers reduce the severity of the pain. I also think, compared to the pain many others face, mine is not something big. I still ponder, "What is the purpose of migraine headaches in me?" "Why am I going through this suffering?" This is not how my life is supposed to be.

---

[3]   C. S. Lewis, *Mere Christianity* (1944; reprint, New York: Simon & Schuster, 1996), 121.

Some children are born with physical disabilities. The child, the family, and the loved ones may have to go through a lifetime of pain dealing with it. Some people deal with mental illness. When loved ones die, it leaves great trauma in some people's lives. Physical pain is probably bearable to many, but the pain in one's heart and mind stays. Along with that, when one loses all hope, it increases the severity of the pain. Some try to end their lives when they go through deep suffering without hope of a cure and when they find it difficult to bear any longer. I know of a person who had deadly cancer in his throat. After several months of diagnosing cancer, he took his life because he did not find any reason to live anymore. Some people deal with depression and anxiety. All these are depressing realities that human beings face in this life. The problem of pain and suffering is real. Why pain and suffering? Can we find meaning and purpose in pain and suffering? Is there a way to suffer well? Is there hope? We need sufficient and satisfactory answers for it.

The Problem of Evil

There are two categories of evil: moral evil and natural evil. Moral evil is something that is caused by individual people. We can notice violence all over the world caused by people. We can see people fighting and killing each other for their own gains of power, money, and pleasure. We always have to keep our belongings secure because we are always cautious that an evil-doer may break into our belongings for his gain. We can notice immoral actions all around. We hear news of rape, murder, betrayal, burglary, oppression, and trafficking. We can see injustices all over the world where humanity is involved.

Some years back, when I lived in London, I saw a group of young people fighting in the street about something, and it ended up with a person fatally stabbing someone. Those are painful, evil actions that are difficult to erase from minds. Was the offender satisfied with his action? Of course not! He ended up in prison with the guilt of committing a homicide. Perhaps he did not intend to do it, but all of a sudden, the anger that arose in him caused him to take another person's life. Along with moral evil, we cannot deny the problem of natural evil.

Natural evil includes earthquakes, storms, tornados, tsunamis, wildfires, and volcanic eruptions. Many people die and are injured due to natural disasters. These are beyond the abilities of human beings to control. However, these natural activities impact the lives of human beings at the locations that hit those. Those bring huge destruction to humanity. That is why these natural activities are considered evil by most people. We all face the effects of moral and natural evil in this life. Why is there moral evil? Is there a purpose for natural evil? We need sufficient and satisfactory answers for these.

Guilt and Shame

Many people deal with the problem of guilt. A guilt complex is a self-conscious emotion that occurs when one has done something wrong or compromised a standard of conduct, which involves a negative evaluation of self. Sometimes, a wrong action may end with terrible consequences. The whole world may be against those people for their bad actions. Maybe they ended up in prison for a lifetime. Various reasons can cause a guilt complex. Some have faced bad childhood experiences. Some have committed wrong actions based on ignorance. Sometimes, anger and revengeful mentality can cause bad actions, which may result in harmful consequences.

There are many people who have committed wrong acts, but nobody knows about them. But it bothers those individuals frequently. Many people feel guilty for actions they have committed unintentionally. Some people have performed shameful acts secretly. Many often end up living lives in tears because of the guilty feeling. Some wealthy people do charity work at some point in life because of the emotional stress they are experiencing deep within their hearts due to some wrong actions they have committed in the past. They think contributing to charities may help them feel a little comfort. Some people donate a lot of money to religious centers.

A guilt complex can make people find it difficult to face the world. Society, family, friends, and all loved ones often avoid such people. Some people isolate themselves from society because they have a feeling that they are bad. Society may view them as if they are bad people. Even if that person has changed his past behavior, society may not accept him. They continue to accuse him of his wrongdoing. A guilt complex can have a severe impact on a person's life. It can lead to anxiety, depression, regret, and shame. Many people become alcoholics and drug addicts. Some people commit suicide. These are painful situations that human beings face.

We all may have guilty feelings about some of our past wrong actions, which may still be bothering us. Many people are hurting so badly deep within them, even if most people don't realize it. Why does the feeling of guilt occur to people in the first place? Is there a solution to overcome the pain of guilt? What is the ultimate solution for those who have done wrong in the past but desire a better life? Do they deserve true love and forgiveness? Or should we separate them from society as bad or evil people? Don't they deserve better lives? Is there an objective solution to it? We need sufficient and satisfactory answers to the problem of guilt.

Long Delays

Long delays are a crucial problem that many people face in reality in one form or another. Some people often desire to do good acts with good intentions, but it never becomes fruitful. Many tragedies chase them one after another. They do not know the reason for those hardships. They find it difficult to get out of those situations even after a long wait. Some people struggle financially. They do everything right and with great, careful thoughts, but things always turn out differently than they planned. Often, they do not receive help from those who can help. Some people avoid those who are struggling. They do not know why things are getting so delayed. Many people move forward with the hope that someday, the situation will change. However, this is not the case for everyone.

Some people lose all hope after waiting a long time. Sometimes it makes them sick, and they cry out loudly with great anguish. Some do it secretly. Their heart is aching miserably, but others around them may not realize that deep pain. They become disappointed and desperate. Sometimes, they no longer know how to face the world. Some people even plan to end their lives when things get delayed too much and become unbearable. We hear news of people ending their lives. These are depressing realities. Those facing these issues ask questions such as: Why is it happening to me? What am I doing wrong? How do I keep moving? Where do I go for a solution? Who can listen to my heart? Where can I find answers? We need sufficient and satisfactory answers for it.

The Problem of Injustices

We see injustices all over the world. Many people in the world are oppressed by powerful people. Some people seek justice on issues they face. They know that they are right, but society may be against them. Sometimes, innocent people face punishment even if the fault is not on their side. But often, they become separated from society because of misunderstandings. They live with the hope that someday, the world will realize their innocence. Some people do not even get justice. We often see unjust people live happily and flourish, but harmless people live in misery. Why all these injustices? Is there an ultimate solution for these injustices? We need sufficient and satisfactory solutions to these questions.

The Brevity of Life

Everyone comes into existence at a finite point in time and space. This is the day we call the 'Date of Birth.' On an average, we may live for about sixty to eighty years. Some live a little longer. Then we die. The duration from birth to death is what we call 'life.' If you are in your twenties, almost one-fourth of your life is over. If you are in your forties, over half of your life is over. If you are in your sixties, the majority of your life is over. If you are healthy and living in a safe environment, you may live for several more years or a few decades. Even knowing the brevity of life, many people live with a lot of confidence and pride that death will not affect them anytime soon. Nowadays, we hear news of the death of young people more often, which is shocking at times.

Several of my friends and known people recently died in their twenties and thirties. One died in a car crash, another of a heart attack, and others for many other reasons. They never expected death at those ages. They all lived with great dreams and expectations. But all of a sudden, they were gone, leaving pain in loved ones. We don't know when we will die. We do not have any guarantee. All we know for sure is that we will die one day, and our life is short. This is an inescapable truth. Groothuis writes, "In one sense, we are alone. No one else will live our life or die our death."[4] Every living being tries to preserve its life because they do not want to die quickly. Are we only here for a short time? Why death? Is death the end? If death

---

[4]   Groothuis, *Christian Apologetics*, 16.

is the end, what meaning do our lives offer? Is there a life after the physical death? Is there hope for humankind? We need sufficient and satisfactory answers for them before the end of our lives. Which worldview can bear the weight of all these problems that human beings face on Earth?

A System of Objective Truth

Our hearts desire to live a meaningful, purposeful, and joyful life, but we live in a world that is mixed with more misery and less joy than we want. Is there a possibility that we can experience more joy and less pain or joy in the midst of all miseries? Is there a purpose for this reality to be the way it is? Who can answer these deep questions with true solutions? People often give advice such as "Believe in yourself," "Stay positive," "Hope the best," "Enjoy every moment," "Forget the past," "Live in the present," "Don't think too much," "Don't worry," etc. However, those are not the ultimate true solutions. Those are just opinions of people that do not produce permanent solutions. A motivational speech may stimulate people for a while, but after some time, they have to face the miseries of reality.

We need a true worldview that can bear the weight of all these questions and real problems that human beings face. That worldview should not be the opinion of a particular person or group. This worldview must be universally true for everyone. This worldview must address the problems of the whole person and a solution to them. It should address the human condition and the problems of the world, such as evil, pain, suffering, the vacuum of human life, the heart's longing, guilt, long delays, and death. It should offer objective meaning, purpose, and hope to human lives. This worldview must be objectively true, rationally compelling, and important to the whole life, as Groothuis puts it.[5] In short, we need a system of objective truth that can bear the weight of all these questions. That is our goal of this journey - to discover this system of objective truth. As we transition to the next chapter, let us consider this question: Are we just a cosmic accident or created by an all-powerful, all-knowing, and all-loving God for a purpose?

❏❏❏

---

[5]   Groothuis, *Christian Apologetics*, 16.

CHAPTER 4

Cosmic Accident or Creation?

We live in a huge universe. All astronomers and physicists agree that there is an incredible level of fine-tuning in the physical constants, laws, and properties so that human life is possible on planet Earth. Astronomer Carl Sagan had the privilege of seeing our home planet, the Earth, from about 6.5 billion kilometers away on the Voyager 1 mission in 1990. An image was taken in which the Earth appears as a tiny dot in the center of scattered light rays (You may search on the internet to see the image). In his book *Pale Blue Dot*, Sagan wrote about the planet Earth:

> Look again at that dot. That's here. That's home. That's us. On it everyone you love, everyone you know, everyone you ever heard of, every human being who ever was, lived out their lives. The aggregate of our joy and suffering, thousands of confident religions, ideologies, and economic doctrines, every hunter and forager, every hero and coward, every creator and destroyer of civilization, every king and peasant, every young couple in love, every mother and father, hopeful child, inventor and explorer, every teacher of morals, every corrupt politician, every "superstar," every "supreme leader," every saint and sinner in the history of our species lived there—on a mote of dust suspended in a sunbeam.

> The Earth is a very small stage in a vast cosmic arena. Think of the rivers of blood spilled by all those generals and emperors so that, in glory and triumph, they could become the momentary masters of a fraction of a dot. Think of the endless cruelties visited by the inhabitants of one corner of this pixel on the scarcely distinguishable inhabitants of some other corner, how frequent their misunderstandings, how eager they are to kill one another, how fervent their hatreds.

> Our posturings, our imagined self-importance, the delusion that we have some privileged position in the Universe, are challenged by this point of pale light. Our planet is a lonely speck in the great enveloping cosmic dark. In our obscurity, in all this vastness, there is no hint that help will come from elsewhere to save us from ourselves.[1]

Sagan was a secular humanist. The first line of Sagan's film (1980) *Cosmos: A Personal Voyage* is memorable. He says, "The cosmos is all that is, or ever was, or ever will be." Sagan held that the 'natural world is all there is.' This is what naturalists and secular humanists believe. These worldviews are equivalent to atheism. Suppose we are just a cosmic accident, and that the natural world is all that exists. What kind of meaning and purpose does such a view offer? Atheist biologist Richard Dawkins exclaimed, "The universe that we observe has precisely the properties we should expect if there is, at the bottom, no design, no purpose, no evil, no good, nothing but pitiless indifference."[2] An atheist professor of biological sciences, William Provine wrote, "There are no gods, no purposes, no goal-directed forces of any kind. There is no life after death… no ultimate foundation for ethics, no ultimate meaning to life, and no free will for humans, either."[3]

Nobel Prize-winning atheist physicist Steven Weinberg said, "The more the universe seems comprehensible, the more it seems pointless."[4] Paleontologist George Gaylord Simpson states, "Man is the result of a purposeless and natural process that did not have him in mind."[5] The atheistic worldview carries no ultimate significance or

---

[1]   Carl Sagan, *Pale Blue Dot: A Vision of the Human Future in Space* (New York, NY: Random House, 1994), 8.

[2]   Richard Dawkins, *A River Out of Eden* (New York: Basic, 1995), 133.

[3]   William Provine, "Darwinism: Science or Naturalistic Philosophy?" *Origins Research* 16, no.1/2 (1994):9.

[4]   Steven Weinberg, cited in James Glanz, "SCIENTIST AT WORK: Steven Weinberg; Physicist Ponders God, Truth and 'Final Theory,'" *New York Times*, January 25, 2000, Accessed April 13, 2021. https://www.nytimes.com/2000/01/25/science/scientist-at-work-steven-weinberg-physicist-ponders-god-truth-and- final-theory.html

[5]   George Gaylord Simpson, *The Meaning of Evolution*. Rev. ed. (Connecticut: Yale University Press, 1967), 345.

objective meaning and purpose for humanity. Scientific credentials combined with eloquence will not make an irrational position rational. It is like making a fruit cocktail salad with slices of bitter gourd added to it. It may look good to our eyes, but we will realize the bitterness once we taste it. This worldview puts one into despair if one thinks about it deeply. Are you satisfied with a purely atheistic, naturalistic understanding of the world and humanity? Think about it carefully!

Atheistic understanding forces us to believe we are just a product of an unguided natural process. If the unguided natural process is true, did it know we need eyes to see, ears to hear, mouths to eat, tongues to taste, teeth to chew, noses to smell, legs to walk, and hands to work? Did unguided natural processes know that all these features must be arranged perfectly for specific functions? What if eyes, ears, mouth, tongue, teeth, nose, legs, and hands exchanged positions in a way that does not function? Wouldn't these become purposeless? If we are just a product of unguided natural processes, wouldn't it devalue our lives in the first place?

How can we trust our thoughts if our mind is not designed for the purpose of thinking but was accidentally formed for no particular purpose? Our thoughts are just some chemical fluctuations, then. When we take atheism to its logical conclusion, we are just an accidental byproduct of blind, unguided natural processes that had no goal of becoming what we are now. We are just thick chunks of meat that happened to exist and have evolved for no reason. In the bottom line, we have no intrinsic value, meaning, or purpose. Would you believe this purely naturalistic (atheistic) conclusion that devalues our very existence? Unfortunately, many people hold this view and think it is an intellectual thing to believe so. What then gives objective meaning, value, and purpose to life?

If the idea of cosmic accident does not offer these, we should consider the idea of the creation of the world and humanity by an all-powerful, all-knowing, and all-loving God for a particular purpose. Does God exist? What if God exists and created the universe for a purpose and knows what is happening in the world now? Can we find meaning, value, and purpose in life if God exists? Philosopher William Lane Craig writes,

> If there is no God, then man and the universe are doomed. Like prisoners condemned to death, we await our unavoidable execution. There is no God, and there is no immortality. And what is the consequence of this? It means that life itself is absurd. It means that the life we have is without ultimate significance, value, or purpose.[6]

Craig also writes, "If life ends at the grave, then it makes no difference whether one has lived as a Stalin or as a saint."[7] We can only find the meaning and purpose of life if we see a balance of temporal and eternal significance. At this point, we may ask, what are the reasons and evidence for the existence of God? How do we know it? We are beginning a deeper intellectual journey as we are about to deal with some big questions to discover the objective truth. Before we delve into this big topic of the existence of God, I must build a classical foundation to make you think properly as you continue this philosophical journey. Let us move to the next part- The journey as a philosopher!

❏❏❏

---

[6] William Lane Craig, *Reasonable Faith: Christian Truth and Apologetics*, 3rd ed. (Wheaton, Ill.: Crossway Books, 2008), 72.

[7] Craig, *Reasonable Faith*, 74.

PART TWO

THE JOURNEY
AS A PHILOSOPHER

SECTION 1:

Preparing for a Philosophical Journey

CHAPTER 5

What is Philosophy?

Many people are familiar with the names of some philosophers, such as Socrates, Plato, Aristotle, Augustine, Aquinas, Pascal, Descartes, Spinoza, Locke, Hume, Kant, etc. Sometimes, when I tell people that I majored in philosophy, some people give me a strange look with their eyes wide open, as if they are looking at an uncommon animal for the first time. They ask questions such as, "Who wants to listen to philosophy in the modern day?" "What kind of job can you find with a degree in philosophy?" "How do you make money?" Many think philosophers are boring, useless, jobless, and financially broken. Others have an exalted view of philosophy as if it is specifically for intellectual elites and not something common people can grasp and enjoy. Unfortunately, most people have misconceptions about philosophy in general. Therefore, many people are nervous about philosophy and philosophers. So, what is philosophy? Who are philosophers?

The Definition of Philosophy

We all think hard about life and the world. We all are philosophers. Philosophy is difficult to define perfectly. The definition of philosophy itself is a philosophical question. There is no generally accepted set of necessary and sufficient conditions for determining philosophy.[1] However, different reasonable definitions can be provided. Etymologically, the term philosophy (Gk: *φιλοσοφία; Philosophia*) comes from two Greek words, "*Phileō*" (means "to love") and "*Sophia*" (means "wisdom"). Philosophy is the love of wisdom. A philosopher (Gk: *φιλόσοφος; Philosophos*) is a lover of wisdom. The credit for coining these terms goes to the ancient Greek philosopher Pythagoras.[2] In the ancient period, when many were in pursuit of wealth and fame, a few individuals closely scanned the nature of things in pursuit of truth and wisdom.[3] They were the philosophers.

Philosophy is the love of knowledge, the love of truth, or the quest for truth. Philosophers William Lane Craig and J.P. Moreland define philosophy "as an attempt to think rationally and critically about life's most important questions in order to obtain knowledge and wisdom about them."[4] Professor of Philosophy Garrett DeWeese writes, "…philosophy is something everyone does. Everyone has beliefs about what is real, what is valuable, and how we come to know such things."[5] Philosopher Peter Kreeft writes, "Philosophy is not confined to philosophers… Everyone has a philosophy. As Cicero famously said, you have no choice between having a philosophy and not having one, only between having a good one and having a bad

---

[1]   J. P. Moreland, *Christianity and the Nature of Science* (Grand Rapids, Mich.: Baker Book House, 1989), 43.

[2]   John T. Fitzgerald, "Greco-Roman Philosophical Schools" in Joel B. Green and Lee Martin McDonald (Editors), "*The World of the New Testament: Cultural, Social, and Historical Contexts* (Grand Rapids, Michigan: Baker Academic, 2013), 136.

[3]   Fitzgerald, "Greco-Roman Philosophical Schools," 136.

[4]   J.P. Moreland, and William L. Craig, *Philosophical Foundations for a Christian Worldview*, 2nd ed. (Downers Grove, Ill.: IVP Academic, InterVarsity Press, 2017), 15.

[5]   Garrett J. DeWeese and J.P. Moreland, *Philosophy Made Slightly Less Difficult: A Beginner's Guide to Life's Big Questions, 2nd ed.* (Downers Grove, Illinois: InterVarsity Press, 2021), 2.

one. And not to admit that you have a philosophy at all is to have a bad one."[6] Groothuis writes,

> Philosophy is not a closed club or a secret society…we all can think about ultimate questions…I propose that the requirements for being a philosopher (whether good or bad, major or minor, professional or layperson) are a strong and lived-out inclination to pursue truth through the rigorous use of human reasoning, and to do so with some intellectual facility.[7]

Philosophers Norman Geisler and Paul Feinberg write, "The indispensable ingredient possessed by a good philosopher is an inquiring or questioning mind."[8] There are good philosophies and bad philosophies. C. S. Lewis famously writes, "Good philosophy must exist, if for no other reason, because bad philosophy needs to be answered."[9] You are a philosopher, too, even though you may not be doing it professionally in the academy. Those who are committed to studying philosophy academically are committed to the study of anything or any subject more systematically.

The Functions of Philosophy

Philosophers love asking questions and finding reasonable answers for them. Philosophy stresses thinking or reasoning. The major event in the life of a philosopher is thinking hard about the most significant questions about life and the world. Philosophers are interested in questions about the nature of existence, truth, mind, causation, space, time, rationality, value, perception, rational justification of theories, explanation, freedom, life, purpose, substance, properties, and so on.[10] Professional philosophers use many technical uncommon

---

[6] Peter Kreeft, *The Philosophy of Tolkien: The Worldview Behind "The Lord of the Rings"* (Ignatius Press, 2009), 13.

[7] Groothuis, *Philosophy in Seven Sentences,* 13.

[8] Norman L. Geisler and Paul D. Feinberg, *Introduction to Philosophy: A Christian Perspective* (MI: Baker Books, 2003), 12.

[9] C.S. Lewis, "Learning in War-Time," *The Weight of Glory* (New York: HarperCollins Publishers, 2001), 58.

[10] Moreland, *Christianity and the Nature of Science,* 43.

terminologies for different concepts, which are difficult for common people to understand. I promise that this book is written in lay-level language as it is written for common people.

Moreland and Craig demonstrate philosophy as if it functions as a second-order discipline in that it reflects on the nature of intellectual disciplines.[11] If philosophy is a second-order discipline, then what is first-order discipline? First-order fields include science (biology, physics, chemistry), religion, law, mathematics, language, education, history, theology, medicine, literature, etc. Every field of study involves philosophy. Philosophy, as a second-order discipline, has something to say about every subject that is a first-order discipline. That is why there are second-order branches of philosophy, such as the philosophy of science, the philosophy of religion, the philosophy of mind, the philosophy of language, the philosophy of mathematics, the philosophy of education, the philosophy of law, and the philosophy of history. It is possible to formulate a philosophy of any first-order field. For example, biology is a discipline that studies living organisms, but philosophy, which works as a second-order discipline, studies the first-order discipline, biology. The philosophy of biology doesn't study the organisms themselves, but asks questions about such things as definitions, methodology, the possibility of teleology or design, and so forth. It is impossible to avoid philosophy.

When philosophers examine the first-order discipline, they ask standard questions about it, analyze and criticize its assumptions, clarify its concepts, and integrate that discipline with other fields.[12] Examples: In the realm of biology, philosophers pose inquiries like "What constitutes life, and how does it distinguish itself from non-life?" and "Does an external world exist, and if so, how can one comprehend it?" They also ponder the ethical obligations involved

---

[11]   Moreland and Craig, *Philosophical Foundations for a Christian Worldview*, 15.
[12]   Ibid.

in performing experiments on living organisms. They explore the concept of DNA information and how it can be interpreted, as well as the connection between the biological understanding of humans as Homo sapiens and the theological belief of being made in God's image.[13] Philosophy is foundational for integrating one field of study with other areas.

Many think scientists have the last word on what their discipline tells us about reality. People tend to listen to scientists' words as authoritative. In reality, it can be dangerous when scientists who are not trained in other fields make authoritative false comments as if they know the other field. It is important to understand what scientists are trained in. They are trained in the first-order discipline. For example, they can study bacteria, quarks, chemicals, and gravity. They are not trained in the second-order practice of studying science as a discipline. They are not generally trained to integrate their findings with other disciplines (for example, theology).

After studying the material world, when atheist scientists make authoritative statements such as "God does not exist" or "the natural world is all that exists," they are not only going outside their field of study but also limiting their source of knowledge to scientific knowledge alone. Such statements come from their worldview (naturalism), not from their field of study. Therefore, people should avoid blindly believing in such statements by outspoken atheist scientists. This doesn't mean scientists cannot make such statements; of course, they can. However, scientists should not limit their knowledge to their field of study. (I will explain the different sources of knowledge and limits of science in part 3.) Integrating one source of knowledge with other fields is the domain of philosophy.

---

[13] Ibid.

Philosophy is a unique domain. There is the realm of rational investigation that is independent and more fundamental than science.[14] That realm is a domain of philosophy. Science (or any subject) is built on a philosophical foundation. What is the full form of the highest academic level, Ph.D.? Yes! "Doctor of Philosophy!" In the academy, there is a Doctor of Philosophy in Biology, a Doctor of Philosophy in Theology, a Doctor of Philosophy in History, a Doctor of Philosophy in Psychology, and a Doctor of Philosophy in "Any field of study." There is also a Doctor of Philosophy in Philosophy and a Doctor of Philosophy in Philosophy of Science.

Philosophy is not only more fundamental than science, but as a mode of learning, philosophy also has authority over scientific disciplines or any other discipline. French philosopher Etienne Gilson writes, "Philosophy is the only rational knowledge by which both science and nature can be judged. By reducing philosophy to pure science, man has... abdicated his right to judge nature."[15] In a philosophical pursuit, you may evaluate the reasons, arguments, and evidence for yourself instead of blindly trusting (many people trust) scientists' authoritative statements based on their worldview.

It is also important to note that when the one who is committed to philosophy judges something, they are not always necessarily right. They can still be wrong. We all can be wrong about many things and right about many things. However, a philosopher's (i.e., your) goal is to arrive at a valid and sound conclusion by evaluating reasons, arguments, and evidence from different sources of knowledge. My role is to equip you with some important tools in philosophy so that they can assist our philosophical journey when we go deeper into some topics. What are the different branches of philosophy?

---

[14]   J.P. Moreland, *Scientism and Secularism* (Illinois: Crossway, 2018), 98.
[15]   Etienne Gilson, *The Unity of Philosophical Experience* (New York: Charles Scribner's Sons, 1937), 223.

The Branches of Philosophy

The classical disciplines of philosophy include *logic, metaphysics, epistemology,* and *value theory.*[16] Logic deals with rules of argumentation and reasoning. Metaphysics deals with the study of the nature of reality or being. Epistemology deals with the study of knowledge. Value theory deals with studying values in areas such as ethics and aesthetics. Human beings are rational beings. Thinking is crucial to everything we do. Thus, we should think before we act. If we learn to reason properly, we can always enjoy freedom of thought. Otherwise, tyrants may try to take over our minds.

Generally, philosophy is dedicated to teaching how to think or reason. Philosophers are interested in the big questions of life and the world and finding true answers to them. An honest truth seeker should desire to find a system of objective truth that can sufficiently and satisfactorily deal with the big questions about reality. The goal is not to formulate an opinion but to arrive at the objective truths that are true from every perspective. As we continue this philosophical journey to find the truth, we draw knowledge from various disciplines such as metaphysics, science, religion, ethics, history, theology, and archeology. The job of a professional philosopher is to critically study and compare these topics and, if necessary, integrate them with other disciplines and draw a conclusion using philosophical tools.

A mechanical engineer or a carpenter keeps their appropriate toolkits to do their work. Similarly, philosophers also keep a toolkit that can assist in drawing valid conclusions from their studies of various subjects. In the next chapter, I will introduce a very important tool (the laws of thought) for valid thinking, as it is required to evaluate the reasons, evidence, and arguments to discover the truth. It is a basic tool that is necessary, undeniable, and very easy to

---

[16]   Moreland and Craig, *Philosophical Foundations for a Christian Worldview,* 16.

understand. Learning the foundations for a philosophical journey can be boring sometimes. It is similar to building a house. Often, the foundation work of a building is boring. However, it gets interesting after laying the foundation. Just like that, the philosophical journey gets more interesting as we move forward. I highly encourage you to press on with the foundational chapters, even if these may seem boring initially.

CHAPTER 6

The Philosopher's Toolkit

We need to learn to reason well to discover the truth with greater clarity. In order to know something, basic laws of thought are inevitable. It is the major tool in a philosopher's toolkit. Any knowledge is impossible without it. Logic is the basis of all valid thinking. Everyone uses laws of logic in daily life, even if most people may not have a formal understanding of the laws. Many people think that the ancient philosopher Aristotle invented the laws of logic. Actually, he did not invent the laws of logic; Aristotle first discovered and put them together in written form. Three fundamental, undeniable classical laws of logic govern our reality and thoughts. These laws are the first principles. These are the *Law of Non-contradiction*, the *Law of Identity*, and the *Law of Excluded Middle*. These are universal laws presupposed by everyone. They are self-evident truths that require no defense. I will try to explain them in plain language.

The Law of Non-contradiction (A is not non-A): No statement can be both true and false at the same time and in the same sense.[1] Example 1, Suppose I say, "It is raining outside," and "It is not raining outside." Both statements cannot be true at the same time and in the same sense because they are contradictory. Example 2: Suppose I say

---

[1]   Aristotle, *Metaphysics* 1005 b19-20.

the statements, "Jacob lives in the US" and "Jacob does not live in the US." Both statements are contradictory at the same time and in the same sense. Example 3: If I say, "Kaiser is a dog" and "Kaiser is not a dog." Both statements are contradictory at the same time and in the same sense. To be "a dog" and "not a dog" is contradictory in this context. Both statements cannot be true. If people say both statements are true, they are violating the law of non-contradiction. Knowledge is impossible if we say contradictory statements. The law of non-contradiction is vital for attaining knowledge and discovering the truth.

The Law of Identity (A is A): the law of identity explains that each thing is identical to itself. Everything is itself and not something else. It is applied to all reality. Everything that exists has a specific nature or identity. Example 1: A tiger is a tiger. A tiger is not a mobile phone. Example 2: The black color shirt is a black color shirt. The black color shirt is not a red color shirt. Example 3: The Earth is a planet. The Earth is not a star (once you know the identity of planets and stars). The Earth is not other than itself. Something cannot exist without an identity. Everything exists in a particular way with some characteristics. Since everything that exists has an identity, it is possible to know about something. If things have no identity, it is not possible to attain knowledge.

The Law of Excluded Middle (either A or non-A): Any statement is either true or false, with no middle alternative. A statement is either true or not true. Example 1: the statements, either "It is raining" or "It is not raining." One of the statements must be true in the same sense. There is no middle option. Example 2: Either "Kaiser is a dog" or "Kaiser is not a dog." There is no middle ground. Example 3: "A woman is either pregnant or not pregnant." One of these statements must be true, referring to the same woman. There is no middle position.

These are three foundational classical laws of thought to have meaningful discussions. If someone denies the basic laws of logic, they are using the laws of logic to deny it. Thus, it self-refutes. To deny the law of non-contradiction requires the law of non-contradiction. If the law of non-contradiction is not binding, then what is true can also be not true. This is self-defeating. Persian philosopher Avicenna (980-1037) commented about Aristotelian logic, "Anyone who denies the law of non-contradiction should be beaten and burned until he admits that to be beaten is not the same as not to be beaten, and to be burned is not the same as not to be burned."[2] Avicenna was not in any way literally advocating beating or burning those who deny the law of non-contradiction, but he was making a point to explain the undeniable and binding rules of logic.

As we continue this journey to discover the truth, these first principles are important in critical thinking. Philosophers use logic as the handmaid to discover the truth. In addition to the above three basic laws of logic, there is *the law of rational inference*. It helps us to draw valid conclusions from premises.

The Law of Rational Inference

Inferences can be made by reasoning. From the given series of premises, a conclusion can be drawn. We need to know what is correct and incorrect. Logic is concerned with whether an argument is good or bad, correct or incorrect.[3] The law of rational inference falls into two broad categories. These are *deductive* and *inductive*. In deductive thinking, if the premises are true, the conclusion must be true. Deductive thinking can provide absolute certainty. These come

---

[2]   Avicenna, *La Métaphysique du Shifa*, ed. Georges Anawati (Paris: J. Vrin, 1978-85), vol. 1, commenting on Aristotle, 1.8, 53. 13-15.

[3]   Virginia Klenk, *Understanding Symbolic Logic* 4th Ed. (NJ: Prentice Hall, 2002), 4.

in different forms (Hypothetical syllogism, Categorical syllogism, Disjunctive syllogism). Here are some examples.

Example 1 (Hypothetical Syllogism[4]):

Premise 1: If it rains, then the road is wet.

Premise 2: If the road is wet, then the road is slippery.

Conclusion: Therefore, if it rains, then the road is slippery.

Example 2 (Hypothetical Syllogism- Modus Ponens[5]):

Premise 1: If I don't either exercise or diet, then I will gain weight.

Premise 2: I don't either exercise or diet.

Conclusion: Therefore, I will gain weight.

Example 3 (Categorical Syllogism):

Premise 1: All men are mortal.

Premise 2: Socrates is a man.

Conclusion: Therefore, Socrates is mortal.

Example 4 (Disjunctive Syllogism[6]):

Premise 1: Either Dobermann is a dog or Dobermann is a cat.

Premise 2: Dobermann is not a cat.

Conclusion: Therefore, Dobermann is a dog.

In deductive reasoning, the truth of the premises absolutely guarantees the truth of the conclusion, but in inductive reasoning, we make specific observations, recognize patterns, and draw a conclusion. The argument in induction is tied to probability. The premises in inductive argument are only supposed to provide some degree of support for the conclusion. For instance, the sun has risen every morning throughout history. Therefore, we may infer that the sun will

---

[4]   Hypothetical Syllogism: if p then q; if q then r; therefore, if p then r.
[5]   Modus Ponens: if p then q; p; therefore q.
[6]   Disjunctive Syllogism: p or q; not p; therefore q. Also, p or q; not q; therefore p.

rise tomorrow. In this case, the conclusion is based on observations of the sun from the past. There is a high probability that the sun will rise tomorrow. Still, it is not certain because what if the world ends today? In inductive reasoning, we make an informed or educated guess based on the information or data that we have.

Another example is that most of the flights have landed safely without accident. Therefore, we may conclude that the next flight will almost certainly arrive safely. However, there is no absolute certainty that the next flight will land safely. It may end up in an accident. Another instance is that my neighbor is in the house because he always parks his black car in front of his house when he is in the house. Based on past observation of the pattern, there is a high probability that the neighbor is in the house. But it is not certain because the neighbor may have had his car parked in front of his house but was picked up by a friend. However, there are also instances where a perfect conclusion can be formed. If every instance can be examined, we can draw a perfect conclusion. In the same example, if I examine another piece of evidence, that is, I knocked on my neighbor's door, and he opened it. Based on more evidence, I can conclude that the neighbor is in the house.

Deductive logic provides certainty; inductive logic provides probable conclusions. A strong argument for induction is well supported by evidence. If the evidence for premises is poor, it can only give a probable conclusion. Now, you may think that logic is just common sense. Therefore, there is no need to teach it. It is true that everyone uses rules of logic in daily life because one cannot think without logic.

Example 5:

> Premise 1: If today is a public holiday, then the bank is closed.
>
> Premise 2: Today is a public holiday.
>
> Conclusion: Therefore, the bank is closed.

Example 6.

> Premise 1: John lives in England.
>
> Premise 2: England is in the United Kingdom.
>
> Conclusion: Therefore, John lives in the United Kingdom.

These are common sense conclusions, and everyone knows them. At this point, some people may ask, 'Why did I include a chapter on logic, as it is simply a matter of common sense?' I have some good reasons for adding this section. Although laws of logic are undeniable and are the way our life operates, when it comes to truth quests, many people fail to apply basic logical principles. Especially in a culture that continues to deny the idea of absolute, universal, objective truth, it is very important to use the basic rules of logic to attain true knowledge and wisdom. Most people are unfamiliar with applying these principles more formally in big questions of life and the world. Finding good reasons and evidence to support a premise is part of the problem, along with a lack of knowledge in applying logical principles correctly from those findings. Therefore, a systematic study is important to arrive at the truth. We must eliminate what is false using these logical principles. It is also important to note that logic is a highly technical subdiscipline of philosophy.[7]

It consists of sub-fields: sentential logic, first-order predicate logic, many-valued logic, modal logic, tense logic, etc. There are many rules to follow under all these sub-fields. I am not presenting a more detailed explanation of all these rules. However, I will be using some of the rules (*modus ponens, modus tollens, disjunctive syllogism*, etc.) in some of the chapters. Those are simple to understand for a layperson. Therefore, do not be worried about the terminologies now. We need the rules of logic to draw valid and sound conclusions since our goal

---

[7]   Moreland, and Craig, *Philosophical Foundations for a Christian Worldview*, 29.

is to discover the objective truth. A glimpse of more interesting and challenging examples of using rules of inference are below.

Example 1:

Premise 1: Either the universe has always existed, or the universe had a beginning.

Premise 2: The universe has not always existed.

Conclusion: Therefore, the universe had a beginning.

Example 2:

Premise 1: Everything that begins to exist must have a cause.

Premise 2: The universe began to exist.

Conclusion: Therefore, the universe must have a cause.

The logical validity of the premises is not the only thing required to arrive at the truth. The argument must be valid and sound. In examples 1 and 2, the weight of the argument lies on premise 2, as it is necessary to show that the universe had a beginning. I did not present the evidence to support premise 2 here. I gave these examples to give a glimpse of the kind of topics and arguments we will be dealing with in the coming chapters, where we will draw valid and sound conclusions by providing solid reasons and evidence. Now we have the "philosophers toolkit" ready. Let's move forward and use the tools where these are necessary. In the next chapter, we will look at the nature of truth.

CHAPTER 7

The Nature of Truth

To discover a system of objective truth, we need to understand the nature of truth. In this chapter, I aim to help you understand the nature (definition) of truth. We need an adequate view of truth as we continue this journey. People are often confused about what is true and what is not true. I will also try to remove some confusion surrounding the nature of truth. What is truth?

Some people understand the truth in terms of what works. This is called the pragmatic theory of truth. According to this view, if an action has the ability to bring beneficial results, it is considered true. However, this is not how truth is understood in everyday life. For example, robbing a bank works for the burglars to make money. But it is not a truthful action. Cheating someone to get a job offer might work for someone, but it is not a true action. Something that works does not always make it true. But a true system of truth must work or be livable. Pragmatism is an inadequate view of truth.

Some people understand the truth in terms of internal coherence or consistency, which means if a belief or statement within a system does not logically contradict other statements or beliefs, it is considered true. This is called the coherence theory of truth. This has problems. For example, fiction can be internally consistent, but it does not mean it is true. Fiction is not reality. A worldview may be internally consistent, but it could still be false. An internally consistent worldview may be in sharp contradiction with another internally consistent worldview. Both opposing internally consistent worldviews cannot be true at the same time logically. Consistency alone does not make something true. It could still be false. A system of objective truth must be internally consistent, given the law of non-contradiction. If the beliefs within a system contradict one another, it is necessarily false. Testing coherence can be used as a negative test for truth. Coherence theory is an inadequate view of truth. There are many other theories of truth, but I do not want to go into all the details, because it is not necessary here. What is an adequate view of truth, then?

The adequate view of truth is the correspondence theory of truth. According to the correspondence view, truth is found in correspondence. Truth corresponds to the object of the referent.[1] Truth corresponds to facts. Something is true if it corresponds to (or matches up with) reality. Truth is telling the way it is in reality. If what you say corresponds to how the world actually is, it is true. If it does not correspond, then it is false. Aristotle defines correspondence theory as, "To say of what is that it is not, or of what is not that it is, is false, while to say of what is that it is, and of what is not that it is not, is true."[2] In simple terms, if you say something (for example, it is snowing) and if it corresponds to reality (i.e., it is actually snowing), then it is true. If you say something (for example, it is snowing) and it does not correspond to reality (i.e., it is not snowing), then that statement is false. The reality must correspond to what is said. The truth claims depend on correspondence.

---

[1]   Norman Geisler, *Systematic Theology in One Volume* (Minnesota: Bethany House, 2011), 81-84.

[2]   Aristotle, *Metaphysics* 1011b25.

Many years ago, when I was working as a Revenue Protection Inspector for a British Railways company, our team sometimes did some special operations to prosecute those who violated rail ticketing policies and committed fraudulent activities. According to the railway ticketing policy, the passengers must purchase valid rail tickets before they board the train unless a station does not have a ticket purchase facility provided. Those who board the train from stations that have no facility are allowed to purchase the ticket on board or when they arrive at their destination. In the state of Wales, there are many stations that have no facilities for ticket purchase. Some people who know this try to do some intentional tricks to avoid paying for tickets.

For illustration, imagine three stations--Station A, Station B, and Station Z. The station B does not have ticket purchase facility. Suppose a man got on the train from Station Z without a ticket, although he had the facility to purchase a ticket at Station Z. He arrived at Station A, which was a long journey from Station Z. Station A is gated, and he cannot get out of the station without his ticket. He goes to the ticket seller and claims a short fare ticket from Station B, saying that he got on the train from Station B. Generally, the ticker seller issues a ticket from Station B by trusting that person's word. But on that specific day of ticket inspection, we blocked Station B and provided a facility to purchase a ticket at Station B itself. No one can get on the train from Station B on that specific day without a ticket. If a person arrives at Station A and tries to purchase a ticket by claiming that he got on the train from Station B, we know that it is not true. We ask more questions, and finally, he will admit that he was lying. Then, we prosecute such offenders according to the Police and Criminal Evidence Act 1984. In this instance, the reasons he gave do not correspond to reality. The facts did not support his false claims. The facts suggest that he was lying.

Facts play the role in determining the truth or falsity of a statement or belief. As Groothuis writes, "for a statement to be true, there must be a *truth-maker* that determines its truth. A statement is never true simply because someone thinks it or utters it. We may be entitled to our own opinions, but we are not entitled to our own facts. Believing a statement is one thing; that statement being true is another."[3] There could be no such thing as truth or falsity without correspondence. Geisler puts it, "In order to know that something is true as opposed to knowing that something is false, there must be a real difference between things and the statements about the things. But this real difference between thought and things is precisely what is entailed in a correspondence view of truth."[4] The truth claims are dependent on the correspondence. The moment when we use the word "is" in a claim, it links the claim to the existence of what we claim.[5] The adequate view of truth is correspondence. This is the objective truth.

It's important to base our beliefs on facts rather than personal (subjective) feelings, false assumptions, or hearsay. This is especially important in today's world, where misinformation and fake news can spread quickly and cause harm. Let us now turn to the relativistic approach to truth.

The Incoherence of Relativism

Today, many people want to avoid accepting the idea of absolute, objective, and universal truth. Instead, they believe all truths are relative by saying, "It might be true for you, but not for me." This approach is called relativism. Relativists hold that there is no such thing as absolute truth, and all truth is specific to its place, culture,

---

[3]   Groothuis, *Christian Apologetics,* 124.
[4]   Geisler, *Systematic Theology in One Volume, 85.*
[5]   This is taken from a lecture slide by one of my philosophy professors, Dr. Bernard James Mauser.

and time. In this view, truth is relative to what an individual believes or thinks, or prefers (in other words, subjective truth). The truth and falsity depend entirely on a person. Let's think about a few examples. Can you identify objective truths (true for everyone) and subjective truths (personal opinion, desires, thoughts, etc.) from this list?

1. $E = MC^2$
2. Washington D.C. is the capital of the United States of America.
3. A pet elephant is better than a pet cat.
4. Cheating is morally wrong.
5. A minimalist lifestyle is the best.
6. Indian food is the best food in the world.
7. The tiger is the most beautiful animal.
8. Narendra Modi was the prime minister of India in 2023.
9. $2+2 = 4$
10. Philosophy is the coolest major.

Here are the answers. In this list, #1, #2, #4, #8, and #9 are objective truths. They are facts. They are verifiable. They are true for everyone. Historical facts, scientific facts, mathematical facts, and logical facts are clear examples of objective truths. On the other side, #3, #5, #6, #7, and #10 are subjective truths. These are personal opinions. It can vary greatly from individual to individual. Did you get the answers right? (You will get extra points if you truly believe opinion #3.)

Our journey is to discover the absolute truth which is universally true for everyone. Everybody believes in absolute truth in real life, even if they say they don't believe in absolute truth. If one declares, "There is no absolute truth," I can ask, "Is it absolutely true that there is no absolute truth?" If the answer is "yes," that person agrees that absolute truth exists because the assertion "there is no absolute truth" itself is an absolute truth statement. Such a claim is a contradiction and plain absurdity. Those who say "There is no objective truth" are making an objective truth claim without realizing it. There are objections to the idea of absolute, objective, universal truth, which come in different forms and can sometimes confuse people instantly.

Many people believe all truth is relative. However, relativism is self-defeating when we apply the claim to itself. If one says, "All truth is relative," I can respond by saying, "That statement itself is not a relative truth; the statement, 'all truth is relative,' is an absolute truth claim." Do you see the self-defeating nature of relativism? Relativism is not only self-defeating but also has many consequences. If all truth is relative, then no book can be truer than any other book. People can have their own reality and define reality in whatever way they want. Then, words cannot have objective meaning. For example, if one sees a bottle labeled 'poison,' does anyone ever take it as "it is true for you, but not for me?"

Communication becomes impossible if everybody defines their own reality. One cannot make objective historical claims. For example, one cannot even say that India became an independent nation on August 15, 1947. A relativist can disagree with the historical truth that the Taj Mahal was built by the Mughal emperor Shah Jahan. Instead, one can say the Taj Mahal was built by a group of red ants with the help of many fishes in the sea and birds in the sky. Isn't this absurd? If relativism is true, one cannot make objective moral statements such as "torturing babies for fun is wrong," "murder is wrong," "Cheating is vice," etc. We can think of other instances: No country ever celebrated an athlete winning a game by cheating. '1+1 =2' is universally true for everyone in every culture.

Some agnostics or skeptics claim, 'You can't know anything.' Then I can ask, 'How do you know that is true?' or 'How do you know "you can't know anything?"' If the statement is true, then that person at least knows that 'you can't know anything,' which defeats itself. Some people say, 'You should not judge me.' The statement collapses itself as it is a statement of judgment. These self-refuting statements are similar to saying, 'I can't write a word in English.'

Truth is absolute. Truth corresponds to the object of reference. For example, I (Aby) am currently in the USA while writing this book. It is a fact that I am not somewhere else. Even if you are now in India or South Africa, it is also true for you that Aby is in the USA when referring to Aby. It is a false claim if someone says Aby is currently in the UK when he is in the USA. Another example: Suppose Aby loves a particular pizza. There are others who do not love it. When referring to Aby, it is absolutely true he loves that particular pizza. It is absolutely true for others who do not love that particular pizza that Aby loves a particular pizza as it is referring to Aby.

Although the truth is absolute, sometimes our understanding may not be absolute. Since we are finite creatures, we continue to grow in our understanding. However, the truth is real and knowable. It is self-defeating to claim that we cannot know the truth. Now, it is clear that everyone believes in absolute, objective, and universal truth. We should not fall into the absurd and incoherent idea of relativism. Many people lean more towards a relativistic approach to truth. But it is important to remove the confusion because truth matters.

The Nature of Truth as Narrow and Exclusive

Many people claim absolutists are narrow-minded because they exclude all other views and regard them as false. Therefore, many believe relativism seems to be a humble approach to showing respect to people of all beliefs. While respecting people regardless of their views is important, it does not necessarily mean what they believe is true. It is important to understand that anything that is opposite to truth must necessarily be false. For example, the statement "it is raining" is true if it corresponds to reality. Then its opposite, "it is not raining," must be false. It cannot be raining and not raining at the same time in the same sense. It violates the law of non-contradiction. The opposite of truth must necessarily be false. Truth excludes its opposing claims. Truth is exclusive and narrow.

Another example: the correct answer for 1+2+3 is 6. The answer is not 1, 2, 3, 4, 5, 7, 8, or any other number. The true answer is 6, which is narrow. The true answer excludes all wrong answers. That is the nature of truth. Even if this principle is applied in any other field, we can see the nature of truth as narrow. Truth excludes all opposing views whether one likes it or not. A truth seeker should accept the nature of reality to discover the truth. Another example: when a medical doctor gives an accurate description of someone's bad health condition, would you say the doctor is narrow-minded? No! We need an absolutely true medical report so that proper medical treatment can be performed. A false medical report may satisfy for that moment, but it leads one to destruction. Accusing absolutists as narrow-minded is not an intellectually virtuous thing to do. Such an accusation is based on ignorance of the nature of truth.

As we continue this journey, we should remember the laws of logic and the nature of truth as *correspondence, absolute, exclusive, and narrow*. We want a system of objective truth, not a mere opinion formulated based on someone's subjective feelings. Objective truth statements are statements about objects that exist outside of personal opinions. If a statement is true, it is true universally for everyone whether or not one likes it, knows it, or believes it. It should be testable. It should be based on reason and facts. For example, if God exists, it is true for everyone, whether or not one accepts, likes, knows, or believes that fact. Truth excludes all opposing views. Truth is narrow and absolute.

We will now shift our gear to the most important questions about God: Does God exist? What are the evidence and reasons for God's existence? Does one require religious texts to justify the existence of God? Is it even possible to know God? What do philosophers have to say about this topic since they study individual disciplines and have authority over every other subject? Can a philosopher rationally demonstrate the existence of God? A philosopher should give the best reasons for God or against God by studying various disciplines. Some of the best thinkers have been defending various arguments for and against God's existence for many centuries. There are several solid and undeniable arguments for the existence of God. In the next section, I will briefly present a few arguments for God's existence. You may then evaluate the reasons for yourselves. Let us turn to this weighty topic: the existence of God.

SECTION 2:

The God of Philosophy:
The Existence of God

CHAPTER 8

The Existence of God Part 1: Cosmological Arguments

In human history, there is no other topic that is greater than the topic of the existence of God. In the book, *The Great Ideas: A Syntopicon of Great Books of the Western World*, Editor in Chief Mortimer J Adler wrote, "More consequences for thought and action follow from the affirmation or denial of God than from answering any other basic question in life."[1] If God doesn't exist, there is no reason for talking about God and special revelation. If God exists, nothing else matters more than God. What does nature teach us about the existence of God? Can one find good reasons for the existence of God without appealing to sacred scriptures? Yes! Natural Theology enables us to successfully argue for the existence of God.

The proponents of natural theology use scientific and philosophical arguments. We will be looking at a few arguments from natural theology in the current section. In this chapter, I will present two cosmological arguments for the existence of God: the Kalam Cosmological Argument and the Leibnizian Cosmological Argument. In the following chapters, I will give a few more

---

[1] Adler, Mortimer, Ed. in Chief. *The Great Ideas: A Syntopicon of Great Books of the Western World*. Vol. 2 (Chicago: Benton/Encyclopeadia Brittanica, 1952), 543.

arguments to strengthen the case for God's existence. I do not intend to explain all these arguments comprehensively. My goal is to give a brief explanation that can help you study further if you are interested in exploring deeper. My arguments should be sufficient for one to believe in God through reason and evidence.

The Kalam Cosmological Argument

The Kalam Cosmological Argument is an argument developed primarily by Arabic philosophers in the Middle Ages.[2] In recent decades, a growing number of thinkers have defended this reasoning for the existence of God and brought clarity to this argument through academic works and public debates. Some of them are Stuart Hackett, Ed L. Miller, William Lane Craig, J. P. Moreland, Douglas Groothuis, etc.[3] This is what the Kalam cosmological argument looks like:

Premise 1: Everything that begins to exist must have a cause (separate from itself.)

Premise 2: The universe began to exist.

Premise 3: Therefore, the universe must have a cause (separate from itself.)

This is a deductive argument. If premises one and two are true, then premise three (the conclusion) must follow necessarily. Let's find out if the first two premises are true or not.

Premise 1: Something cannot come from nothing without a cause unless someone takes a blind leap of faith that nothingness has causal properties. But that does not make sense. If something does not exist, it does not exist; it has no causal properties. That is the bottom line. Premise 1 is a self-evident truth that does not require

---

[2]   William Lane Craig, "Historical Statements of the Kalam Cosmological Argument," in *The Kalam Cosmological Argument* (Oregon: Wipf & Stock, 2000).

[3]   Groothuis, *Christian Apologetics*, 214.

further explanation. It is important to note that many people make an elementary mistake by avoiding the term 'begins' from premise 1. The term 'begins' is crucial because only whatever begins to exist requires a cause. That which is eternal does not require a cause because there is no beginning and end to something eternal. And we will see that only God is eternal.

Premise 2: The major strength of the overall argument rests on this premise. 'The universe began to exist' has modern scientific and philosophical reasons to support it. I will present the scientific evidence before the philosophical reasons.

The Scientific Evidence for the
Finite Beginning of the Universe

For many centuries, great thinkers in the past wondered whether the universe had a beginning. Those who believed that 'the universe is all that exists' denied an absolute beginning. They held that the physical universe has no beginning or end (in other words, 'eternal') and is self-existent. Therefore, there was no need for a Creator explanation. Only if the universe had a finite beginning does it require a causal explanation outside of the universe. While this view was in place, modern science made an unexpected discovery that the universe had an absolute beginning. Astronomer Robert Jastrow wrote, "This is an exceedingly strange development, unexpected by all but the theologians."[4] If the universe began to exist a finite time ago, it lends support to creation 'out of nothing.'

Some of the modern scientific evidence that supports the finite beginning of the universe are The Big Bang Cosmology, The Second Law of Thermodynamics, Einstein's Theory of General Relativity, Cosmic Microwave Background (CMB) Radiation discovery, many

---

[4]   Robert Jastrow, *God and the Astronomers* (New York: Norton, 1978), 116.

space-time theorems of General Relativity, the Hawking-Penrose singularity theorem, BVG theorem, etc. (Please note: There are overlaps in some of these theories). I will briefly explain the Big Bang Cosmology and the Thermodynamic properties of the Universe to show that the universe had a beginning.

(1) The Big Bang Cosmology

Prior to the 1920s, scientists assumed that the universe was stationary and eternal.[5] In 1917, Einstein's general theory of relativity assumed an eternal universe that exits in a steady state without expansion. Russian mathematician Alexander Friedmann noticed an elementary mistake in Einstein's calculation, and when corrected, the theory predicted an expanding universe.[6] In 1927, a Belgian priest and astronomer, Georges Lemaitre, also suggested a beginning to space-time by using Einstein's theory independently of Friedmann.[7]

In 1929, astronomer Edwin Hubble discovered a phenomenon known as the redshift in the light coming from galaxies, indicating that the universe is expanding.[8] Like dots on the surface of an inflating balloon, the galaxies are moving away from each other. If you reverse the process by deflating the balloon, it will return to its original point. Just like that, if you reverse the current expanding universe (in imagination), it will bring you back to a singular point: the beginning of space, time, matter, and energy.[9] It cannot go back forever but to that finite point of beginning. Physicists John Barrow and Frank Tipler write, "At this singularity, space and time came into existence; literally nothing existed before the singularity, so, if

---

[5]   Craig, *Reasonable Faith*, 125.

[6]   Groothuis, *Christian Apologetics*, 224.

[7]   Ibid.

[8]   Moreland, *Christianity and the Nature of Science*, 33.

[9]   Moreland, *Scientism and Secularism*, 138.

the Universe originated in such a singularity, we would truly have a creation *ex nihilo*."[10] This discovery that the universe had a beginning was eventually jokingly called "the Big Bang" by the cosmologist Sir Fred Hoyle.[11] The great theoretical physicist Stephen Hawking said that "almost everyone now believes that the universe, and time itself, had a beginning at the Big Bang."[12] The Big Bang theory is not an explanation of how everything began to exist in the first place.[13] It is a label that says there was a beginning. Hawking never believed in God personally (just like all atheist scientists), but he knew the philosophical implication of the need for a Creator according to the Big Bang cosmology. Hawking initially challenged by writing,

> So long as the universe had a beginning that was a singularity, one could suppose that it was created by an outside agency. But if the universe is really self-contained, having no boundary or edge, it would be neither created nor destroyed. It would simply be. What place, then, for a creator.[14]

Hawking's challenge did not grow roots. Physicist Alexander Vilenkin writes, "With the proof now in place, cosmologists can no longer hide behind the possibility of a past eternal universe. There is no escape, they have to face the problem of a cosmic beginning."[15] The Big Bang cosmology has an undeniable philosophical implication that there must be a cause behind that event. Another piece of evidence comes from the second law of thermodynamics.

(2) The Thermodynamic Properties of the Universe

Thermodynamics is a science that deals with energy. A concept

---

[10] John Barrow and Frank Tipler, *The Anthropic Cosmological Principle* (Oxford: Oxford University Press, 1986), 442.

[11] Lennox, *Can Science Explain Everything?* 71.

[12] Stephen Hawking and Roger Penrose, *The Nature of Space and Time*, The Isaac Newton Institute Series of Lectures (Princeton, N.J.: Princeton University Press, 1996), 20.

[13] Lennox, *Can Science Explain Everything?* 71.

[14] Stephen Hawking, *The Theory of Everything* (California: New Millennium, 2002), 126.

[15] Alexander Vilenkin, *Many Worlds in One* (New York: Hill & Wang, 2006), 176.

known as entropy is involved in the second law of thermodynamics.[16] Entropy is understood in terms of energy, disorder, or information. The second law states that there is an increase in the entropy of the universe. The energy is being uniformly distributed, and the energy available is decreasing. Moreland puts it, "The universe is moving irreversibly towards a state of maximum disorder and minimum energy."[17] The second law of thermodynamics states that if the universe is infinitely old, all the useful energy would have already been used up. This points out that the universe must be finite in duration. As theoretical physicist Paul Davies puts it, "The sun and stars cannot keep burning forever: sooner or later they will run out of fuel and die."[18] Davies also writes,

> If the universe has a finite stock of order and is changing irreversibly towards disorder – ultimately to thermodynamic equilibrium–two very deep inferences follow immediately. The first is that the universe will eventually die, wallowing, as it were, in its own entropy. This is known among physicists as the 'heat death' of the universe. The second is that the universe cannot have existed forever, otherwise, it would have reached its equilibrium end state an infinite time ago. Conclusion: the universe did not always exist.[19]

Additionally, the scientific world holds that the universe has an age of approx. 13.73 billion years.[20] If it has an age, it is not eternal by definition. It should have a starting point. From these scientific arguments, we can conclude that the universe had a beginning in the finite past. For detailed scientific knowledge, I recommend the books by astrophysicist Hugh Ross.[21]

---

[16]   Moreland, *Christianity and the Nature of Science*, 34.

[17]   Ibid.

[18]   Paul Davies, "The Big Bang—and Before," a paper presented at the *Thomas Aquinas College Lecture Series*, Thomas Aquinas College, Santa Paula, Calif., March 2002.

[19]   Paul Davies, *God and the New Physics* (United Kingdom: Simon & Schuster, 1984), 11.

[20]   Hugh Ross, *Why the Universe Is the Way It Is* (Grand Rapids: Baker, 2008), 44.

[21]   Ross, *Why the Universe Is the Way It Is* and Hugh Ross, *The Creator and The Cosmos: How the Latest Scientific Discoveries Reveal God*, fourth ed, (CA: RTB Press, 2018).

The Philosophical Evidence
for the Finite Beginning of the Universe

Craig put forth two philosophical arguments[22] to support premise 2. One, the impossibility of an actually infinite number of things. Two, the impossibility of forming an actually infinite collection of things by adding one member after another. Readers interested in more details of these philosophical reasonings should see the comprehensive work by Craig. Here is a simple philosophical illustration showing that there were only finite moments before today:[23]

1. An infinite (endless) number of moments/days cannot be crossed. An infinite number of moments/days has no end. It is impossible for an actual infinite to exist in the actual world. Infinity is conceivable theoretically in mathematics but not in the actual world.

2. If there were infinite moments/days before today, then today would never have come. (Something infinite has no end. Today is the end of all previous moments/days. So, an infinite number of moments/days could not have occurred before today.)

3. But today (or the present) has arrived.

4. Hence, there were only finite moments/days before today (i.e., the beginning of time).

Philosophers Groothuis and Andrew Shepardson explain the idea of the 'actual infinite' in an easily understandable way using an illustration.

---

22   Craig, *Reasonable Faith*, 116.
23   Geisler, *Systematic Theology in One Volume*, 23.

> Consider a library with an actually infinite number of books. Half of the books are blue, and the other half are red. If a library had one million books, there would be no problem. Five hundred thousand would be red and five hundred thousand would be blue. But if the holdings of the library were actually infinite, the number of blue books would be actually infinite and the number of red books would be actually infinite. That means that each half of the holdings of the library ends up being equal to its entire holdings, which is impossible, since a whole is greater than the sum of its parts.[24]

Groothuis and Shepardson also give another illustration to show that an actual infinite cannot be crossed in time:

> If dinner is served at 6:00 p.m. and it is now 12:00 p.m., there are six hours until dinner… But if you are told dinner will be served an actually infinite number of hours from 12:00, you will starve to death because that moment never arrives.[25]

The philosophical reasons alone are sufficient to support premise 2. The universe is not infinitely old. It had a finite beginning.

Premise 3: If premises 1 and 2 in the Kalam Cosmological Argument are true, premise 3 (the conclusion) will follow necessarily. The universe must have a cause separate from itself because the universe cannot cause itself into existence. Since the physical universe (time, space, matter, energy) is what we are trying to explain, and it began to exist, it cannot explain itself. Therefore, the cause of the origin of the universe must transcend the physical universe. When there is no material cause (because there is no matter or space), the only kind of cause available must be a rational agent. The cause of the physical universe must be an uncaused, beginningless, timeless, spaceless, changeless, immaterial, enormously powerful, intelligent, and personal being. Groothuis puts it, "if natural law indicates a beginning of the universe and will not take us beyond the beginning of the universe, then that beginning should be explained on other, non-natural grounds."[26] The cause must therefore be supernatural. A 'supernatural cause' (God) explanation is the best fit.

---

[24] Douglas Groothuis and Andrew I. Shepardson, *The Knowledge of God in the World and Word: An Introduction to Classical Apologetics* (Michigan: Zondervan, 2022), 87.

[25] Groothuis and Shepardson, *The Knowledge of God in the World and Word*, 87-88.

[26] Groothuis, *Christian Apologetics*, 226.

Some people do not like to call this causal agent "God." Instead, they give some other names; for example, once, an atheist scientist called that agent "Supercomputer" because he did not want to give credit to God. But they give God-like attributes to whatever label they give to that agent. The cause of the universe cannot be impersonal either. An impersonal principle cannot choose to create. If the cause of the universe is impersonal, it would simply be a cause-and-effect relationship. If that is the case, the universe has to be eternal. Since the universe is not eternal, the cause of the universe cannot be impersonal.[27] The cause of the universe must be personal.

From all the evidence we have, it is impossible to deny the existence of a causal agent (in other words, God). If one cannot accept God as the causal agent, one should have a blind leap of faith in nothingness with causal properties, which is not something that a properly thinking person does. The Kalam Cosmological Argument is only one among the many arguments for the existence of God. Some people find it difficult to believe in the eternality of God but do not have a problem holding an eternal universe.

Something Must Exist Eternally

Something must exist eternally, and it must be self-existent. It must not require a causal agent. If the universe is eternal and self-existent, then, that is the end of the conversation. No more explanation is needed. If the universe is not eternal and self-existent, something outside of the universe must exist eternally, and it must be self-existent. We have seen that the universe had a finite beginning. Therefore, an outside agent must necessarily exist. This agent must be God because only God fits that category with properties to bring

---

[27]   Ibid, 235.

something into existence out of nothing. If I put it into a logical syllogism (*Disjunctive Syllogism*):[28]

Premise 1: Either the universe is eternal and self-existent, or God is eternal and self-existent.

Premise 2: The universe is not eternal and self-existent (Scientific and Philosophical support.)

Premise 3: Therefore, God is eternal and self-existent.

From the above syllogism, it is clear that God is eternal and self-existent. God does not require further explanation because something's (God's) eternal existence is necessary. Those who previously found it easy to attribute eternality to the universe should push one step backward based on the evidence that the universe is finite. Then they can attribute the eternality to the agent (God), who is self-existent and requires no more explanation.

If I frame one more philosophical syllogism for greater clarity, there are two options to choose from. Either the universe is eternal and self-existent, or God caused the universe into existence. If the universe is eternal and self-existent, then God's existence is not necessary for explanation. But if the universe is not eternal, there must exist an eternal being or causal agent (God) who can bring the universe into existence. Although few hold this, a third option we can think of is the possibility that the universe is eternal but eternally dependent on God's existence. From scientific and philosophical points of view, we know that the universe is not eternal but had a finite beginning. Therefore, I am only laying two options to choose from. If I put the options into syllogism.

---

[28]   Rule of inference: Disjunctive Syllogism: p or q, not p, therefore, q.

Premise 1: Either the universe is eternal and self-existent, or God caused the universe to come into existence.

Premise 2: The universe is not eternal and self-existent (Scientific and Philosophical support.)

Premise 3: Therefore, God caused the universe to come into existence.

The only option left is to accept the existence of an eternal being/agent who transcends the space-time dimension. Therefore, an eternal God must exist as the causal agent of the universe. Now, let's turn to the Leibnizian Cosmological Argument.

Leibnizian Cosmological Argument

'Why is there something rather than nothing?'[29] This is a question that German philosopher and mathematician Gottfried Leibniz first posed concerning the existence of the universe. A simpler rendering of the question would be, 'Why is there a universe instead of no universe at all?' This is a simple yet powerful question you may want to pose and think about for some time. Perhaps now you are thinking, "Hmm! This is an interesting question that I have never seriously thought about before." Well, it is not too late to think about it; now is the right time as you are on a philosophical journey.

It is important to note that the universe does not necessarily have to exist. There could have been nothing at all. If so, we would not even be here to ask such a deep question. However, it is self-evident that the universe exists. Moreover, we, the thinking beings exist on the planet Earth within this vast universe to posit such a question. We do not necessarily have to exist, either. The universe exists contingently. Things that exist contingently are caused to exist by something else that exists necessarily. Contingent things exist only

---

[29]   G.W.F. von Leibniz, "Principles of Nature and Grace," in *Leibniz Selections*, ed. Philip P. Wiener (New York: Charles Scribner's, 1951), 527.

because something else caused them to exist. As the universe itself does not necessarily have to exist, according to Leibniz's famous 'Principle of Sufficient Reason,' there must be a necessary, sufficient reason for the existence of the universe in the first place because 'nothing happens without a sufficient reason.'[30]

Since the sufficient reason for the existence of this contingent physical reality (i.e., the universe) is what we need, a higher being beyond the physical world is necessary. Leibniz attributed God as the necessary, sufficient reason because the universe cannot be the reason for its own existence. The universe is contingent; the universe is not necessary. God's existence is necessary to bring the contingent universe into existence. This is the Leibnizian cosmological argument for the existence of God. God's existence requires no explanation because God is not contingent. Only the contingent things require explanation. God is eternal and self-existent and requires no outside causal agent. God cannot not exist.

The goal of the Leibnizian argument was not to examine whether the universe had a finite beginning or to explain the first cause. But it was just looking for a necessary, sufficient reason for the existence of the universe. For a more comprehensive explanation of the Leibnizian cosmological argument, I recommend the work of philosophers William Lane Craig and Douglas Groothuis.[31]

Both the Leibnizian and the Kalam Cosmological arguments build a strong case for the existence of God, who brought the universe into existence out of nothing a finite time ago. The fact that the universe had a finite beginning was supported by philosophical and scientific reasons. Since the universe began to exist, which requires a causal agent outside of the universe, God's existence is necessary.

---

[30]   Leibniz, "Principles of Nature and Grace," 527.
[31]   Craig, *Reasonable Faith*, 93. Douglas Groothuis, *Christian Apologetics: A Comprehensive Case for Biblical Faith*, 2nd ed. (Downers Grove: IVP Academic, 2022), Chapter 11.

This explanation also sufficiently answers the question raised by Leibniz. The evidence for the existence of God rests on several lines of arguments. As we move forward, we will look into a few more arguments for the existence of God that can make the overall case more robust. Next, we will look into the Cosmic fine-tuning argument.

CHAPTER 9

The Existence of God Part 2:
Cosmic Fine-Tuning Argument

We live in a vast universe. Every human being appreciates the splendor of nature. It is beautiful to gaze at the night sky, experiencing a sense of marvel and astonishment, seeing the stars, the moon, the planets, and all other visible objects moving through the solar system. People travel worldwide to experience nature's wonder, even though most do not know how nature functions. On the other hand, scientists who study the cosmos aim "to unveil the inner workings of nature, the rules, and properties."[1] Consequently, the results continue to give mind-blowing data of fine-tuning in the universe's operation in order for advanced life to be possible on Earth, as if the universe is placed on a razor edge for that possibility of life. If there is a slight change in the physical properties of the universe, advanced life would not be possible on planet Earth. In his book, *A Brief History of Time*, Hawking stated,

> The laws of science, as we know them at present, contain many fundamental numbers, like the size of the electric charge of the electron and the ratio of the masses of the proton and the electron. … The remarkable fact is that the values of these numbers seem to have been very finely adjusted to make possible the development of life.[2]

---

[1]   Geraint F. Lewis and Luke A. Barnes, *A Fortunate Universe: Life in a Finely-Tuned Cosmos* (Cambridge: Cambridge University Press, 2017), 1.

[2]   Stephen Hawking, *A Brief History of Time* (NY: Random House, 1998), 129.

It is important to note that when physicists use the term 'fine-tuning,' they do not mean whether a fine-tuner exists or not. 'Fine-tuning' is a metaphor which is a technical term in physics that refers to the contrast between a wide range of possibilities and a narrow range of a particular outcome or phenomenon.[3] Craig defines "fine-tuning" as follows:

> By "fine-tuning," one means that a small deviation from the actual values of the constants and quantities in question renders the universe life-prohibiting or, alternatively, that the range of life-permitting values is extremely narrow in comparison with the range of assumable values.[4]

According to the *anthropic principle*, the universe appears fine-tuned for the existence of human life. Astronomy and physics show that the emergence of humans and human civilization requires physical constants, laws, and properties in a narrow range. This razor-edge fine-tuning applies to the entire universe and the local features of the galaxy, the solar system, and the planet Earth. Many scientists have pondered this question, 'Is there life outside the planet Earth?' This question encouraged many scientists to search for extraterrestrial planets. The exoplanet research has contributed to our understanding of the nature and design of our solar system's planets. It became more evident that our solar system is incredibly fine-tuned, so advanced life is possible on Earth. It is also clear that no other planets in the solar system can support advanced life.

In his book, *How to Find a Habitable Planet,* NASA's Geoscientist James Kasting points out that another habitable planet has not yet been discovered in 20 years of search.[5] Kasting demonstrates the advanced methodologies used to discover another habitable planet from his experience working with NASA on this particular mission.

---

[3]   Lewis and Barnes, *A Fortunate Universe, 04.*

[4]   Craig, *Reasonable Faith,* 58.

[5]   James F. Kasting, *How to Find a Habitable Planet.* (Princeton, NJ; Woodstock: Princeton University Press, 2012).

Although no other habitable planet has been discovered, it does not necessarily mean scientists will not find one in the future. Even if life is found on other planets, that would not dilute the power of the fine-tuning argument, since the cosmos would have to be fine-tuned for that life to exist as well. However, the more scientists study the universe, the more evident it becomes that it will be less likely to find one. Ross states, "the probability for finding a planet or rock anywhere in the universe with the capacity to support long-lasting microbial physical life, independent of divine miraculous intervention, has shrunk from 10^{-53} to 10^{-144} to 10^{-556}."[6] Ross puts,

> the probability of finding, without divine intervention, a single planet capable of supporting physical life is much less than one in a quadrillion, quadrillion quadrillion, quadrillion, quadrillion, quadrillion, quadrillion quadrillion, quadrillion, quadrillion, quadrillion, quadrillion quadrillion, quadrillion, quadrillion, quadrillion, quadrillion quadrillion, quadrillion, quadrillion, quadrillion, quadrillion quadrillion, quadrillion, quadrillion, quadrillion, quadrillion quadrillion quadrillion, quadrillion, quadrillion, quadrillion, quadrillion quadrillion, quadrillion, quadrillion, quadrillion, quadrillion quadrillion, quadrillion, quadrillion, quadrillion, quadrillion.[7]

All the evidence points out that humanity is the central theme of the cosmos. The more astronomers look at the data, the more apparent it becomes that many features must be fine-tuned with great precision to accommodate human life. Here is an illustration. Imagine you are forced to stay inside a cage in a standing position with both hands lifted up. Two extremely sharp spears are placed on the front (chest) and backside. Two long pointed needles are placed on both sides below the rib cage. Both hands are tied with a string attached to a bomb; a slight movement of hands triggers the bomb that can immediately explode. A little movement of the foot can touch an electric line which electrocutes you to death. If you remain extra-ordinarily unmoving, it can keep you alive. The slightest degree of movement can put you to death. The life we experience on the planet Earth has such kind

---

6   Ross, *The Creator and the Cosmos*, 219.
7   Ibid.

of fine-tuning from a bigger perspective. A razor edge fine-tuning makes it possible to accommodate human life. I have only included a few factors in the illustration. In the universe, there are multiple hundred fine-tuning parameters that scientists already discovered. Any slight variation would make advanced life impossible.

A simple example is that if the Earth were closer or away from its position from the Sun, advanced life would not be possible. It would be too hot (Venus) or cold (Mars). Earth is located in a habitable zone (also called the Goldilocks zone). Now let us take a look at the fine-tuning parameters.

List of Fine-Tuning Parameters

In the book, *The Privileged Planet: How Our Place in the Cosmos is Designed for Discovery*, Astrophysicist Guillermo Gonzalez and philosopher Jay Richards point out several widely recognized fine-tuning factors.[8] Richards summarized the various fine-tuned features that are necessary conditions for the existence of complex life.[9] The features include (A) the cosmic constants, (B) the initial condition and "brute facts," and (C) the local features of habitable planets.

(A) The cosmic constants include

1. *Gravitational force constant*: If it were too weak, planets and stars could not form. If it is too strong, stars will burn too quickly.

---

[8]   Guillermo Gonzalez and Jay W. Richards, *The Privileged Planet: How Our Place in the Cosmos is Designed for Discovery* (Washington D.C: Regnery Gateway, 2020).

[9]   Jay W. Richards, "List of Fine-Tuning Parameters," *Discovery Institute*. January 14, 2015, Accessed April 12, 2021. https://www.discovery.org/a/fine-tuning-parameters/.

2. *Electromagnetic force constant*: a stable chemical bond is not possible if the ratio of electron to proton mass is much stronger or weaker.

3. *Stronger nuclear force constant*: if it were weaker, it would eliminate several chemical elements essential to life.

4. *Weak nuclear force constant*: a stronger or weaker of this could stop forming life-essential stars.

5. *Cosmological constants*: This controls the expansion speed of the universe. If the rate of expansion is slightly lower or higher, the universe will collapse.

(B) Initial Condition and "Brute Facts"

1. *Initial condition*: The ratio of the initial distribution of mass/energy at the beginning of the universe should be fine-tuned. Chance alone cannot explain this initial condition. Physicist Roger Penrose estimates that the odds by chance alone is 1 in $10^{10^{(123)}}$, which is beyond our power of comprehension. Along with the initial condition, the brute facts include:

2. *The ratio of masses for protons and electrons*: DNA could not be formed if slightly different.

3. *The velocity of light*: Stars would be too luminous or not be luminous enough if they were larger or smaller.

4. *Mass excess of neutron over proton*: there would be too few heavy elements for life if it were greater. Stars would quickly collapse if they were smaller.

(C) The Local Feature of Habitable Planets

Gonzalez and Richards point out twelve widely recognized fine-tuning factors required to build a single, habitable planet.[10] The basic list of twelve ingredients for building a single, habitable planet are (1) Steady plate tectonics with the right kind of geological interior; (2) Right amount of water in crust; (3) Large moon with right planetary rotation period; (4) Proper concentration of sulfur; (5) Right planetary mass; (6) Near the inner edge of the circumstellar habitable zone; (7) Low-eccentricity orbit outside spin-orbit and giant planet resonances; (8) A few, large Jupiter-mass planetary neighbors in large circular orbits; (9) Outside spiral arm of the galaxy; (10) Near co-rotation circle of the galaxy, in a circular orbit around the galactic center; (11) Within the galactic habitable zone; (12) During the cosmic habitable age.[11] All twelve factors can be found together on Earth. The vast majority of the universe is unsuited for life.

Gonzalez and Richards argue that the fine-tuning of these features for habitability suggests that the universe is designed not only for complex life but also for scientific discovery. Ross points out that the Earth is prepared for physical life through many finely tuned characteristics of our galaxy cluster, galaxy, star, planet, planetary partners, collider, moon, and belts of asteroids and comets.[12] He also lists hundreds of fine-tuning parameters in his book *Why the Universe Is the Way It Is*.[13] As the study continues, it may be possible to see a longer list of fine-tuning parameters.

---

[10] Guillermo Gonzalez and Jay W. Richards, *The Privileged Planet: How Our Place in the Cosmos is Designed for Discovery* (Washington D.C: Regnery Gateway, 2020), 195-218. See Richards, "List of Fine-Tuning Parameters."

[11] Ibid.

[12] Ross, *The Creator and the Cosmos*, 217.

[13] I recommend the website (reasons.org), where the researchers list the growing number of fine-tuning parameters. Also, see the books by Ross, *Why the Universe is the Way it is* and *The Creator and the Cosmos*.

Scientific evidence in support of the anthropic principle fills several books. Astronomer Robert Jastrow writes, "The anthropic principles...seems to say that science itself has proven as a hard fact, that this universe was made, was designed, for man to live in. It's a very theistic result."[14] All research astronomers agree that the universe manifests exquisite fine-tuning for advanced life to be possible. Theoretical physicist and mathematician Freeman Dyson stated, "The more I examine the universe,... the more evidence I find that the universe in some sense must have known we were coming."[15] Where does the scientific discovery of fine-tuning point us?

Fine-Tuning Requires a Designer

When philosophers study the information from the scientific data, a proper interpretation can conclude that there must be a 'Fine-Tuner' behind the operation of the universe because all the researches point to an intelligent fine-tuning agent. There are three options to choose from to explain the fine-tuning features. Either fine-tuning is due to *chance, necessity,* or *design.* Given the finite cosmic beginning and features of the universe, chance and necessity cannot bring fine-tuning of this precision. The only option left is design. By understanding many spectacular examples of fine-tuning in nature, Davies exclaimed, "the impression of design is overwhelming."[16] Some scientists try to use a "multiverse (or many universes)" to account for evidence for the beginning and design of the universe. What about this claim? Does the multiverse argument defeat the need for a Creator?

---

[14]   Robert Jastrow, "A Scientist Caught Between Two Faiths: Interview with Robert Jastrow" *Christianity Today* (August 6, 1982).

[15]   Freeman J. Dyson. *Disturbing the Universe* (United States: Harper & Row, 1979), 250.

[16]   Paul Davies, *The Cosmic Blueprint,* (United States: New York, Simon and Schuster, 1988), 203.

In his book, *Who's Afraid of the Multiverse?* Astrophysicist Jeffrey Zweerink argues that there are good scientific reasons that a multiverse might exist. Multiverse has several meanings, but each definition requires the existence of regions beyond the observable universe.[17] There are many multiverse models, which are mainly categorized into four levels. However, some unbelieving scientists use multiverse theory to argue against the existence of God and his involvement in the universe. At first look, it seems like a threat to the theistic arguments, but when multiverse theories are put to the test, they fail to deny the existence of God. Moreover, it supports the existence of God more strongly. The real problem is not the multiverse but the naturalistic interpretation of the multiverse. It is naturalism that gets into more trouble as we explore the evidence of the multiverse. Zweerink argues that many criteria need to be met to adequately explain the universe and our existence for a strictly naturalistic understanding of the multiverse model.[18] He argues that these criteria are not met. Below are some of them.

First, the naturalistic multiverse model must be self-contained. Scientific theories and models mandate a cosmic beginning based on general relativity and Hawking-Penrose theorems. The inflation-generated multiverses exhibit expansion on average, which implies a beginning that points to a Creator. A multiverse must have a beginning in the first place, according to the Borde-Vilenkin-Guth theorem. Moreover, the mechanism that generates the multiverse must exhibit fine-tuning, which points to a fine-tuning Designer.

Second, the multiverse model must account for all relevant observations and data. Current evidence falsifies the models. *Third*, the naturalistic multiverse model must provide a mechanism that produces a sufficient variety of universes. Otherwise, it cannot

---

[17]   Jeffrey A. Zweerink, *Who's Afraid of the Multiverse?* (CA: Reasons to Believe, 2008),14.
[18]   Zweerink, *Who's Afraid of the Multiverse?*,30.

address the physical laws, constants, and other fine-tuning parameters observed in the known universe. No such mechanism is currently known. *Fourth*, our universe must be one of the possible universes in a naturalistic multiverse model. Future testable evidence must support this hypothesis. *Fifth*, a purely naturalistic multiverse implies that human life is completely physical. It cannot account for justice, free will, laws of logic, metaphysical truth, mathematics, aesthetics, etc. It undermines the intrinsic value and meaning of human life.

A multiverse is a metaphysical assumption. Multiverse may or may not exist. Even if the multiverse exists, it explains nothing about who created the multiverse, why there is a multiverse at all in the first place, why there is fine-tuning, and several other life questions. The multiverse does not affect the cosmological and teleological argument for the existence of God. There are plenty of scientific challenges to multiverse advocates when they try to exclude the cosmic designer. Moreover, there is a huge philosophical objection against anything growing from finite to infinite. The naturalistic multiverse model fails to answer many criteria. Only a supernatural explanation can sufficiently answer many big questions. The naturalistic multiverse undermines the whole scientific enterprise when considering every possible situation. A large portion of the scientific community disagrees with multiverse theory. Many scientists think these models are unscientific as they offer no testable predictions. Zweerink writes,

> Scientific studies into the multiverse greatly strengthen the cosmological case for the universe having a beginning. Though some multiverse models appear to undermine the teleological argument, they still exhibit design and fine-tuning. Granted the design argument is more subtle and complex if a multiverse actually exists. However, as with the cosmological argument, studies of the multiverse ultimately make the teleological arguments more robust.[19]

---

[19]   Zweerink, *Who's Afraid of the Multiverse?* 51.

Former atheistic astronomer Alan Sandage writes,

> The world is too complicated in all of its parts to be due to chance alone. I am convinced that the existence of life on Earth with all its order in each of its organisms is simply too well put together... The more one learns of biochemistry, the more unbelievable it becomes unless there is some kind of organizing principle- an architect for believers.[20]

Hoyle writes, "The probability of life originating on Earth is no greater than the chance that a hurricane, sweeping through a scrapyard, would have the luck to assemble a Boeing 747."[21] Regarding the fine-tuning data, Hoyle summarized, "A common sense interpretation of the facts suggests that a super intellect has monkeyed with the physics, as well as the chemistry and biology, and there are no blind forces worth speaking about in nature."[22] The fine-tuning discovery by scientists led atheist philosopher Antony Flew to denounce his atheism and conversion to belief in God. Flew began to ask, 'Did the universe know we were coming?'[23] He knew that matter could not know anything, so it had to be God who knew we were coming. Hawking writes, "It would be very difficult to explain why the universe should have begun in just this way, except as the act of a God who intended to create beings like us."[24]

Fine-tuning points to a Designer. What can we infer about the Designer, then? After tackling several objections to fine-tuning and designing agent, Groothuis writes,

---

[20]   Alan Sandage, "A Scientist Reflects on Religious Belief" in *Truth*. Volume 1. Dallas: Truth Incorporated, 1985.

[21]   Fred Hoyle, *The Intelligent Universe* (New York: Holt, Rinehart, and Winston, 1984), 18-19.

[22]   Fred Hoyle, "The Universe: Some Past and Present Reflections," *Engineering and Science* (1981):12.

[23]   Antony Flew, *There Is a God: How the World's Most Notorious Atheist Changed His Mind* (New York: HarperCollins, 2007), Chapter 6.

[24]   Hawking, *A Brief History of Time*, 131.

> This Designer is…singular, outside of the universe (transcendent), a personal agent (having a mind to conceive the fine-tuning and the will to bring it about), and immensely powerful (given the complexity and scope of the universe).[25]

An honest evaluation of evidence points to the existence of God, who is not only the causal agent but also the fine-tuner of this universe for a purpose. We will now look into a few more arguments for the existence of God.

---

[25]   Groothuis, *Christian Apologetics,* 264-65.

CHAPTER 10

The Existence of God Part 3: Design & Moral Arguments

Design Argument

Everyone can recognize evidence of design themselves in nature. For example, if you are driving by the Mount Rushmore National Memorial in South Dakota, you can see the giant carved faces of the past few American presidents (George Washington, Thomas Jefferson, Theodore Roosevelt, Abraham Lincoln) on a mountain surrounded by the beauty of the Black Hills. By seeing them, you will never think it was formed by soil erosion or wind. You will never conclude that natural law or chance produced them. Instead, your common sense will tell you that a sculptor purposefully designed those faces because you can notice complexity (human faces) and specificity (past presidents). Complexity and specificity are properties that indicate design. This is a simple illustration of design detection. One does not need to believe in God or a religious text to understand design. We can see a lot of examples through our naked eye.

The evidence for design is overwhelming in every area of life and nature. An innocent four-year-old child can understand the hallmark of design with common sense better than many adult atheists who blindly believe that the natural world is all there is and that everything they see is just a cosmic accident. We see the fine-tuning design in the universe (we covered it in the last chapter). We can think of many other examples: the structure of DNA, the human body and every purpose-filled arrangement, molecular machines, etc. Design points to a Designer. Obviously, if something is designed, it has a philosophical implication to find out the designing agent. This requires further philosophical reasoning. The one who is committed to the discipline of philosophy takes the scientific data and uses reason to make a further argument for the designing agent by integrating it with theology.

If I put it into a logical syllogism (*Modus Ponens*),[1] here is how it follows:

Premise 1: If we can detect design in life and nature, then there must be a designer.

Premise 2: We can detect design in life and nature.

Premise 3: Therefore, there must be a designer.

An honest evaluation of evidence points to a designing agent (in other words, God) who not only brought the universe into existence and fine-tuned it for life but also designed everything else, even at the molecular level. Now, let's look at the moral argument for the existence of God.

Moral Argument

Everybody has a sense of moral conscience that one should do good and avoid evil. It is a universally accepted principle. Everyone recognizes that there are certain things we should and should not do in society. For example, if someone cheated on you, you know it

---

[1]   Rule of Inference. *Modus Ponens* (If p then q; p; therefore q).

was wrong. Then, you may seek justice for the wrong that has been done to you. We know that what Hitler did through the Holocaust was wrong and that what Mother Teresa did was good. The moral arguments for God's existence have been demonstrated in many ways by many philosophers. A basic structure of the argument can be stated like this (*Modus Ponens*):

Premise 1: If objective moral law exists, then there is an objective Moral Lawgiver.

Premise 2: Objective moral law exists.

Premise 3: Therefore, there is an objective Moral Lawgiver.

Premise 1: Premise 1 is self-evident. Every law requires a lawgiver. Geisler argues that the moral law is a prescription as it prescribes how one should and should not behave. They are not descriptions of the way people behave but prescriptions for human beings on how to behave. Prescriptions can only come from prescribers.[2] The objective moral law transcends humanity. If objective moral law exists, this universal law requires an objective Moral Lawgiver (God) who prescribes this in humanity.

Premise 2: It is possible to demonstrate Premise (2) -- the existence of objective moral law that binds all humanity. There are certain moral values and duties that exist. Examples: "Murder is wrong," "It is wrong to torture innocent babies for fun," "Betrayal is wrong," "Do not rape," "Do not steal," "Loyalty is good," "Greed is bad," etc. No culture has ever celebrated an athlete winning a trophy by cheating another player. As Lewis wrote, "Think of a country where people were admired for running away in battle, or where a man felt proud of double-crossing all the people who had been kindest to him. You might as well try to imagine a country where two and

---

[2]   Geisler, *Systematic Theology in One Volume*, 29.

two made five."[3]   If moral law does not exist, there is no way one can distinguish between right and wrong or good and bad. If moral law does not exist, there is nothing wrong with breaking into one's neighbor's house and stealing all their money so that one can enjoy a luxurious life. If all moral laws are subjective (personal feelings), it is okay to steal from someone if that is what one likes to do. If morality is purely subjective, there will be a conflict with other people's opinions or feelings.

Indeed, there are certain things in which cultures behave differently. For example, in India, we take off our shoes when we enter a house. It will be a dishonor if one violates it. In America, keeping shoes on when one enters a house is not considered bad. There are many other etiquettes that are subjective to a specific culture. But objective moral laws are principles that bind all of humanity. They are not based on an opinion, culture, or place. The objective moral law is prescribed to us, which we can recognize naturally. In this short chapter, I did not present the objections to Premise 2 since it is a vast topic to be discussed. However, we can recognize the objective moral law. Even atheists can indeed be good without God.

Premise 3: If Premises 1 and 2 are true, then Premise three (the conclusion) must follow necessarily. The existence of the objective moral law points to the objective Moral Law Giver. This is a version of the moral argument for God's existence. If an Objective Moral Lawgiver (God) does not exist, there is nobody to judge, ultimately. No matter how I live, I will end up at the grave. I can live like Hitler, or I can live my whole life stealing from people, or I can live like a saint by practicing forgiveness and charity. However, whatever way one lives, it does not matter if God does not exist with an eternal plan for humanity.

---

[3]   C. S. Lewis, *Mere Christianity* (New York: HarperOne, 2015), 7.

The problem of evil is raised against a perfect Moral Law Giver to deny the existence of a perfect God. This is something that should be answered by the different worldviews. A worldview system of objective truth must be able to answer the reason sufficiently and satisfactorily for the presence of evil in the world. This is a topic for part three. At this point, we can conclude that God (Moral Law Giver) exists.

Section Conclusion

In this section, I have presented several arguments for the existence of God. The cosmological arguments demonstrate the need for a causal agent, the fine-tuning argument shows the need for a fine-tuner, the design argument proves the need for a designer, and the moral argument attests to the need for a moral lawgiver. All arguments contribute to making the case for the existence of God stronger. Since space is limited, I did not comprehensively treat each argument by presenting objections and responses to the objections. A lot of work has been done on these topics by prominent scholars. I have included some references and suggestions for your deeper study. I also want to point out that the arguments I presented are not the only arguments for the existence of God.

There are many other arguments, such as ontological arguments, different forms of teleological arguments, different forms of moral arguments, arguments from religious experience, the argument from the truth, the argument from human finitude, the argument from beauty, the argument from perception, existential arguments, the argument from blessedness, the argument from innate idea, the argument from mysticism, Aquinas' Five Ways, Pascal's anthropological argument, etc.

If one argument for the existence of God does not satisfy you fully, you may move to the next one. If that argument does not satisfy you, move to the other one and to the next one. If none of them or a group of arguments together does not yet convince you of the existence of God, I do not think any more arguments and reasons can convince you. It simply proves a person's rebellion against God. Some of the most brilliant philosophers hold on to one or the other arguments as undeniable. In the next section, we will depart our journey from the existence of God to the knowledge of God. It deals with the topic of comprehending God through reason and special revelation. We will also evaluate the major worldviews.

SECTION 3:

The God of Philosophy: The Knowledge of God

CHAPTER 11

Knowing God

Every intentional action has a purpose. From the moment we wake up in the morning, every intentional action in our lives is for a purpose, whether for good or bad. We brush our teeth, exercise, shower, put on clothes, eat food, work, travel, and engage in many activities throughout the day. When we do something, we know in our hearts the purpose of that action. We do activities out of love for something or someone. It could be for our family, society, or out of compassion for ourselves. For instance, when we drink some water or eat some food, it is to nourish our body. When we take a shower and put on clean clothes, it is to keep us clean and look presentable. We keep our phone with us so that we can communicate with someone or use its features for the appropriate purposes. We go to college to gain knowledge for a higher purpose. We work hard to earn money or career growth. We create things for different purposes.

A friend of mine may know why I do an action in a particular way, but he may not know the purpose of every action in my life. For instance, suppose I see a friend of mine driving by my house. But I have no idea where he is going because it is not something that he regularly does. All I know at that point is that he passed by my house, and he had a destination in mind. Unless he stopped and explained it to me, I wouldn't know his purpose. What can we think about the great act of creation? What is the purpose behind it? Have we tried to know it? Is there a way we can know it? How do we know it? Have we really tried to gain some knowledge of the divine being? Or have we just ignored this question by concluding that there is no way we can know the divine being and his purpose?

Many people think that there is no way we can know God even if he exists. If that is the case, we are left abandoned without knowing where our life is heading. It is similar to becoming stuck with an extremely complicated, confusing puzzle without knowing the end and the next step, which can ultimately put us in despair when we see no hope of a solution. We might be able to gain some knowledge about God by considering the great act of creation.

We can assume that the act of creation must be for a great purpose. It has to be considered a great act because, unlike any other actions within the universe, we would not be here if the act of creation of the universe did not happen. We know that we do not necessarily have to exist. It could have been nothing at all. We are contingent beings that depend on a necessary being (God) for our existence. From the fact that God has given us existence, we can conclude that it must be for a purpose. If God does not have a purpose, he does not have to provide us with the gift of existence in the first place. If God exists and gives us existence, we have good reasons to conclude that we can know him to a certain extent. Unlike a human-to-human interaction, there is a huge epistemic gap between the infinite divine being and a finite human being. There is always a limit to what a finite mind can comprehend about the infinite being. How can we gain the knowledge of God, then?

We can think of at least two methods to attain the knowledge of God: (1) Knowledge based on Rational Demonstration and (2) Knowledge based on Credible Authority.[1]

---

[1]   I owe partial credit to one of my professors of philosophy, Dr. J.T Bridges, whose

The Knowledge of God Based on Rational Demonstration

In the previous chapters, I have presented a few classical arguments for the existence of God as a necessary being to explain the universe and the life we experience. In philosophical terminology, God is a metaphysically[2] necessary being. The knowledge of the existence of God is objectively accessible to all people as it is evident in nature, history, and conscience. We can evaluate evidence by studying the natural world and from our experience. Then we can reason back to an Agent who created everything out of nothing. Philosopher Henri Renard wrote,

> The knowledge of the God of philosophy is a scientific, and objectively evident knowledge; consequently it is communicable. It will supply a rational, secure basis which man, any man, must require, if not in its entirety, at least indirectly, as a fundamental estimation of the existence of a Supreme Being. This rational basis, human reason must possess at least implicitly in the formation of the act of faith… the objective presentation of the philosopher in presenting a formal demonstration of the existence of God paves the way towards faith, for it proposes a necessary foundation for the acceptance of the God of religion,… [3]

A philosopher does not need religious texts to establish the existence of a Being or an Agent or First Cause, whom we call God. Reason and various pieces of evidence are sufficient to affirm this objective knowledge with certainty. So far, we have gained reasonable knowledge of the existence of God. How can we comprehend God?

Comprehending God

It is important to note that we are created beings with finite and limited abilities. In contrast, God is not created. God is infinite and limitless. God is beyond our ability to comprehend fully (i.e., to an infinite

---

lectures helped me formulate this section.

[2] Metaphysics comes from the Greek word "*metaphysica*," which means "after physics." Metaphysics deals with the study of the nature of reality or being.

[3] Henri Renard, *Foreword*, in Maurice Holloway, *An Introduction to Natural Theology* (Eugene, OR: Wipf and Stock Publishers, 1959), X.

degree). We can definitely think of some knowledge about the divine being using natural reason, but not fully. We can use some analogies for God talk. I do not intend to enter into the deeper philosophical debates surrounding this topic. The bottom-line is, using reason, there is always a limit to what a finite mind can comprehend about infinite God. Using reasoning and evidence, we have established the existence of God. An attempt to fully comprehend an infinite God to an infinite degree with our finite mind is mere stupidity because a finite mind cannot comprehend an infinite mind to an infinite degree. Philosopher Thomas Aquinas writes quoting Augustine, "It is impossible for any created intellect to comprehend God; yet 'for the mind to attain to God in some degree is great beatitude.' as Augustine says."[4] Aquinas also states, "…no created intellect can know God infinitely… since… any created intellect cannot be infinite, it is clearly impossible for any created intellect to know God in an infinite degree. Hence it is impossible that it should comprehend God."[5]

A simple illustration may help us understand better. We know from studying nature that time, space, matter, and energy came into existence at a singular point. You may ask these questions: What is it like to be timeless? What is it like to be spaceless? What is it like to be immaterial? We cannot even imagine what it is like to be in a timeless, spaceless, immaterial state. We find no clue what it is like to be in such a state because our experience with the world is bound by time, space, and matter. The God-- who is timeless, spaceless, immaterial, infinite, all-powerful, etc.,-- is beyond our ability to comprehend fully by our finite mind. So, we all have to keep a great humility in God-topics. However, the concept of such a being is logically coherent and has been established through arguments that we can understand. But we should not elevate ourselves in a God-

---

4   Thomas Aquinas, *Summa Theologica*, 1, 12, 7; (De Verb. Dim., Serm. xxxvii)

5   Aquinas, *Summa Theologica*, 1, 12, 7.

like position, claiming to know everything about God. Since it is impossible to fully comprehend God with finite human reasoning, how do we know God and his plan for humanity, at least to some degree? The only solution is that *the infinite God must reveal himself to us in a way our finite mind can understand.*

God Must Reveal

To know God's personality, character, nature, and purpose of creation, God himself must reveal to us in a special way unless he does not want humans to know him. If I meet a stranger and want to know him personally, he has to introduce himself. If I test him in a laboratory, I may be able to identify his body's complex structure. Still, it never explains his personality at all. Silence never explains anything. If God created everything and if he remains silent, we wouldn't know him personally. We would not understand why he created us if he decided not to reveal himself. Such a concept gives no meaning to life. If God created everything, including human beings, that must be for a purpose only God can reveal. Therefore, a special revelation is necessary to know that.

Moreover, the infinite God must reveal knowledge about him in a way that the finite mind can understand. For example, we use language to communicate truth. We use symbols to convey a message. We invent language. An analogy may help to understand. When a child is born into this world, its parents do not use high-level vocabulary to communicate because that baby cannot understand their complex language yet. Once the baby grows a little more, they try to communicate simple messages using their language (perhaps using a medium-level vocabulary). As time passes, he will grow to a level when he can grasp complex language. A father and mother know how to communicate at a lower level by adapting to a lower level. And then eventually raise the standard as the child grows up. However, adapting to a lower level is important in the initial stage.

As I have written, there is no way the finite mind can comprehend the infinite God to an infinite degree. The only way God can reveal himself is by *adapting to finite levels*. A divine adaptation to finitude is necessary if there is to be a union between God and human beings.[6] We can suppose that God, who is all-knowing, knows how to communicate his message to finite minds without error. It is vital to note that error-free communication is necessary to understand the truth. It is possible to have error-free communication if God is involved in the process. God cannot say one thing to a particular group of people and another to another group of people that contradicts the first group. Such a contradicting revelation will get us in trouble because we cannot have true knowledge of God then. We can assume that God knows how to do his job in all perfection.

If God can create the universe out of nothing and fine-tune the physical laws to accommodate human life as if placed on a razor's edge, we can assume that he can easily communicate his truth to human beings in all perfection and beauty. God does not necessarily have to give all knowledge about him. He only needs to provide what is necessary for the human to know for their good and for the glory of God. However, human beings are responsible for carefully studying and analyzing what has been revealed if the goal is to understand the truth given by the divine being. Whatever God reveals will be true because it is God who reveals them. The knowledge that God reveals is truth. All truth is God's truth. Truth is absolute. Although the truth is absolute, our understanding of truth may not be absolute. To know the absolute truth, we have to carefully evaluate reasons

---

6   Norman Geisler, *Systematic Theology in One Volume* (Minnesota: Bethany House, 2011), 194-95.

and evidence. We can indeed draw a reasonable conclusion if we do such an exercise.

Even our knowledge of the world is finite. We do not have to know every single detail of the universe to live our daily lives. Those who study the universe reveal that knowledge as the study progresses. But there is also knowledge about the universe that we can believe with certainty. For example, I know with certainty that if a coconut falls on my head, it hurts. Therefore, I have to be wise to stay away from a coconut tree to avoid getting hurt by a falling coconut. I do not have to know every detail of coconut to have that knowledge; a reasonable experience with coconut trees is enough. Similarly, we do not have to know every detail about God to understand God's plan of creation. But it is important to know the significant truths that are clearly revealed by God about his plan for humanity and the world. If we neglect that, it can really lead us to destruction.

We have learned that the knowledge of the existence of God is objectively demonstrable. We have understood several arguments for the existence of God through reason and evidence. By affirming the existence of God, we can conclude that it is also possible for God to demonstrate who he is and his plan for humanity through special revelation so that the finite mind can understand the infinite God to a certain degree. We should have this firm conviction that it is possible for God to do what is necessary to make him known to us without error.

The Knowledge of God Based on Credible Authority

To gain knowledge about something, we need credible authority or trustworthy sources. If I have a serious health problem, I will consult credible medical doctors who have knowledge about the human body. I will not go to a random person on the street. If I need to know history, I need to refer to historians who have studied that particular topic of history. If I need to gain scientific knowledge, I will go to scientific journals; I will not believe the opinions of random people on the internet who have no credible authority about a particular field of study. I will also do more detailed research from various credible journals to see if the knowledge is trustworthy. I will look into arguments and counter-arguments before I trust that knowledge. What about the knowledge of God?

We live in a pluralistic world with many religions and ideologies. Many claim to know the truth of God. We have the availability of many religious texts that are considered by many people groups as credible authorities that reveal the knowledge of God. Can all those religious ideologies be true? Absolutely not, because many of their essential claims sharply contradict. We know that God will not give contradictory information. So, we need to find out the objectively true revelation of God. We need credible authority to put trust in. If it is possible that God can reveal his truth through special revelation without error, we need to identify the credibility of that authority to have the true knowledge of God. If we can identify the credible authority, we can indeed gain true knowledge of God based on the authority of that special revelation. At the point when the authority or a trustworthy source can be established, we will have access to the highest possible knowledge about God because it comes from God. How do we establish the credible authority of the true sacred revelation?

Reason and evidence assist us in demonstrating the trustworthy source. So far, we have been able to demonstrate the existence of God through various arguments and reasoning. In order to identify the trustworthiness of God's special revelation, we have to use information from different disciplines such as history, archeology, science, etc. We must be able to verify the claims, events, and details from an objective perspective. We need to put some effort into conducting various tests to establish the trustworthiness of the source.

Now, in our philosophical journey, I want to shift the gear to move forward to a more complex and controversial route—worldviews, which include religion. Among the various concepts of God, we have to embrace the true concept of God and exclude the concepts of God that are not true. Knowledge from various sources can assist us in eliminating what is false.

In the next chapter, we will distinguish the true concept of God among various concepts through rational demonstration. After establishing the true concept of God, we will do some further tests using different truth test criteria. The trustworthiness of the source will be demonstrated by reason and evidence by using various fields of study. Let's see how philosophical tools can assist us in gaining the true concept of God. Remember that our goal is to discover a system of objective truth, not a subjective opinion.

CHAPTER 12

The Worldviews on Trial Part 1

We live in a pluralistic world. Everyone has a worldview and these worldviews may differ radically from one another. Our worldview is the lens through which we view the world. It impacts our perception and comprehension of life and our surroundings, ultimately forming the basis for our actions and choices. American thinker and academic James Sire defines worldview as follows:

> A worldview is a commitment, a fundamental orientation of the heart, that can be expressed as a story or in a set of presuppositions (assumptions that may be true, partially true, or entirely false) that we hold (consciously or subconsciously, consistently or inconsistently) about the basic constitution of reality, and that provides the foundation on which we live and move and have our being.[1]

Discovering our essential worldview matter, and it is valuable in everyone's life. It is a significant step toward self-awareness, self-knowledge, and self-understanding.[2] It shapes who we are and what we do.[3]

A Personal Note

I am well aware that discussing worldviews that include religion can

---

[1]   James W. Sire, *The Universe Next Door: A Basic Worldview Catalog*, 5th ed. (Downers Grove, Ill.: InterVarsity Press, 2009), 20.

[2]   Sire, *The Universe Next Door*, 20.

[3]   Groothuis, *Christian Apologetics*, 75.

be a sensitive matter. I would like to share a bit about my background to provide more insight. As I mentioned earlier, I was born and raised in Kerala, India until I was nineteen years old. Since then, I have been studying and residing overseas (in the UK and USA) for about fourteen years. At 33, I am a product of mixed cultures and take great pride in my homeland, India. India boasts a vast diversity, and I hold dear certain values of Indian culture. I am privileged to have loyal and supportive friends with different religious beliefs. Interestingly, my closest friends happen to be either agnostics or atheists. Despite our differing worldviews, we respect and value one another. Occasionally, we engage in friendly debates and discussions on various topics, but we always approach these conversations with respect and love. Although we have several generations of Christian history in my family, the record indicates that my ancestors have roots in Hinduism. I have a huge respect for people of all faiths.

Having had the opportunity to travel internationally at a young age, I gained valuable experience interacting with people from diverse cultures and religions. I want to make it clear that the purpose of this chapter is not to disrespect or cause harm to any religious beliefs. I do not intend to force my beliefs onto others or suggest that other belief systems are inferior to mine. I honor and uphold objective truth above all else, whether or not one likes, knows, or believes it. This became my focus in my early twenties as I recognized the immense value and significance of truth as the foundation of reality. Rather than blindly adhering to a worldview simply because it was the one I was raised with; I sought to analyze and compare various perspectives in my pursuit of truth. I acknowledge that all religions contain elements of truth and share common ground. However, this does not mean that everything taught by every religion is objectively true from a broader perspective. Is there an objectively true worldview? How do we arrive at what is absolutely true? My aim is to provide a concise overview of the major worldviews.

As this is a philosophical journey, we must evaluate it honestly. I don't intend to judge a worldview based on its negative aspects or the behavior of certain religious groups or individuals. I can acknowledge and appreciate the good works of people from different religions, especially Hindus, Muslims, and Christians, as they are prevalent in my state, Kerala. Similarly, I can also critique the bad actions of individuals from every religion. My evaluation is based on facts and reason, not based on bad behaviors of people. Many renowned scholars have written books on religious worldviews comprehensively.[4] My approach to evaluating worldviews for this book is simple. This chapter evaluates the subject from a logical standpoint, and the next chapter explores it through the lens of the big questions. Before evaluating the worldviews, I will briefly explain the major ones.

The Major Worldviews

We can identify seven major worldviews. These are *Atheism, Theism (Monotheism), Pantheism, Panentheism, Finite Godism, Polytheism, and Deism.*[5] I will give a short description of each of them.

Atheism: Atheism denies the existence of God or gods. Atheism holds that only the natural world exists and that there is nothing outside the physical universe. 'All is matter' for atheism. There is no God who exists beyond or in the universe. Those who hold naturalism, secular humanism, etc., are logically equivalent to atheism. Some atheists, such as Sinnott-Armstrong and Erik Weilenberg, believe in moral truths that are non-natural states.

---

[4]   To know about world religions, see the work of professor of philosophy and religion, Winfried Corduan, *Neighboring Faiths: A Christian Introduction to World Religions* (IL.: InterVarsity Press, 2013. Also see Douglas Groothuis, *World Religions in Seven Sentences: A Small Introduction to a Vast Topic* (IL: IVP Academic, 2023).

[5]   Geisler, *Systematic Theology in One Volume,* 17-18; Also see Groothuis, *Christian Apologetics,* 50.

Pantheism: Pantheists hold that God is the universe (God is all) and the universe is God. They do not believe in a creator beyond the universe. Creator and creation are two different ways of viewing one reality, which is ultimate. In pantheism, all is mind. All things are God, and all things can be worshipped. Pantheism holds that the universe is eternal. Some forms of Hinduism, Zen Buddhism, Christian Science, New Age religions, mind-science movements, and others, represent pantheistic worldviews.

Theism (Monotheism): Theism holds that there is one infinite personal God who exists both beyond and in the universe. This one infinite personal God (either unitarian or Trinitarian) created the physical universe (time, space, matter, energy) and acts within it. He is both transcendent (presence of God beyond the universe) and immanent (indwelling presence of God in the universe). Theism holds that the universe is not eternal. Traditional Judaism, Islam, and Christianity represent theistic worldviews. There are also some other religious worldviews that use the Bible but have interpretations differing from the original traditional interpretation.

Panentheism: Panentheism holds that the physical universe is within God. There is another pole to God other than the physical universe. This pole is God's eternal and infinite potential beyond the material universe. Panentheism holds that the physical universe is eternal. In classical panentheism, God and the physical universe are necessarily and eternally dependent on each other. Panentheists hold that God is constantly changing; therefore, it is also called *process theology*. Some liberal Christians hold this view. Major proponents of this view include Alfred North Whitehead, Charles Hartshorne, John Cobb Jr., Schubert Ogden, Lewis Ford, and Henri Bergson.

Polytheism: Polytheists hold that there are many finite gods beyond the world and in it. Each finite god has its own domain. Polytheism holds that the universe is eternal. This view is represented by some forms of Hinduism, early Greeks and Romans, ancient nature religions, Mormonism, and witchcraft. Epicureans were polytheistic but didn't think gods interacted with the world.

Finite Godism: According to Finite Godism, there is a finite god who exists beyond and in the universe, but the god is limited in his nature and power. They also deny the miraculous intervention of god in the universe. They believe that it is because of the limited power of god that evil is still present. The proponents of this view include Plato and John Stuart Mill.

Deism: Deism closely resembles Theism. Deists hold that God is exclusively transcendent over the universe but does not intervene in the world personally. They hold a purely naturalistic operation of the world, although they believe that a Creator created the universe in the first place. But the Creator plays no role in the universe after it was created. The proponents of this view include Voltaire, John Toland, Thomas Paine, Thomas Hobbes, Charles Blount, Antony Flew, and Lord Herbert of Cherbury.[6]

Evaluation on the Logical Ground

We do not need to study all the thousands of religions and non-religious ideologies available in the world to draw a valid and true conclusion about the true worldview. Every religious person believes in some kind of supernatural force, God, gods, or a sacred state. Most of the major worldviews fall into these three categories: *Atheism* (no God at all), *Theism* (God made everything), and *Pantheism* (God is everything). All worldviews hold that either universe is eternal or not eternal. It is important to note that all these worldviews cannot

---

[6]   H. Wayne House and Joseph M. Holden, *Charts of Apologetics and Christian Evidences* (Grand Rapids, Michigan: Zondervan, 2006), Chart 27.

be true simultaneously on logical grounds. Now we can do a simple logical evaluation.

For example, either there is one God (theism), or God is everything (Pantheism), or no god (Atheism). If it is true that "God exists," its opposite claim, "God does not exist," must be false necessarily because God cannot exist and not exist simultaneously. We have to exclude one of them. Both cannot be true. If "God is infinite," then its opposite, "God is finite," is false. The universe cannot be both "eternal" and "not eternal." God cannot be "one" and "many." We have to exclude what is not true. The opposite of true is false. Truth excludes its opposite. If atheism is true, all other opposing worldviews must be false. If theism is true, all other contradicting worldviews must necessarily be false. If pantheism is true, all other worldviews (except polytheism have some overlap) must necessarily be false. Only one of these can be true, logically. All others must be false because they make opposing claims.

Every worldview claims to be the truth. Every worldview excludes its opposing claims. For example, Atheists claim that atheism is true and exclude all other non-atheistic worldviews. That means they are narrow in their view. Truth is narrow. The nature of truth as narrow is not my opinion. Narrowness is the nature of the truth.[7] A worldview that accepts all truth claims is not actually making a truth claim. It may be painful to accept the nature of truth, but that is the fabric of reality that is undeniable. Let's use the rule of rational inference to draw a clear conclusion.

Through the Kalam Cosmological argument (Chapter 8), we have established that the universe had a finite beginning. Now, let us do a logical evaluation by putting some information into syllogism (*Modus Ponens*).[8]

---

[7]	See Chapter 7.

[8]	Modus Ponens: If p, then q; p; therefore, q.

Premise 1: If X is a worldview that holds that the universe is eternal, then X must be rejected or excluded.

Premise 2: X is a worldview that holds that the universe is eternal.

Conclusion: Therefore, X must be rejected or excluded.

You may assume "X" as any worldview. Based on philosophical reasoning and scientific evidence, we have good reasons to conclude that the universe had a finite beginning.[9] Any worldview that claims its opposite must be false necessarily. This information helps us to exclude what is not true. Which worldview is true? Where does the evidence lead?

Theism: The True Concept of God

All reason and evidence suggest that we live in a theistic universe. I have presented several classical arguments for the existence of a theistic God.[10] We learned that the universe began to exist a finite time ago. Therefore, a causal agent beyond the universe (space, time, matter, and energy) must bring it into existence. God also continues to act in creation. He sustains the universe. All evidence points to theism. Since truth necessarily excludes its opposite, we have to eliminate all other worldviews on logical ground. If the evidence leads us to theism, then that is the identity of God (the law of identity). God cannot be anything other than his true identity. That is the bottom line.

So far, we have established that theism is true based on evidence and reason. We have excluded opposing worldviews on purely logical grounds. Philosophy and science assisted us in eliminating what was not true. However, we have yet to evaluate which among the traditional theistic worldviews is objectively true. It requires

---

9   See Chapter 8.
10   See Chapters 8, 9, 10.

further reasoning. In many ways, the claims of these theistic religions sharply contradict each other in many areas. Islam, Judaism, and Christianity are theistic belief systems. If one among them can be proven to be objectively true, we have to exclude all others because contradictory claims cannot be true simultaneously. The only thing is to show that one is objectively true. It must be supported with good reasons and evidence. It must be objectively verifiable. Before I reason in that route, I also like to analyze the worldview from a different perspective-- by asking big questions.

CHAPTER 13

The Worldviews on Trial Part 2

A true worldview must make sense of our life and the world around us. It has to address and sufficiently answer some big questions. Questions vary slightly in individuals. Some of the questions many thinkers find important are: *What is the ultimate reality? How did everything originate? What gives life intrinsic value? What is the meaning and purpose of life? Why is there evil and suffering in this world? What gives ultimate hope? Is there a life after death? How should we live?* You can add as many questions as you like and see which worldview provides sufficient and satisfactory answers. It may require some genuine research and an unbiased mindset.

Over the millennia, philosophers have been searching and formulating answers to make sense of this world and humanity in particular. Every worldview attempts to answer some or all of these questions. Many worldviews have attempted to explain ultimate reality and human problems. Some worldviews are successful in giving some plausible answers to a few questions, but they fail to answer other questions sufficiently. So, the plausible answers they have given to some of the questions do not necessarily have to be objectively true, although they may sound suitable for temporary satisfaction. Therefore, such worldviews cannot be trusted.

For example, naturalists claim that the ultimate reality is matter/energy, the natural world is all that exists, and we are the product of blind natural processes. However, they fail to give sufficient answers to the questions about humanity, the meaning and the purpose of life, morality, and more. If we are just a product of unguided, blind natural processes, it devalues our lives in the first place. Such a worldview does not make good sense about life and the world. We also have good reasons to believe that the universe began to exist a finite time ago, which requires God as the causal agent, which excludes all non-theistic worldviews. Some worldviews teach about the reality of suffering in this world and some possible temporary solutions, but they fail to answer many other questions. Every worldview has to deal with the big questions. An objectively true worldview can sufficiently answer all the most pertinent questions. How do we test which is objectively true in all senses and can adequately answer all the big questions?

Testing Worldviews

Truth must correspond to reality. Truth is saying the way it is. If something is true, it must correspond to the facts. If the claims in a worldview do not correspond to the facts, we can reject that worldview in the first place. For example, we have good reasons to conclude that theism corresponds to reality. It is verifiable. Therefore, all non-theistic worldviews must be rejected because these do not correspond to the facts. Any worldview that is non-theistic has to be eliminated at this point because the opposite of truth cannot be true. We also have to test a worldview for coherence.

When we test coherence within the worldview, we must test if there is *logical consistency, factual adequacy,* and *experiential relevance.*[1] The

---

[1]   See Groothuis, *Christian Apologetics,* 52-60.

worldview must be *internally consistent* in its claims. There cannot be contradictions within the worldview. Internal consistency is necessary for the truth of a worldview but not sufficient by itself. For example, fiction can be written with internal consistency. But after all, it is fiction; it is not fact. A worldview must be *factually adequate.* The factual claims must be verifiable. Various disciplines can help verify facts. Various scientific disciplines, such as physics, astronomy, biology, and chemistry, can help empirically verify scientific claims. The discipline of archaeology can help verify past events. Historians can verify historical data.

For example, if Jesus Christ existed, historians can verify it. If Jesus Christ died on the cross and was raised from the dead, history should give evidence. Within the theistic worldview, we have Judaism, Christianity, and Islam. Islam rejects Jesus' death on the cross; Judaism holds that Jesus died on the cross but was never resurrected; Christianity (Judeo-Christian worldview) claims that Jesus died and was resurrected. All three cannot be true simultaneously. One of these must be true. Another example is that Christians believe in the deity of Jesus Christ. Islam and traditional Judaism deny it. Either Jesus is divine or not divine. There is no middle option. One must be rejected. The claims of Jesus must be tested from various viewpoints.

Another test within the coherence is to test it from an *experiential relevance* standpoint. We have to test if the worldview is livable. Maybe a worldview is livable for someone because it works for him (pragmatism), but that does not make it objectively true. An objectively true worldview must explain the human condition, meaning, value, and purpose of life. It must sufficiently and satisfactorily answer all the questions concerning the problem of suffering, pain, and death. The worldview must give true hope and assurance for living.

All these truth test criteria must be met. When all the major questions I listed above are tested in each worldview, a true worldview must pass these criteria of the truth tests. An objectively true worldview must be able to answer all these questions sufficiently and satisfactorily. All worldviews cannot be true simultaneously. If one among the possible worldviews can be proven to be objectively true, we have to exclude all opposing views, even if it hurts.

It is important to note that our journey is to discover the objective truth--that which is not based on the opinion of a particular group of people. Even though this journey may possibly make you reject your current worldview, you are not a loser but a winner. You are winning the truth. You are getting an opportunity to turn from what is not true. It is good because the truth has eternal significance. Anything that is not true must be rejected. It may be a life-death game if one does not evaluate the truth and does not reject what is not true. In the end, we should rejoice in what is true, good, and beautiful. We should realize it as soon as possible.

Our Journey So Far as a Philosopher

In our journey as philosophers, we learned the importance and role of philosophy in trying to discover the truth. We also learned the basic laws of thought. Moreover, we learned the nature of truth as absolute, exclusive, and narrow. We have established the existence of God by looking at several arguments. We also learned that it is impossible for the finite mind to fully comprehend the infinite God through reason alone. There is always a limit to what a finite mind can do. In order to know God and his plan for humanity, it is necessary that God reveal it to us in a special way in our finite language. We concluded that it is possible for God to reveal the truth without error. We then looked into worldviews. We have evaluated seven major worldviews. All evidence and reason point us to a theistic universe. Theism is an objective truth that is based on reason and evidence. If theism is true, all opposing worldviews should be excluded as part of the journey of discovering the objective truth because truth excludes its opposing views. Now, we have to find out which of the theistic worldviews is true and makes sense. This requires further analysis.

Since we have established the existence of a theistic (monotheistic) God, I suggest saying a prayer from your heart to the God of the universe because God must be able to listen to you since he is God. Here is a simple yet powerful prayer you can pray from an honest, skeptical mind that desires to find the truth.

> ***Dear God of the Universe: I am a sincere truth seeker. I want to know the objective truth with clarity. So far, I am convinced that you exist. Since you exist, I believe that you can listen to my heart. Now, I desire to know which worldview is objectively true in all senses. Please help me understand who you are and convince me of the truth. Amen!***

From here, I am shifting to defend the Judeo-Christian worldview as objectively true, rational, and important to our whole life. You may evaluate the reasons and evidence for yourself.

Transition to Part Three:
Journey as a Judeo-Christian Apologist

Now, let us turn to the next part--the journey as a Judeo-Christian Apologist. My goal is to show the evidence for the Judeo-Christian worldview (or simply call it the Christian worldview). We can call it the Judeo-Christian worldview because Jesus Christ is the promised Messiah of Judaism. God's work of redemption has been performed through the Jewish nation in that God used that nation to bring forth the Messiah, Jesus. I am not defending Christianity because of my interest in it or my personal spiritual experience. I am defending it because Christianity is objectively true, rational, and important to whole life. The claims are verifiable. It corresponds well with reality and gives a coherent set of answers when all the big questions are put together with logical consistency, factual adequacy, and experiential relevance. I have two main purposes for the next sections.

1. The first is to show non-Christian believers that the Judeo-Christian worldview is objectively true by presenting the reason and evidence for it.

2. The second is to show many Christians that the Christian faith is founded on reason and evidence. Many anti-intellectual Christians think that faith does not get along with reason and, therefore, we should avoid reasoning. My goal is to remove some of the misconceptions of many Christians about the role of reason in faith. Undoubtedly, it is possible to have knowledge of God without considering all reason and evidence. If Christianity is true, the Holy Spirit can convict a person of the truth without evaluating reasons and evidence. That is exactly what happened in my life initially. I came to the faith in Christ by reading the Scripture, and I experienced a spiritual encounter with Jesus Christ. After that, it was my Christian faith that encouraged me to dive into the rational side as I desired to have a deeper knowledge of God. We cannot reject the intellectual side because the question "Is the Bible reliable?" should be demonstrated with reason and evidence. We can indeed demonstrate with reason and evidence that the Bible is a trustworthy source. Therefore, with reasons for reliability, the Bible should be considered the ultimate credible authority to gain true knowledge of God.

PART THREE

THE JOURNEY AS A JUDEO-CHRISTIAN APOLOGIST

SECTION 1:

Preparing for an Apologetic Journey

CHAPTER 14

What is Apologetics?

The terms 'Apologetics' and 'Apologist' are not widely known. Most of the time, when I introduce myself to someone as an apologist, I find myself having to explain what 'apologist' or 'apologetics' means because most people have never heard these terminologies. People often mistake them for the word 'apology,' which means expressing regret. In my group of friends in North Carolina, one friend always apologizes, even for some matters where an apology is not necessary. He's very polite and well-behaved, but we often tease him for excessively apologizing. My friends also know that I'm an apologist by training. One day, another friend in our group joked, 'We have two apologists in our group.' I couldn't stop laughing thinking about it, although the term 'apologist' has nothing to do with expressing regret. So, what is apologetics?

Apologetics is not about apologizing; it is a word that comes from the Greek word *apologia* (Gk: ἀπολογία), which is translated as defense. Apologetics is the act of providing a defense for something. An apologist is an individual who performs this task. Groothuis defines Christian apologetics as "the rational defense of the Christian worldview as objectively true, rationally compelling, and existentially or subjectively engaging."[1] A Christian apologist defends Christian

---

[1]   Groothuis, *Christian Apologetics,* 24.

truth claims from various attacks from the outside and heresies from within.

Apologetics removes intellectual obstacles so that one can hear the most important message of God more clearly. Philosopher Garrett DeWeese says, "We believe things for reasons. The stronger the reasons, the stronger the conviction. The stronger the conviction, the stronger the commitment. The stronger the commitment, the more consistent the spiritual growth."[2] The Bible commands us to do apologetics (1 Peter 3:15; Jude 3). Apostle Peter wrote in plain language, *"But in your hearts revere Christ as Lord. Always be prepared to give an answer to everyone who asks you to give the reason for the hope that you have. But do this with gentleness and respect"* (1 Peter 3:15). Apologetics is a branch of theology that deals with giving a reasoned defense of the Christian worldview. Apologetics walks arm-in-arm with philosophy. Philosophy assists the task of apologetics.

Philosophy is a discipline that has undergone heavy skepticism in general and within the Christian community. Many Christians, including scholars and lay preachers, view philosophy and philosophers as threats to Christianity. This is due to many misunderstandings about philosophy. While it is true that bad reasoning is dangerous to Christian theology, one cannot neglect sound reasoning to construct good systematic theology. It is inevitable for the true intellectual growth of the Christian community. A prolific writer and Christian intellectual, C.S. Lewis, famously writes, "Good philosophy must exist, if for no other reason, because bad philosophy needs to be answered."[3]

---

[2] I have quoted this from the lecture slide prepared by Professor of Philosophy Dr. Garrett DeWeese. I've had the privilege of taking my first apologetics class with Dr. DeWeese at Denver Seminary, Colorado.

[3] C.S. Lewis, "Learning in War-Time," *The Weight of Glory* (New York: HarperCollins Publishers, 2001), 58.

This chapter briefly illustrates how philosophy can be understood as the handmaiden to theology and demonstrates the danger of neglecting philosophy in theology and Christian life. Through this, I aim to defend the discipline of apologetics and philosophy. I believe a defense for apologetics is important because of so much opposition within the Christian community. You may skip this chapter if you are not interested in reading a defense for apologetics. In Chapter 5, I have given definitions of philosophy in general. In this chapter, I connect philosophy and apologetics and their roles in Christian theology and spiritual life.

In Defense of Philosophy/Apologetics: My Personal Journey

When I accepted Christ as Lord and Savior at the age of 24, I didn't know all the intellectual grounds of the Judeo-Christian worldview. I have never heard the term 'apologetics.' My initial journey to the Christian faith was truly experiential, as I have presented in my testimony. The Holy Spirit convinced me of my sin and confirmed the truth to me. My love for knowledge, wisdom, and truth led me to pursue a major in apologetics to learn God's truth in depth intellectually and systematically. At that time, I didn't know how to define apologetics. I wasn't familiar with most of the names of major apologists. I have never read apologetics works previously. I was simply a lay-level Christian who desired to begin a deeper intellectual journey.

I have always had a huge respect for all servants and ministers of the Lord. I loved to listen and spend time with them so that I could gain some wisdom of God from them. However, some of the experiences I had with some theologians and ministers were not encouraging, especially when they heard I was going to study apologetics. Some of them discouraged me from pursuing it. They made comments like these, "I would lose my faith if I tried to reason about God," "Those who go into rational studies come back as atheists," "People who try to reason are great problems to the Christian community," "Faith is not something we can reason," "Faith and reason are against each other," etc. Since I didn't know how to refute them or defend apologetics at that time, I remained silent. Those were potentially discouraging words from some church leaders. Those words may have possibly influenced me to turn away from the apologetics journey. But I decided to take a risk. An analogy that came to my mind strengthened me to pursue this intellectual journey.

Suppose a car and truck collision occurred at a crossroad where the truck was coming from the east, and the car was coming from the north. Perfectly working CCTV cameras (Camera A, B, C, D) were placed at four different corners of the crossroad. The collision event (the truth) should correspond to the fact if it truly occurred. The CCTV cameras should have captured the footage. If such an event truly occurred, all the evidence should be consistent in a way that it truly happened. Therefore, one of the CCTV cameras cannot show the image of a bus instead of the truck in the accident. All working cameras will show the footage of that same incident at that specific time from different viewpoints. If the police officers need to find out how exactly the collision occurred, they can verify it by checking each CCTV camera footage from different angles. These are proofs that will be presented in court or make an insurance claim.

However, simply by looking into the CCTV footage, the police officers may not be able to immediately find out where and when both these vehicles originated their journeys, their final destinations, how the drivers lost control (whether one of the drivers was drunk or had a heart arrest, or the vehicle had brake issue or the driver fell asleep), etc. Finding out such information requires more investigation with the support of experts who can perform such tasks. Collecting all those data from different resources makes it possible to build a case for the truth of that collision event. This takes effort and time. One can gather information from different CCTV camera viewpoints to gain knowledge of that particular event. One can also gather information from other resources for more comprehensive details to make a case.

Just like this illustration, when we investigate or test a truth claim, we can gather data from different viewpoints and resources. A truth seeker draws knowledge from all resources and all viewpoints and evaluates it with an open mind. Sometimes, we may find vague evidence. The absence of clear evidence of an event is not necessarily evidence against an event. But if there is clear evidence, we can infer that such an event had occurred in history. Just like that, we can test the truth about God and his revelations from different sources of knowledge. This takes time, commitment, and great effort. We can gather evidence for truth from historical records, archeology, many scientific disciplines, theology, and philosophy. If truth is what we are investigating, we can keep confidence that these must be verifiable. This illustration that came to my mind gave me the confidence to pursue the study of apologetics without fear. So, I ignored all the discouraging words from anti-intellectual church leaders.

I was very honest in my truth search. I thought that if what I was studying was truth claims, no matter how I investigated or tested it, the truth would remain the truth. Sometimes, it may be a little difficult to connect all the dots initially, but eventually, it will make sense if it is true. Truth corresponds to the facts. My presupposition was that if Christianity is objectively true, then my tests of it from different perspectives will show it as objectively true. That is the nature of truth. In one sense, I was taking a risk because if it turned out that Christianity is built without reason and evidence, I would get into trouble about my faith and confidence in Christ. It would even make me doubt about the experience I had with Christ. There was even a possibility that I may even consider my spiritual experience as some kind of delusion.

My thought was that if Christianity turned out to be false, I would not spend my life defending it. I will keep all my spiritual journey to myself. However, I also decided that if it turned out to be true, I would spend the rest of my life defending it. After several years of study, the latter happened. The reason and evidence for the Christian faith are abundant. It brought a lot of tears of joy as it helped me grow strong in my spiritual journey with Christ. It helped me build a strong intellectual foundation for my faith in Christ. Now, I feel so confident and joyful to share the truth with others so that they can find the truth and have confidence in Christ.

Apologetics is an aspect of the philosophy of religion. Apologetics is connected to philosophy because philosophy is an aid in the apologetics task. The foundation of apologetics is the very character of God because philosophy assists in expressing God's image on human beings by reasoning. The theological doctrine of human beings made in the image of God implies an ability to reason because God is a rational Being. God wants his people to love Him with all their minds (Matt. 22:37). Philosophical reflection is an important aspect of loving God with all their minds. What are the roles of philosophy and apologetics in Theology?

Roles of Philosophy and Apologetics in Theology

What is Theology? Theology is rational discourse[4] or reasoning or philosophizing about God. The etymology of the word *theology* comes from two Greek words, "*Theos*" (which means "God") and

---

4   Geisler, *Systematic Theology: In One Volume*, 13.

"*logos*" (which means "reason" or "discourse"). The theological concept of God as Creator is studied as a philosophical concept. If theology is the reasoning about God and philosophy is teaching how to reason, then we cannot understand theology correctly and clearly without understanding philosophy. Philosophy is inherent to the task of systematic theology to present an organized Christian worldview. It is crucial to defend Christian theology from external attacks.[5] To accomplish this apologetics task, one needs to use the tools of philosophy. Constructing a systematic theology requires a clear definition of terms and logical argumentations, which are philosophical tools.

Philosophy can establish the foundations of systematic theology. Before one begins to reason about God's attributes and plan for the world and humanity, it is vital to have a solid philosophical foundation. For example, it is necessary to have the metaphysical foundation that God exists. There is no reason to talk anything about God if he does not exist. In that case, there is no point in building a systematic theology. As I have argued in a previous chapter, philosophy aids in demonstrating the existence of God and the true concept of God by taking data from various other disciplines. After establishing the existence of a theistic God, philosophy can further defend supernaturalism. A defense of supernaturalism is important because biblical theology is built on supernatural acts of God in history, especially the resurrection of Christ. To accomplish the task of systematic theology, the foundation of logic, which is the rational precondition, is necessary.

Logic deals with the method of valid thinking, which is a prerequisite for all thinking, including theology.[6] All theological claims are subject to the fundamental laws of thought. Deductive and

---

5   Geisler, *Systematic Theology in One Volume*, 14.
6   Ibid, 61.

inductive logic are methods used in systematic theology. Further, it is important to have a foundation of truth, as I argued in a previous chapter. This is the epistemological precondition for doing systematic theology. In a culture that overly adopts relativism, pluralism, and inclusivism, it is crucial to show the nature of truth. It is also important to defend objectivity in meaning because the objectivity and universality of truth depend on it. This view is widely rejected by many contemporary linguistics.

When doing systematic theology, it is essential to show that we can have positive knowledge of God and that finite language is capable of meaningful expression of the nature of God. Philosophy can assist in our talk about God--what should we take literally, metaphorically, figuratively, etc. One must know hermeneutics to interpret the Bible. Hermeneutics is the philosophy of interpretation. The rules of reason and interpretation used in hermeneutics come from philosophy. It is important to show that an objective interpretation of God's revelation is possible, and it helps refute subjective interpretation.[7] Philosophy can help to deal with difficult passages and confusions. It can assist in showing that there are no contradictions in the Bible.

Philosophy can help to safeguard the doctrines of theology—for example, the doctrine of the attributes of God. Philosophy can clarify the meanings of theology. For example, the meaning of the word "nature" in the two natures of Jesus and the meaning of "flesh" vs. "spirit." Philosophy can help to tackle disputes about the inerrancy of the Bible, and disputes about the nature of God. Philosophy can help to clarify different theological concepts, such as the Trinity and Incarnation.

Philosophy can help to integrate theology with any other field. For example, scientists, as they study nature, find patterns of

---

[7]   Ibid, 117.

design. Complex and specified design requires a designer. This has a theological implication. A philosopher who studies scientific data and theology can conclude that God is the designer. A philosopher who has studied religion can further demonstrate that the God of the Bible is the designer, as I have argued. Philosophy assists the task of polemics. Polemics deals with the mission of criticizing and refuting other false views of the world,[8] and defends the Christian faith from heresies and false teachings of doctrines.

Theology is the knowledge of God, which is the supreme knowledge. Philosophy can and should assist theology. There are things that philosophy has to bring to the conversation that can help theology to do what it needs to do. In short, philosophy is not trying to remove theology but assisting theology. That is why philosophy works as a handmaiden to theology. Philosophy is indispensable in this task. What are some of the common objections about apologetics and philosophy?

Common Objections to Philosophy and Apologetics

Many Christians have a misunderstanding about philosophy and apologetics. One of the primary objections most people bring forth is Colossians 2:8, where Apostle Paul warns against philosophy. When one interprets the verse in its context and looks at the bigger picture of the biblical worldview, it becomes clear that Paul's warning is against the false, hollow, deceptive, and vain philosophy, which is against the truth. A kind of Gnosticism circulated in that period, which denied the deity of Christ. There was also a kind of legalism that was plaguing during that time. Paul's warning is against these particular false philosophies.

---

[8]   Moreland and Craig, *Philosophical Foundations for a Christian Worldview*, 17.

It is important to note that there are false ideologies out there that must be avoided. One cannot identify false philosophy unless one knows it is false. When a doctor treats a patient, that doctor should have studied about sickness so that he can treat that patient correctly. Just like that, people need to understand false philosophies well to know how to refute and stay away from them. Paul's warning is not against good philosophy. It is also clear from the Bible that Paul used apologetic reasoning throughout his ministry (Acts 17:16-34.)

Another objection to philosophy is that philosophical tools are borrowed from pagan Greek philosophers such as Plato and Aristotle. It is a claim that church fathers were trying to infiltrate pagan thoughts into theological discourse. As a response, it is important to note that truth will always be true, even if a pagan says it. All truth is God's truth. Even if a pagan or Christian discovers that truth for the first time, it is still true. For example, gravity is not something that Isaac Newton invented, but he first discovered it. Even before discovering it, the world operated with the law of gravity. Just like that, Plato and Aristotle did not get everything wrong. They did not invent the laws of logic.

Plato and Aristotle did an intense analysis and came up with many conclusions. For example, they discovered that contradictions cannot be true. Laws of logic are not human-invented but self-evident. Aristotle developed it formally for a clear understanding. Pagan philosophers speculated many things about some things. Church fathers such as Augustine, Aquinas, and many others reflected on what the ancient philosophers speculated, made corrections to the errors, and used them in theological discourse. Moreover, even the apostle Paul cited pagan thinkers in Acts 17 to make his case.

Another objection to philosophy is the claim that all philosophy leads to heresy. They claim that many people who studied philosophy came out as atheists, agnostics, or pluralists. It is true that many people who have studied philosophy have gone in the wrong direction. Bad philosophical presuppositions can produce bad theology. But one cannot generalize it because only false philosophy leads to heresy. Just because false philosophy has led many people to heresy, one should not reject the discipline of philosophy as bad because good philosophy is necessary to refute bad theology.

Another objection is the claim that there is no point in studying reasoning because Christianity is irrational. They claim that the doctrines of the Trinity, Incarnation, the deity of Christ, miracles, and predestination vs. free will are not areas one can reason. However, it is important to show that Christianity is not irrational or contradictory. It can be shown that miracles are possible if theism is true. It is possible to show that the Trinity is not contradictory. Nothing in the Bible goes against the basic laws of thought. However, there are things that we cannot fully comprehend with our finite and limited minds (Romans 11:33-36). These are mysteries that are legitimate philosophical stopping points. Philosophers can demonstrate that there are things that go beyond reason, but nothing goes against reason.

Another objection is the claim that only intellectual people require philosophical arguments. While this is not true, I can accept it for the sake of argument. It is equally important to influence great minds and public intellectuals so that they can influence the culture for a better society. In addition, many lay people have honest doubts which need to be cleared to hear the truth of the gospel. Philosophy and apologetics help achieve that goal. Do we have historical and biblical support for using philosophy?

Historical and Biblical Support for Using Philosophy

Philosophy has always played a great role in the church's growth. Philosophically-minded Christians were great defenders of the faith throughout church history by articulating the doctrines clearly. They equipped the church against heresies. Some of the important theologians and apologists are Justin Martyr, Augustine, Anselm, Thomas Aquinas, John Calvin, Jonathan Edwards, John Wesley, Blaise Pascal, C. S. Lewis, Francis Schaeffer, and Carl Henry.[9]

In the Old Testament, prophets often appealed to broad arguments from the nature of the world to justify the religion of Israel (Isaiah 44-45).[10] Prophets often used moral reasoning to criticize the immorality of pagan nations (Amos 1-2). Prophets gave rational defenses for their claims. Even the Genesis creation account can be seen as a polemic or defense against the mystical cosmologies of the ancient Near Eastern culture. Genesis's emphasis on the one Creator who is separate from His creation contradicted the polytheism of nearby cultures. In the New Testament, the apostles engaged in philosophical reasoning to proclaim the gospel to unbelievers (Acts 17:2-4, 17-31; 18:4; 19:8). Paul was well educated and engaged in philosophical reasoning throughout his ministry. He quoted philosophy and poetry in his conversations.

Moreover, Jesus engaged in philosophical reasoning. In his book *On Jesus*, Groothuis argues that Jesus uses significant logical arguments worthy of a philosopher.[11] Jesus often marshals empirical evidence to support his claims. He regards non-contradiction and existential viability as necessary tests for truth. He also emphasizes the importance of imagination and character for knowing in the context of God's revelation.[12] Here is one example of Jesus as a philosopher: Once, John the Baptist sent messengers to ask Jesus the question,

---

[9]   Moreland and Craig, *Philosophical Foundations for a Christian Worldview*, 19.

[10]   Ibid, 16.

[11]   Douglas R. Groothuis, *On Jesus* (South Melbourne, Australia: Thomson/Wadsworth, 2003), 23.

[12]   Groothuis, *On Jesus*, 51.

"Are you the one who was to come, or should we expect someone else?" (Matt. 11:3). Jesus responded by giving much evidence of his messianic identity instead of a plain "yes, I am one!" From that evidence, one can conclude that Jesus is the Messiah. Groothuis puts it into an explicit *modus ponens* form of argument:

(1) If one does X-kind of actions, then one is the Messiah.

(2) I am doing X-kind of actions.

(3) Therefore, I am the Messiah.[13]

Groothuis argues that Jesus reasoned using *tertium quid, a fortiori, modus ponens*, appeals to evidence, *reduction ad absurdum*, and many more.[14]

The Danger of Neglecting Philosophy in Theology[15]

It is clear to any thinking person that true philosophy is indispensable in theology. However, the importance of philosophy has often been neglected by most church leaders, theologians, Christian scholars, and preachers. Anti-intellectualism is one of the greatest threats to the Christian faith, causing more problems in Christianity.

Many heresies are plaguing theology. Many theologians and scholars have been influenced by false philosophical presuppositions, which led them to develop bad theology. This also led to the sprouting of many cult movements. The Christian culture is becoming more relativistic. Many Christians have accepted a pluralistic approach. Truth is no longer considered absolute. Some people think there

---

[13]   Ibid, 31.

[14]   Ibid, 35.

[15]   Some of these insights come from public talks of Philosophers Dr. Norman Geisler and Dr. Richard G. Howe. Moreover, several insights come from the lectures of Professor of Philosophy Dr. Bernard James Mauser. I've had the privilege of taking some classes with Dr. Mauser at Southern Evangelical Seminary, North Carolina.

is no such thing as objective, absolute, universal truth. All truth is based on culture, time, and place. One can develop their own truths. Many Christians think there are multiple ways to God, and Christ is just one of many ways.

Progressive Christianity is on the rise. Many kinds of sexual immoralities are practiced and encouraged in many churches. Many have denied the miracle claims in the Bible, including the resurrection of Jesus Christ. Christianity is considered a mere opinion and must be accepted with blind faith. Many people claim that reason and faith do not get along. Due to bad philosophical presuppositions, many concluded that the Bible is not the inspired, inerrant, and infallible word of God. It is vital to show that the Bible is the inspired, inerrant, and infallible word of God. But unfortunately, by having false presuppositions, problems such as anti-supernaturalism, liberalism, and neo-orthodoxy have entered into theological discourse. Objective morality is widely denied. Many think that Christianity is not livable in the modern day. All these issues happened because good and true philosophy was neglected.

If philosophy is neglected, good theology becomes impossible. Good and right theology is necessary because that is what we believe. For example, if one denies the deity of Christ, then he cannot remain a true Christian. If one considers Christ only as a guru (as Hindus believe) or only sees Christ as a moral teacher, then we have no gospel message left to preach.

If philosophy is neglected, Bible study becomes difficult. Growing in the knowledge of God is a spiritual discipline. It is a form of an act of worship. Philosophy can assist in theological study personally and as a community. Good hermeneutics is necessary to do bible study, which is the philosophy of interpretation. If everybody interprets Scripture in their own ways to fit their needs, that is not a sound theology. It does not help one grow in the true knowledge of God.

A serious Bible student must be a good thinker. He should be able to learn to interpret the Bible correctly by following the correct principles and methods and must apply them in his own life.

If philosophy is neglected, the apologetics task becomes impossible. The Bible commands us to give the reason for the hope (1 Peter 3:15; Jude 3). One cannot have an apologetic conversation without philosophical tools. If philosophy is neglected, evangelism becomes difficult. Apologetics is, in one sense, a pre-evangelism. Especially in Asian countries like India, there are many major religious worldviews. They have their own sacred texts; some think they come from God. It is necessary to have pre-evangelism so that their minds can be prepared to receive the gospel. Philosophy and apologetics help to remove intellectual obstacles that stop people from pursuing Christ. It is important to show why one should accept Christ for salvation. Theologian J. Gresham Machen warned, "False ideas are the greatest obstacles to the reception of the gospel."[16]

If philosophy is neglected, integration with other disciplines becomes difficult. For example, one of the significant problems that Christianity faces is a common claim that science and Christian theology are in conflict. Many people leave their faith because of this reason. Philosophy can show how science and faith are not in conflict. I will explain this topic more in the section "scientific apologetics."

If philosophy is neglected, moral issues cannot be tackled. It is possible to show philosophically that many problems, such as abortion and homosexuality, are immoral without even appealing to Scripture. It is also possible to show that Scripture also teaches the same. Philosophy can assist in ethical matters by adequately analyzing theological doctrines. If philosophy is neglected, Christians

---

[16] J. Gresham Machen, "Christianity and Culture," *Princeton Theological Review* 11 (1913): 7.

will become a laughingstock for the public. It is important to show that Christianity is true, rational, and important to whole life. The significant objections, such as the problem of evil and suffering, must be answered with philosophical tools.

Those not trained in philosophy cannot deal with deeper theological and philosophical issues. Therefore, it is important to have philosophers dedicated to such an important task. Churches and Christian organizations should hire philosophically trained Christians to commit to such tasks so that they can face internal and external attacks. Philosophers help to develop the boldness and self-image of the Christian community. In return, Christianity can penetrate the culture to make big changes in society.

In conclusion, it is important to note that we are made in the image of the rational God. So, it is important to use the God-given ability of reasoning to bring glory to God. Philosophy and apologetics are indispensable in witnessing Christ truly. Apologetics goes arm-in-arm with philosophy. I have attempted to define philosophy in general, its role in the task of doing good systematic theology and intellectual growth of the Christian community, and the great danger of neglecting philosophy. We have seen that philosophy is indispensable in theology and that bad philosophy can affect the entire theology. Philosophy is a handmaiden to theology. Good philosophy is sacred. Good philosophers are front-line armies of the Lord. Christian churches should hire and support philosophers and apologists who can commit their lives to this complex, painful, and challenging task. Philosophy matters because truth matters. Next, we will think about the topic "faith and reason."

CHAPTER 15

Faith and Reason

There is a popular opinion that all religion depends on faith and that religious beliefs are without reason and evidence. Many people define faith as a blind belief in something that has no evidence. Prominent atheist biologist Richard Dawkins defines faith as "blind trust, in the absence of evidence, even in the teeth of evidence."[1] American educator George Smith wrote, "Reason and faith are opposite, two mutually exclusive terms: there is no reconciliation or common ground. Faith is belief without, or in spite of reason."[2] Some leave religion and turn to science because they think science relies on evidence and reasoning, requiring no faith. In fact, this is a misconception. As we tackle the matter of faith and reason, it is important to understand the meaning and nature of 'faith.' *Oxford English Dictionary* defines faith as "complete trust or confidence in someone or something." Faith is not essentially a religious phenomenon, but faith is deeply involved in our daily lives. Everybody has faith in something, a person, or a fact. What are some instances?

---

[1] Richard Dawkins, *The Selfish Gene* (Oxford: Oxford University Press, 2006), 198.

[2] George Smith, *Atheism: The Case Against God* (New York: Prometheus Books, 2010), 98.

A wife keeps faith in her husband because she has good reasons for it. One does not blindly trust total strangers. We always make sure that our car is locked when we leave it in a public parking space because we cannot blindly trust strangers. If we have been invited to a friend's house for a meal, we don't do a scientific test to see if poison is contained in the meal; we trust them. We travel on airplanes by putting faith in the pilot. We trust that pilot because we have good reasons, such as the credibility of the airline operator. A credible airline company will not hire a pilot without flying experience. An airline company hires a pilot based on good reason and evidence that he can operate an airplane. We buy a car from a credible motor company and put all our faith in that car that the car can perform sudden breaks in emergencies.

When I lived in England, I worked as a London Travel Information Advisor at Gatwick Airport. When I gave information to the travelers, they took my advice and planned their travel on my word. No one ever told me to "prove it" when I gave them travel information because I was a reliable authority for them to put faith in my words. We believe in medical reports from doctors and medical labs. It is rational to trust those authorities because the sources of those reports are trustworthy. We have to accept their words by faith. Our faith or trust or belief in those reports is reasonable. We also take action based on their report, such as whether to conduct surgery or consume medicines. On the other hand, we don't blindly trust a stranger to perform surgery on our bodies. It is irrational to put faith in someone who has no credible authority. In all these instances, we have good reasons for our faith. Faith is very much involved in scientific works as well.

When scientists do experiments, they have faith that these can be performed. Scientists need faith in presuppositions of the universe's rational intelligibility. The pioneers of modern science believed that science could be done because they knew that the universe has order and regularity.[3] We believe in theories developed by scientists. We believe those theories because credible scientists provide evidence for their findings. Since my area of expertise is not in biology or astrophysics, I do not go and test what is contained in the DNA or how stars are formed. I have to trust those who have researched those fields that are also reviewed by others in those particular fields of study.

Our trust in their findings is based on their credible authority. Nobody can have first-hand experience in every field of scientific discipline. All studies are mutually dependent on trust in other authorities. This teaches us that faith is very much involved in science as well. In short, faith is deeply involved in every area of our lives, and they are reasonable. We mostly live by inductive reasoning, where we see several lines of evidence and reasons and draw a conclusion. The more reasons we have, the more confidence we have in something, a person or a fact.

Without trying to understand the meaning and nature of faith, many think that faith is a belief for which there is no evidence. Such faith is blind faith and irrational. For many religions, faith is blind. In some parts of the world, people perform dangerous practices because of their blind faith in religious ideologies. Examples include walking over the fire, piercing the body, facing the raging bull, using sticks to cast out demons, torturing someone for the sake of blind religious beliefs, killing someone to satisfy their gods, suicide bombings, killing people of other faiths, etc. Such faith is dangerous and irrational. Such practices are harmful to society. That is not the case with the Christian faith. Christian faith is not blind faith but

---

[3]　See the chapter "The Rise and Fall of Theistic Science" in Stephen Meyer, *Return of the God Hypothesis: Three Scientific Discoveries That Reveal the Mind Behind the Universe* (New York: HarperOne, 2021).

evidence-based and reasonable. Christian claims are verifiable. The God of the Bible does not want people to believe blindly.

There are indeed many Christians who think that faith should not be dependent on reason. They believe that the Bible should be accepted blindly and that what is written in the Bible should be trusted blindly, and these are not reasonable. This anti-intellectualism is one of the greatest threats to Christianity. Groothuis notes, "While some have pitted faith against reason, the Bible does not endorse blind leap of faith in the dark but rather speaks of the *knowledge of God* gained through various rational means."[4] The God of the Bible is rational. Humans are made in God's rational image. Humans possess the capacity for rational thinking. For instance, the purpose of John's Gospel is written in John 20:30-31, that is, "Jesus performed many other signs in the presence of his disciples, which are not recorded in this book. But these are written *that you may believe* that Jesus is the Messiah, the Son of God, and that by believing you may have life in his name."

Medieval philosopher and theologian Thomas Aquinas (St. Thomas) has some great insights on faith and reason, which can illuminate our understanding of faith and reason as two different modes of knowing. They are (a) *the beliefs based on rational demonstration* and (b) *the beliefs based on the authority of a trustworthy source*. Let's explore.

Two Modes of Knowing[5]

We can gain some reason for our beliefs based on *rational demonstration* alone. For example, Natural theology enables us to

---

[4]   Groothuis, *Christian Apologetics*, 96.

[5]   This section is heavily indebted to the lecture by the professor of philosophy, Dr. J. T Bridges. I will be using a lot of wisdom from his lecture. Dr. Bridges draws wisdom from the works of Thomas Aquinas and the commentaries on the works of Aquinas. I recommend the Youtube Channel 'A Considerate Life' by Dr. Bridges.

demonstrate the existence of God (monotheism) through reason and evidence. We have done these earlier in part two. We can also demonstrate through reason and evidence that the Bible is trustworthy. (I deal with it in the biblical apologetics section.) We can demonstrate the evidence for the Bible from history, archeology, authorship of the biblical books, and the textual evidence for the Bible. All these are clearly demonstrable Christian beliefs. By demonstrating that, we can hold without a doubt that the Bible is the special revelation of God to humanity and that it could be used as a genuine authority for the rest of our beliefs.

Based on the *authority* or testimony of this trustworthy source (the Bible), we can believe what God reveals to people. While there are some Christian beliefs that we cannot rationally demonstrate fully using unaided reason alone, we can trust them based on the credibility of the authority. What are some examples of those non-demonstrable beliefs? The doctrine of the Trinity is one of them. Aquinas notes,

> There is a twofold mode of truth in what we profess about God. Some truths about God exceed all the ability of the human reason. Such is the truth that God is triune. But there are some truths which the natural reason also is able to reach. Such are that God exists, that He is one, and the like. In fact, such truths about God have been proved demonstratively by the philosophers, guided by the light of the natural reason.[6]

The doctrine of the Trinity is something that we can only understand in reliance on special revelation. This does not mean we should not try to explain the Trinity at all. The Trinity is an important doctrine. For example, the Trinity explains the reality of love; one cannot understand the Incarnation without understanding the doctrine of the Trinity. The doctrine of the Trinity makes perfect sense. In this book, I do not intend to go into greater detail about the Trinity. However, the major point I want to make is that if God had not revealed that he

---

[6]   Thomas Aquinas, *Summa Contra Gentiles* I.3.2.

is Triune, we would not know it. The Trinity is something that God revealed to us in the Scripture, which is a credible authority. It has to be accepted by trusting this credible source. Using unaided natural reason, natural theology enables us to understand the existence of a theistic God, but it cannot demonstrate the Triune nature of God. Therefore, we cannot arrive at the doctrine of the Trinity using natural reason alone. What I am trying to point out is Aquinas's approach to the doctrine of the Trinity as a non-demonstrable belief. That means natural theology will not enable us to understand the Trinity, but we have other good reasons to hold it: the Bible teaches it, and it can be rationally explained without contradiction.[7]

Since faith is trusting a credible authority, in the first place, our understanding of (or belief in) the doctrine of the Trinity is based on the credible authority of the Scripture. It is God who testifies that he is triune. Therefore, when we accept his testimony, faith is at work. We see a lot of debates on the doctrine of the Trinity, trying to demonstrate it using reason alone. Aquinas considers the doctrine of the Trinity as a non-demonstrable belief. He thinks that the Trinity can be rationally discussed, but it cannot be rationally demonstrated. Perhaps this is one of the theological doctrines that most people have difficulty explaining in a convincing way. Oftentimes, people go unconvinced. Why? As Aquinas puts it,

> Those who try to prove the Trinity of persons by natural powers of reason detract from faith in two ways. First on the point of its dignity, for the object of faith is those invisible realities which are beyond the reach of human reason... Secondly, on the point of advantage in bringing others to faith. For when people want to support faith by unconvincing arguments, they become a laughing stock for the unbelievers, who think that we rely on such arguments and believe because of them.[8]

---

[7]   See Millard J. Erickson, *God in Three Persons: A Contemporary Interpretation of the Trinity* (United States, Baker Books, 1995); "God's Unity and Triunity" in Norman Geisler, *Systematic Theology* in One Volume (Grand Rapids, Michigan: Bethany House Publishers, 2011), 537-564.

[8]   Thomas Aquinas, *Summa Theologiae*, Ia. 32. 1; Quoted in Brian Davies, *The Thought of Thomas Aquinas* (New York: Oxford University Press, 1993) 190.

Aquinas thinks it is impossible for the finite mind to fully comprehend the infinite God. There is a limit to what one can imagine what God is like using natural reason alone. There is an infinite gap between a finite mind and an infinite mind. There are three persons in Godhead, which is beyond our ability to imagine. Aquinas believes that philosophy assists us in showing that the Trinity is not contradictory and not impossible. Many theologians, including Aquinas, have discussed the doctrine of the Trinity. They use various analogies to explain the Trinity. Aquinas's approach is that he provides reasons to believe in the doctrine of the Trinity and shows that the objections to the belief fail.

Aquinas believes that the Trinity is a mystery. For him, the word "God," when considered apart from the doctrine of the Trinity, is more mysterious than the doctrine of the Trinity itself.[9] He thinks that the moment when we use the word "God," our reason falls short in one sense because what "God is" is always beyond our ability to understand using reason alone. What God *is* like? I think about it this way—can someone imagine what it is like to be timeless, spaceless, and immaterial? Our experience of this world is bound to the dimensions of time, space, and matter. The God—who is timeless, spaceless, and immaterial—is beyond our ability to imagine using the power of natural reason alone. But we have good reasons for the existence of such a being as a metaphysical necessity. That God not only revealed his existence through nature, history, and conscience, but also revealed in the Scripture that he is Triune. We believe in the Trinity because Scripture is a reliable testimony from God. Faith or trust in a credible authority is at work. Even if the doctrine of the Trinity is non-demonstrable using natural reason, it is reasonable to trust the authority. As Pascal writes, "Faith certainly tells us what

---

9　Davies, *The Thought of Thomas Aquinas,* 188.

the senses do not, but not the contrary of what they see; it is above, not against them."[10]

Maybe the right question to be asked is, "Is the Bible a trustworthy source?" to put our trust in what is revealed. If we have good reason to accept that the Bible is a trustworthy source, then we have good reasons to believe the doctrine of the Triune nature of God based on the authority of the Scripture. Whenever I discuss the doctrine of the Trinity with others, Aquinas's approach has always helped me satisfy people more easily than most other theologians' approaches. Aquinas's approach is simple and reasonable. I agree with Aquinas that the Trinity can be rationally discussed, but it cannot be rationally demonstrated using reason alone apart from special revelation.

There is a relationship between "faith" and "reason" in discussing the doctrine of the Trinity. Natural reason alone cannot prove the Trinity. An analogy may help. Suppose I am a car mechanic. If I use a heavy spanner where a hammer should be used, it may not give the perfect result. Just like that, if I use the tool "reason alone" where "faith" is the right tool, it doesn't produce the right result. When it comes to the discussion of the doctrine of the Trinity, even to start the conversation of the doctrine of the Trinity, faith or trust in God's testimony is at work in the first place. The tool "reason" assists us in further discussion to make sense of this important doctrine. However, if we try to tackle the doctrine of the Trinity using "reason alone," it doesn't produce great results because the object of discussion is the Godhead. I think we have to discuss this doctrine with a lot of humility because God is infinite, and we are finite. We have to trust what God says about him. Philosopher Henri Renard writes,

> The knowledge of the God of philosophy is a scientific, and objectively evident knowledge; consequently it is communicable. It will supply a rational, secure basis which man, any man, must require, if not in its entirety, at least indirectly,

---

[10]   Blaise Pascal, *Pensees* (Penguin Classics) (p.56), Penguin Books Ltd. Kindle Edition.

as a fundamental estimation of the existence of a Supreme Being. This rational basis, human reason must possess at least implicitly in the formation of the act of faith… the objective presentation of the philosopher in presenting a formal demonstration of the existence of God paves the way towards faith, for it proposes a necessary foundation for the acceptance of the God of religion, *of the Triune God.*[11]

The doctrine of the Trinity goes well with other beliefs that we have good reasons to accept based on the authority of the Scripture. In order to discuss and understand the doctrine of Incarnation, the doctrine of the Trinity is important. The doctrine of Incarnation is also a non-demonstrable belief using reason alone. We can definitely rationally discuss the Incarnation and show historical support for the unique birth of Jesus Christ. Indeed, the Incarnation was necessary for man's salvation, and it was proper for God to communicate his divine perfection in the best way through the Incarnation.[12] However, there is still a mystery about the Incarnation that we cannot fully comprehend using reason alone. For example, in the doctrine of the Incarnation, there is a union of two natures (divine and human) in one person. I am not going into the details surrounding the Incarnation in this book either.[13] Geisler writes, "Theologically, a mystery is something that does not go against reason, but beyond reason."[14] What are the other non-demonstrable Christian beliefs we can think of?

We can think of Atonement as a non-demonstrable belief. Apart from the special revelation, we cannot rationally demonstrate how the death and resurrection of Jesus satisfied God the Father's justice. It also requires special revelation that the event undeniably satisfied

---

[11]   Henri Renard, *Foreword*, in Maurice Holloway, *An Introduction to Natural Theology* (Eugene, OR: Wipf and Stock Publishers, 2018) [emphasis added].

[12]   Lecture slide "The Incarnation" by professor of philosophy and theology, Dr. J.T Bridges.

[13]   See the chapter "Defending the Incarnation" in Douglas Groothuis, *Christian Apologetics: A Comprehensive Case for Biblical Faith*, 2nd ed. (Downers Grove, IL: InterVarsity Press, 2022), 549-566. Groothuis defends the rational coherence of the Incarnation.

[14]   Norman Geisler, *Systematic Theology*, Vol. 2 (Grand Rapids, Michigan: Bethany House Publishers, 2003), 251.

God the Father's justice. We have to accept this belief based on the credible testimony of the Scripture. There is indeed a logic to the Atonement; it makes sense given the character of God, the work of Christ, and the fact of sin. I suggest the work of Groothuis, who has done a comprehensive treatment of this topic.[15]

Another non-demonstrable belief is our personal end. We cannot rationally demonstrate our destinies (Heaven or Hell) apart from special revelation. God revealed to us his desire for us to be with him in heaven by accepting Christ as our Lord and Savior. He also revealed that those who die apart from Christ will be forever separated from God and will be in Hell. These are non-demonstrable beliefs apart from the Scripture. We can only accept these beliefs based on the credible authority of the Scripture. Indeed, Heaven and Hell[16] make sense (Matt. 25:46). But we needed a trustworthy source to confirm that it truly exists. Can you now see how faith and reason work together for Christian beliefs? Some of these Christian beliefs are non-demonstrable using reason alone, but these are reasonable beliefs because we have good reasons to trust the authority of the Scripture. It is important to note that these beliefs are not irrational. There are 100% trustworthy beliefs, without a doubt.

Aquinas writes on faith, "Sometimes what we assent to is insufficiently convincing, and our assent is determined by a voluntary choice between alternative positions. If the choice is made tentatively, we call it *opinion*, but if with certainty and without doubt, we call it *faith*."[17] Based on the authority of the Scripture, we can have beliefs with certainty and without a doubt. This is why Aquinas calls "faith" a mode of knowing the truth about God as we trust the trustworthy source given by God. For example, Jesus Christ promised his return.

---

[15]   See Groothuis, *Christian Apologetics*. Groothuis has two chapters on Atonement.
[16]   See the chapter "Hell on Trial" in Groothuis, *Christian Apologetics,* 709-716.
[17]   Thomas Aquinas, *Summa Theologica,* 2a2a, Q.1, a.4.

Can we believe it with certainty and without doubt? Yes, because we can rely on the testimony of the Scripture. We have good reasons to trust that authority. So what can we conclude from our understanding of faith and reason as two modes of knowing?

Faith and reason are two modes of knowing the truth about Christian beliefs. We have seen that some beliefs are rationally demonstrable using reason alone, and some beliefs are based on the authority of the credible source or testimony of God. Faith is complete trust or confidence in someone or something with credible authority or good reasons. Faith in God is complete trust (i.e., without doubt) in what he says. What God says in the Scripture is true and fully trustworthy, even if some things are beyond human reason.

In the next section, I will try to elevate "faith" above "reason" using Aquinas's thoughts. This is for practical life application. My goal with the next section is to make you trust God's Word more than your own thoughts in real life. Through that I want to encourage readers in two things: to make you desire to (a) *Hunt for heavenly wisdom and knowledge*. If properly understood, this section offers motivation to dig deeper into the Scripture, which enables you to gain treasures of heavenly wisdom and knowledge; (b) *Listen to God, who knows better*: If properly understood, this will strengthen your spiritual life, especially in the midst of uncertain situations where you have no idea of how to navigate forward in life. The goal is to make you listen to God, who knows better than what you know through reason. Let's explore.

Faith above Reason

Hunt for Heavenly Wisdom and Knowledge

Human reasoning helps us to know several truths about our world and our lives without a doubt. For example, the laws of logic,

God's existence, scientific knowledge, moral knowledge, historical knowledge, etc. Human reasoning is naturally capable of learning and grasping those with great clarity. This knowledge is great and important for our lives, and we should not deny that knowledge. However, it is far better to gain heavenly wisdom and knowledge from a trustworthy source (the Bible). There are great treasures of wisdom and knowledge revealed in the Scripture. As we dig deeper into the Word of God, we can gain these treasures of wisdom and knowledge and apply them in our lives. Some of the truths that we gain from the Scripture touch the highest realities that the human mind is naturally incapable of grasping. Such higher knowledge is more desirable than the knowledge we can gain through human reason.

Many truths that are revealed in the Scripture are not as clear to the human mind as those that we can understand through reason. For example, we have never had a chance to meet Christ face-to-face yet. Those who are saved by faith in Christ will indeed meet him face-to-face in all glory when the time comes, and they will be with him forever. Until then, we do not know the full extent of what that experience would be like. However, even by digging deeper into the Scripture itself, we can have treasures of wisdom and knowledge about Christ. We may even be able to experience Christ's beautiful presence more powerfully if we do that.

We also do not know what the heavenly realm looks like. God has indeed revealed truths about it,[18] but until we access that realm, many things will remain unclear to human minds. However, we can gain treasures of heavenly wisdom and knowledge by digging deeper into the Scripture. Faith is at work when we go deeper into the Scripture as our thoughts are attempting to gain higher (godly) knowledge and wisdom by trusting his words.

---

[18]   See the Scriptures Rev. 21 & 22; 1 Cori. 2:9; 1 John 3:2; John 14:2, etc.

With this higher view of Scripture in mind, French philosopher Etienne Gilson writes, "Faith is above reason, not in what concerns its mode of learning, for indeed its knowledge is of an inferior kind because of its very obscurity, but in that it puts human thought in possession of a truth which is naturally incapable of grasping."[19] Gilson also writes, "… the slightest knowledge touching the highest realities is far more desirable than the most absolute certitude touching minor objects…"[20]

What Gilson means is that if one can gain knowledge about things that reason by itself is naturally incapable of grasping, it can be considered an extraordinary achievement. While it is great to obtain knowledge without doubt through reasoning, it is far more desirable to gain knowledge about higher realities from a credible source. This is only possible through faith in what God—who knows better—has revealed in the Scripture. In short, accepting what God says just the way it is even if some things are beyond reason. In that sense, the knowledge and wisdom we can gain from the Scripture through faith are above the knowledge and wisdom we can gain through reason.

If one digs deeper into the Scripture, it gives treasures of godly wisdom and knowledge. The more one digs, the more one can gain. This will bring us closer to the Lord. God knows more about the higher realities, our world, lives, and future. The knowledge and wisdom that comes through the Scripture provide the greatest satisfaction to the most devout human because they come from God. Let this be our greatest desire. Let us dig deeper into the Word of God for treasures.

---

[19] Etienne Gilson, *The Christian Philosophy of St. Thomas Aquinas* (New York: Random House, 1966),18.

[20] Gilson, *The Christian Philosophy of St. Thomas Aquinas*, 24; citing *Summa Theologica*, I, 1. 5, ad 1; ibid. I, II, 66, 5 ad 3; Sup. Lib. De Causis. I.

Listen to God, who knows better

In Christian life, we often face challenging and dark situations when we do not know what to do. Indeed, wise thinking is good in situations where a solution can be found by our own thinking. In such a situation, our actions may bring a solution. But there are situations when we see dead ends, and we have no idea what to do next. At that time, we think too much and often stress out too much, fearful of not knowing the future. We think about all the possible negative consequences that may come to our lives in such situations. Stress never brings a solution either, but it can damage our health. This is the situation when we should trust God's Word more than letting ourselves think too much unnecessarily. Our own sight of a situation may be blurry, which leaves us uncertain. However, God knows things with certainty because he has a better picture. Aquinas writes,

> Other things being equal, sight is better than hearing; but if the one we are listening to can see more, then hearing gives the better certainty. So what we hear from God, who cannot be mistaken, is much more certain than what we can see by reason, which makes mistakes.[21]

Aquinas is demonstrating that God has a better picture of the world and our lives. Our reasoning may make mistakes, but God cannot make mistakes. The Word of God is infallible; our own reasoning may be fallible. So, it is always better to listen to the Word of God that is infallible. Professor of Philosophy J. T. Bridges shared an analogy of faith in one of his lectures, which goes well with Aquinas's thoughts. Bridges shared,

> One summer, a man was out for a dip in the lake at the end of the day. As the sun was setting, a thick fog descended upon the lake. Well away from shore, he soon lost his sense of direction as the sun's light was diffused through the fog. He began to panic and would strike out in one direction, only to lose confidence

---

[21]   Aquinas, *Summa Theologica*, 2a2ae. 4.8.

and strike out in another. After half an hour, someone came to look for him; he heard him calling and swam to safety.[22]

In this analogy, the person who is in the lake has no idea which direction to swim because he has lost his sight and sense of direction. But when he heard the person who had a better picture of the situation, the one in the lake swam in that direction and got saved just by listening to that authority. Sometimes, everything may look foggy in our life journey, and we don't know which direction to go. But we can listen to the Word of God with certainty because God has a better picture of the world. His promises and guidance given in the Scripture cannot fail. It also comforts us. Listening to the one who knows more is the only solution in this situation. Faith in God's Word is better than reasoning too much in such situations. We could use another analogy.

At some beaches, there are lifeguards that monitor for sharks to help people. They use drones or simply watch from their tall stands for a better view. Those who are swimming in the ocean cannot spot sharks easily. But the lifeguard who can see more can give warnings when sharks come closer to people. In this instance, hearing from the lifeguard is more reliable than trying to find sharks with our own eyes. The wise people listen to the lifeguards to avoid getting into danger. Just like that, if we have good reasons to trust the authority of the Scripture, hearing from the Word of God is the best solution to navigate our lives. This is something to be applied not only in times of trouble but also in regular life.

We live in a time when many young people are drawn to secular ideologies and opinions. We should not listen to or let those ideologies control our lives. It is always best to walk in the ways of the Lord by

---

22   This analogy was shared in a lecture by Dr. Bridges. He owes credit to another sermon. See also appendix ""Faith" versus Faith" in Francis *Schaeffer's He is There and He is Not Silent, 30th Anniversary ed.* (IL: Tyndale House Publishers, 2001), 87.

listening to what is revealed in the Scripture. Our lives must always be aligned with what the Scripture says is true, good, and beautiful. These would give the best result in our lives. God's ways are always perfect. God would be more pleased if we listened to his Word because faith is in exercise as we trust him. The Scripture is given by God who has the better picture of the world.

There are times when we have to stop reasoning fully and practice trusting the Lord instead. In times of heavy darkness, sometimes our own reasoning might not bring any light, but we have good reasons to have faith in God, who has a better picture of our individual lives. Gilson writes, "Reason is meant to throw its light wherever it can, but when darkness becomes invincible, reason gives way to love, and there is the beginning of the mystical life."[23] I can relate to what Gilson says. Ever since I obeyed God's calling about six years ago, my future began to seem like a mystery. It is still the same. But there is a thrill in such a mystery because nothing is mysterious to God, who chose me to be part of his mission. As the Scripture says, "For we walk by faith, not by sight" (2 Cor 5:7).

God, in his timeline, keeps unlocking those mysteries little by little. The mystery is a legitimate philosophical stopping point. "Reason" played the most significant role in determining if I could trust such a divine mystery. Then comes the need for great faith in the God of the Bible, whom I have good reasons to trust. At this point, "faith" plays the greatest role over "reason." This mystical journey is truly challenging, but the fruit it produces is incredible. This brought tears of joy as I came personally closer and closer to the Creator of the cosmos throughout these years.

---

[23] Etienne Gilson, *The Unity of Philosophical Experience* (San Francisco: Ignatius Press, 1964), 86.

Six years ago, I didn't know I had to go through a mountain of uncertainties and pain in the following years. The journey has been rough. There were times when I lost sight of which way to go. When I began this journey, if I had known ahead of time that I would go through such a dark time, I would have probably tried a better route that was smoother. In the midst of all darkness, whenever I attempted to "reason," it only brought despair into my life. But I decided to trust the one who was in control because I had good reasons to trust that authority. Now, when I reflect on those mystical routes, I realize that those were the best learning experiences.

If I had not walked through those dark mystical paths, I would have never gained the wisdom and experience that I have now, which cannot be gained from a book. Even in those dark paths, God's light was shining brightly within my heart. It was the most meaningful and purposeful journey. I always thank God for letting me go through such dark paths where I had no sight. In fact, I saw more when I lost my sight. God opened my inner eyes. What I saw and experienced was the divine presence. I learned to trust God, and I gained more confidence in God. Those are the most beautiful experiences in my life.

The entire book deals with reasoning. I love reasoning; there is no doubt about it. My faith is grounded in reason and evidence. My pursuit of truth gave me abundant reasons for my faith in God and his Word. Since I know that the Bible is the Word of God, I decided to try an adventurous faith journey. At this point in life, I am living the most adventurous and exciting journey of faith. This is my favorite section in my book because these thoughts elevated how I see the Bible and the elevated trust that I have in the Scripture without a doubt. This journey has been extremely life-transforming ever since I began practicing such an adventurous faith life. There is nothing in my life that is as exciting as this beautiful journey of faith.

Maybe most people cannot understand the depth of what I say, but I often feel like I am in a wonderland. This has always helped me build a much closer relationship with the Lord by exercising faith in practice. It not only brought me closer to the Lord, but it helped me hunt amazing treasures of heavenly and Christly wisdom and knowledge. I will end this chapter with one more thought from the Scripture.

Throughout the Bible, it talks about "faith." What can we learn from the lives of many biblical characters? Their faith was tested! Does this mean God wants an individual to live the whole life without knowing what is ahead? No! This is not the point. But sometimes God wants to test one's faith deeply before he changes one's life. It brings greater glory to God once the test is passed. The tougher the test of faith, the greater glory it brings. For instance, God tested Abraham's faith (Genesis 22); God did not test how much Abraham can reason when it comes to his relationship with God. God wanted Abraham to trust what God said to him, and Abraham did. Earlier, when God promised Abraham that Sarah would conceive and bear a son at that age, it was difficult for them to have faith in God's promise (Genesis 17). Throughout the Scripture, God wanted his people to have faith in his words. Many failed to trust God or listen to God's instructions in many instances, and God was not pleased.

Even today, when it comes to a personal relationship with God and our approach to the Scripture, our faith should be elevated above reason. There are times in life when we should discern to stop reasoning and have faith in God instead. As a young man, I only desire to grow more in this area. Of course, I use reason in many areas of life if it helps. I also use reason for my mission (e.g., this book!). However, I always make sure to stop reasoning when it is not the appropriate tool in some situations when it comes to my relationship with God. Because of this, I have experienced miracles and God's providence and provisions throughout my life. An adventurous faith is the most wonderful journey a devoted Christian should try to put into practice because its final fruits are the sweetest and greatest. Again, dig deeper into the Scripture for treasures and listen to what God says. That would be the most perfect thing.

SECTION 2:

Biblical Apologetics

CHAPTER 16

Evidence for the Bible
and the Resurrection of Jesus

EVIDENCE FOR THE BIBLE

The Bible is a historically reliable document. If the Bible is the true word of God, one should expect truthfulness in its claims. There is a common thread that passes through the entire Bible, from Genesis to Revelation, that points to Jesus Christ. Judeo-Christianity is a historically grounded worldview. There is an abundance of evidence for the places, events, and people mentioned in the Bible. These are verified by archeological discovery. Both the Old Testament and the New Testament are historically reliable documents. A lot of critical studies have been conducted by scholars on the reliability of the Bible. My goal is not to give comprehensive details but to give some basic scholarly information and some suggestions for your further study.

The Historicity of the Old Testament

The historicity of the Old Testament is important because many of the most crucial teachings of the New Testament are based on it.[1] Geisler points out that the historicity of the Old Testament is based on two major factors: *The reliability of the Old Testament manuscripts*

---

[1] Geisler, *Systematic Theology*, 329.

and *the reliability of the Old Testament authors*. The Old Testament manuscripts are considered historically reliable based on three factors. They are the discovery of an abundance of manuscripts, the dating of the manuscripts, and the accuracy of the manuscripts.

In the book, *Evidence That Demands a Verdict*, Josh McDowell and Sean McDowell give a detailed explanation of some of the Hebrew and non-Hebrew resources for the manuscripts.[2] Both Hebrew and Non-Hebrew biblical manuscripts date from c.650 BC. to c. AD 1100. Among ancient Hebrew resources, scholars have access to the Masoretic Text, the Dead Sea Scrolls, the Samaritan Pentateuch, the Nash Papyrus, and the Silver Amulets. Among the Non-Hebrew resources, scholars have access to the Greek translation of the Hebrew Bible known as Septuagint (LXX). Other Greek translations include Hexapla, Theodotion, and Symmachus.[3]

H. Wayne House and Joseph M. Holden list several other Old Testament manuscripts that scholars have access to. This list includes the Dead Sea Isaiah Scroll, Dead Sea Scroll 1 Samuel, Rylands Papyrus 458, Peshitta, Chester Beatty Papyri, Targum of Onkelos, Codex Vaticanus (B), Codex Ephraemi Rescriptus, Codex Sinaiticus, Latin Vulgate, Codex Alexandrinus, British Museum Oriental 4445, Codex Cairensis (C), Aleppo Codex, Lenigrad Codex, Codex Leningradensis B-19A (L), etc.[4] Old Testament scholar Richard Hess writes about the silver scroll discovered in 1979:

> The earliest manuscript of any recognizable part of the Old Testament is a text of part of Numbers 6: 24-26 found incised on two small silver scrolls discovered... during the excavation of Jewish burial sites at Ketef Hinnom, immediately southwest of the City of David in Jerusalem... Although they were discovered

---

[2]   Josh McDowell and Sean McDowell, *Evidence That Demands a Verdict: Life-Changing Truth for A Skeptical World* (Nashville, Tennessee: HarperCollins Publishers, 2017), 100.

[3]   McDowell and McDowell, *Evidence That Demands A Verdict, 100-107.*

[4]   H. Wayne House and Joseph M. Holden, *Charts of Apologetics and Christian Evidences* (Grand Rapids: Michigan: Zondervan, 2006), Chart 40.

in a burial context that dates from the years immediately before the destruction of Jerusalem in 586 BC, it is likely that the actual composition of these silver manuscripts should be assigned an earlier date, in the seventh century BC.[5]

There are a total of 42,300 Old Testament scrolls and codices.[6] The dating of the manuscripts also support their accuracy. Textual criticism demonstrates that the texts have been reliably transmitted.[7] There is also strong evidence for the reliability of the Old Testament authors, which scholars accept.[8]

Archeologists have unearthed an abundance of evidence for the historicity of the Old Testament narratives. Some of them are the Adam and Eve Seal, Amarna Tablets, Babylonian Chronicles, Behistun Inscription, Belshazzar Inscription (Nabonidus Chronicle), Black Obelisk of Shalmanaser III, Code of Hammurabi, Cyrus Cylinder, Ebla Tablets, Gilgamesh Epic, Goliath Inscription, Hittites, House of Yahweh Ostracon, Karnak Inscription, Merneptah Stele, Moabite Stone, Nuzi Tablets, Siloam Inscription, Tayler Prism, Tel Dan Inscription, Temptation Seal, Weld-Blundell Prism, Yehuchal Bulla, etc.[9] Here are some of the statements by scholars in the field. A world-renowned archeologist, William F. Albright, wrote,

> There can be no doubt that archaeology has confirmed the substantial historicity of the Old Testament tradition.[10]

Albright also writes,

> Aside from a few die-hards among older scholars, there is scarcely a single biblical historian who has not been impressed by the rapid accumulation of data supporting the substantial historicity of the patriarchal tradition.[11]

---

[5] Richard D. Hess, *The Old Testament: A Historical, Theological, and Critical Introduction* (Grand Rapids: Baker Academic, 2016), 10.

[6] McDowell and McDowell, *Evidence That Demands A Verdict*, 54.

[7] see Geisler, *Systematic Theology*, 330-331.

[8] Ibid., 331.

[9] House and Holden, *Charts of Apologetics and Christian Evidences*, 41.

[10] William F. Albright, *Archaeology and the Religion of Israel* (Baltimore: The John Hopkins Press, 1953), 176.

[11] William F. Albright, *The Biblical Period from Abraham to Ezra* (New York: Harper & Row, 1960), 2.

Biblical scholar Donald J. Wiseman writes,

The geography of Bible lands and visible remains of antiquity were gradually recorded, until today more than 25,000 sites within this region and dating to Old Testament times, in their broadest sense, have been located.[12]

Biblical scholar Millar Burrows writes,

The Bible is supported by archeological evidence again and again. On the whole, there can be no question that the results of excavation have increased the respect of scholars for the Bible as a collection of historical documents. The confirmation is both general and specific.[13]

Archeologist Joseph P. Free writes,

In addition to illuminating the Bible, archeology has confirmed countless pages which have been rejected by critics as unhistorical or contradictory to known facts.[14]

Historian Edwin M. Yamauchi writes,

Until the breakthrough of archeological discoveries, the stories about the biblical patriarchs- Abraham, Isaac, and Jacob- were subject to considerable skepticism... In the last thirty years, however, a steadily increasing flow of materials from Mesopotamia and Syria-Palestine- from Mari, from Nuzi, from Alalakh- has convinced all except a few holdovers, of the authenticity of the patriarchal narratives.[15]

Burrows also writes,

The excessive skepticism of many liberal theologians stems not from a careful evaluation of the available data, but from an enormous predisposition against the supernatural.[16]

It is important to note that supernaturalism is undeniable if God exists.

---

[12]   Donald J. Wiseman, "Archaeological Confirmation of the Old Testament," Carl F.H. Henry, ed., *Revelation and the Bible: Contemporary Evangelical Thought* (Grand Rapids: Baker, 1958), 301.

[13]   Millar Burrows, "How Archeology Helps the Student of the Bible," in *Workers with Youth* (April 1948): 6, as cited in House and Holden, *Charts of Apologetics and Christian Evidences*, Chart 45.

[14]   Joseph P. Free, *Archeology and Bible History* (Wheaton, Ill.: Scripture Press, 1969), 1.

[15]   Edwin M. Yamauchi, *The Stone and the Scriptures* (New York: J. B. Lippincott, 1972), 36.

[16]   Millar Burrows, *What Mean These Stones?* (New York: Meridian, 1956), 176.

Archeologist Nelson Glueck has asserted,

> As a matter of fact… it may be stated categorically that no archeological discovery has ever controverted a biblical reference. Scores of archeological findings have been made which confirm in clear outline or exact detail historical statements in the Bible.[17]

In short, we can have confidence in the historicity of the Old Testament. Let's turn to the historicity of the New Testament. In the end, I have included some recommendations for a comprehensive understanding of the Bible (both Old Testament and New Testament).

The Historicity of the New Testament

There is an abundance of evidence for the historicity of the New Testament. The historical reliability of the New Testament is based on two major factors: *the reliability of the New Testament manuscripts* and *the reliability of the New Testament witnesses*.[18] The reliability of the manuscripts is supported by the overwhelming number of manuscripts, early dating of the manuscripts, accuracy of the manuscripts, and the confirmation of the manuscripts by early church fathers. There is an abundance of evidence for the reliability of the account of the life of Christ.

The New Testament manuscripts that scholars have access to include John Rylands Fragment (P52), Chester Beatty Papyri (P45, 46, 47), Bodmer Papyri (P66, 72, 75), Codex Vaticanus (B), Codex Sinaiticus (a), Codex Alexandrinus (A), Codex Ephraemi (C), Codex Bezae (D), Magdalen Payrus, Codex Claramontanus (D2), Codex Washingtonianus, The Diatessaron, etc.[19] There is a total of 5856 Greek Manuscripts of the New Testament. There is also a total of 18,130+

---

17 Nelson Glueck, *Rivers in the Desert: A History of the Negev* (New York: Farrar, Strauss & Cudahy, 1959), 31.

18 Geisler, *Systematic Theology,* 346.

19 House and Holden, *Charts of Apologetics and Christian Evidences,* 42; McDowell and McDowell, *Evidence That Demands A Verdict,* 60-63.

non-Greek translation Manuscripts. The translated languages include Armenian, Coptic, Gothic, Ethiopian, Old Latin, Vulgate, Syriac, Georgian, and Slavic.[20] There is also a total of 36,389 citations by early church fathers. Some of them include Justin Martyr, Irenaeus, Clement (Alex.), Origen, Tertullian, Hippolytus, Eusebius, etc.[21]

There are more than 66,000 Biblical manuscripts and scrolls combining both the Old and New Testaments.[22] Compared to the Biblical manuscripts, there are only 4062+ surviving other ancient works. This includes Homer's *Iliad*, Herodotus' The Histories, Sophocles' Plays, Plato's Tetralogies, Caesar's Gallic Wars, Livy's History of Rome, Tacitus's Annals, Pliny the Elder's Natural History, Thucydides' History, Demosthenes' Speeches.[23] New Testament scholar and the founder of the *Center for the Study of New Testament Manuscripts* Daniel B. Wallace notes, "A stack of extant manuscripts for the average classical writer would measure about four feet high; this just cannot compare to the more than one mile of New Testament manuscripts and two-and-a-half miles for the entire Bible."[24]

Some of the important archeological discoveries that help confirm the New Testament include the earliest records of Christianity, the pavement, the pool of Bethesda, the Nazareth Decree, the Yohanan crucifixion, the Pilate inscription, the Erastus Inscription, New Testament Coins, the Gallio Inscription, Gabbatha, Meggido Church, Zeus and Hermes, the pool of Siloam, etc.[25] As the study continues, the numbers may increase as we gather more evidence. Some of the statements by scholars are below.

---

[20]   McDowell and McDowell, *Evidence That Demands A Verdict*, 52.

[21]   Ibid, 64.

[22]   McDowell and McDowell, *Evidence That Demands A Verdict*, 53.

[23]   Ibid, 56.

[24]   Cited by McDowell and McDowell, *Evidence That Demands A Verdict*, 53. This is an insight from Wallace's lecture at Discover the Evidence, Dec. 6, 2013.

[25]   McDowell and McDowell, *Evidence That Demands A Verdict*, 89-91.; House and Holden, *Charts of Apologetics and Christian Evidences*, 44.

Historian A.N. Sherwin-White states,

> For Acts the confirmation of historicity is overwhelming. Yet Acts is, in simple terms and judged externally, no less of a propaganda narrative than the Gospels, liable to similar distortions. But any attempt to reject its basic historicity even in matters of detail must now appear absurd. Roman historians have long taken it for granted.[26]

Archeologist and New Testament scholar Sir William M. Ramsay writes,

> Luke is a historian of the first rank; not merely are his statements of fact trustworthy... this author should be placed along with the very greatest of historians.[27]

New Testament Scholar John A.T. Robinson states,

> The wealth of manuscripts, and above all the narrow interval of time between the writing and the earliest extant, make it the best attested of any ancient writing in the world.[28]

Early Non-Christian Confirmations of New Testament History

There is overwhelmingly convincing evidence that the New Testament records are historically reliable. All events, people, places, and details of the New Testament are historically accurate. No discovery has ever overturned any claim of the New Testament.[29] There are also many other early Christian resources that give important, valuable insights. In addition to that, there are more than a dozen credible independent non-Christian sources that attest to the historicity of Jesus. New Testament scholar Gary Habermas lists 17 ancient non-

---

[26]   A. N. Sherwin- White, *Roman Law and Roman Society in the New Testament* (Grand Rapids: Baker, 1963), 189.

[27]   William Ramsey, *The Bearing of Recent Discovery on the Trustworthiness of the New Testament* (Grand Rapids: Baker, 1953), 222.

[28]   John A. T. Robinson, *Can We Trust the New Testament?* (Grand Rapids, MI: Eerdmans, 1977), 36.

[29]   Quoted from a lecture on the Historicity of the NT by Dr. Bernard J. Mauser at Southern Evangelical Seminary, 2022.

Christian resources and provides a detailed explanation. The list includes:

(1) Josephus (Jewish historian);

(2) Tacitus, Suetonius, and Thallus (Roman historians);

(3) Pliny the Younger, Emperor Trajan, and Emperor Hadrian (Roman Government officials);

(4) Lucian of Samosata and Mara Bar-Serapion (Greek writers);

(5) The Talmud and Toledoth Jesu (Jewish Resource);

(6) The Gospel of Truth, The Apocryphon of John, The Gospel of Thomas, and The Treatise on Resurrection (Gnostic Sources);

(7) Acts of Pontius Pilate and Phlegon.[30]

In the *Baker Encyclopedia of Christian Apologetics*, Geisler puts the following details about gospel accounts from non-Christian resources alone:

(1) Jesus was from Nazareth;

(2) Jesus lived a wise and virtuous life;

(3) Jesus was crucified in Palestine under Pontius Pilate during the reign of Tiberius Caesar at Passover time, being considered the Jewish king;

(4) Jesus was believed by his disciples to have been raised from the dead three days later;

(5) Jesus' enemies acknowledged that he performed unusual feats they called "sorcery";

---

[30]   Gary R. Habermas, *The Historical Jesus: Ancient Evidence for the Life of Christ* (Joplin, Missouri: College Press, 1996), 187-228.

(6) Jesus' small band of disciples multiplied rapidly, spreading as far as Rome;

(7) Jesus' disciples denied polytheism, lived moral lives, and worshipped Christ as Divine.[31]

Ancient Historical Data Assessment

Habermas examined evidence from four non-New Testament categories concerning Jesus' life, person, teaching, death, and resurrection. These four categories are:

(a) Ancient creeds and facts

(b) Archaeology

(c) Non-Christian sources

(d) Christian sources other than the New Testament.

Habermas lists 129 reported facts concerning Jesus's and disciples' message by examining 45 ancient sources, which include 19 early creedal, four archeological, 17 non-Christian, and five non-New Testament Christian sources.[32] Out of the 45 sources, 30 sources report that people believed Jesus was God. This teaching is reported by seven of the 17 non-Christian sources.

Out of 45 ancient resources, 28 specifically mention the death of Jesus. Out of 28, 12 of the sources are non-Christian. 14 of the 28 sources give more detailed information about that crucifixion event. Habermas puts it, "This is one of the best-attested facts in ancient history."[33] The resurrection of Jesus is another important event that is recorded by 18 of these 45 sources. In addition, 11 provide many facts surrounding this event.

---

[31] Norman Geisler, *Baker Encyclopedia of Christian Apologetics* (Grand Rapids, Michigan: Baker Books, 1999), 384.

[32] Habermas, *The Historical Jesus*, 243-255.

[33] Ibid, 252.

What Can We Conclude from this Evidence?

The Bible is historically reliable. Anyone can do a study on this topic because these are historical data that are accessible to everyone. As a young man, Josh McDowell set out to prove that Christianity is false. He traveled through many libraries in the US and Europe as part of his goal of disproving Christianity. However, he came to the conclusion that the Bible is trustworthy and historically reliable.[34] American atheist journalist Lee Strobel set out to prove that Christianity is false because of his wife's conversion to the Christian faith. His investigation not only converted him to Christianity but also became a staunch defender of the Christian faith today. American cold case detective J. Warner Wallace, who was a devout atheist, investigated the claims of the New Testament using his skills as a detective. It turns out that Wallace became a Christian and is now an amazing Christian apologist. All these individuals' works are available today.[35] Many have conducted similar investigations and come to the same conclusion. You may do an honest investigation, and you will come to the same conclusion. The Bible is indeed historically reliable.

For a more comprehensive understanding of the Bible, here are some scholarly resources: K. A. Kitchen, *On the Reliability of the Old Testament*, Richard D. Hess, *The Old Testament: A Historical, Theological, and Critical Introduction*; Douglas Groothuis and Andrew I. Shepardson, *The Knowledge of God in the World and Word*; John D. Meade and Peter J. Gurry, *Scribes & Scripture*; Paul Copan, *Is God a Moral Monster?*; Craig Blomberg, *Can We Still Believe the Bible?*; Craig Blomberg, *The Historical Reliability of The New Testament*;

---

[34]   McDowell and McDowell, *Evidence That Demands A Verdict*, 91.

[35]   See Lee Strobel, *The Case for Christ: A Journalist's Personal Investigation of the Evidence for Jesus* (Grand Rapids: Zondervan, 2016). J. Warner Wallace, *Cold-Case Christianity: A Homicide Detective Investigates the Claims of the Gospels* (Colorado Springs: David C Cook, 2013).

D. A Carson and Douglas J. Moo, *Introduction to the New Testament;* Paul D. Wegner, *The Journey from Texts to Translations.*[36]

THE RESURRECTION OF JESUS

Biblical Theology is built on the supernatural acts of God. The historical events, such as the virgin birth of Christ and his miracle-filled ministry, are beyond nature's power to produce. The central claim and grand miracle of Christianity is the bodily resurrection of Jesus Christ from the dead. Without the resurrection, there is no Christian message of hope and a new life. Apostle Paul wrote, "If Christ has not been raised, our preaching is useless and so is your faith. More than that, we are then found to be false witnesses about God.… And if Christ has not been raised, your faith is futile; you are still in your sins. Then those also who have fallen asleep in Christ are lost" (1 Cor. 15: 14-18). Are miracles really possible? This is a question that many people raise nowadays. Can one rationally believe in the miracle claims in the Bible during an era of modern science? Before I give historical evidence surrounding the resurrection of Jesus Christ, I aim to give a philosophical defense on the possibility of miracles.

---

[36] Full information about the book titles: K. A. Kitchen, *On the Reliability of the Old Testament,* (Grand Rapids: Eerdmans, 2003); Also see Richard D. Hess, *The Old Testament: A Historical, Theological, and Critical Introduction* (Grand Rapids: Baker Academic, 2016); Douglas Groothuis and Andrew I. Shepardson, *The Knowledge of God in the World and Word:* An Introduction to Classical Apologetics (Michigan: Zondervan, 2022), 182-193; John D. Meade and Peter J. Gurry, *Scribes & Scripture: The Amazing Story of How We Got the Bible* (IL: Crossway, 2022), (You may also follow the *Text & Canon Institute* of Phoenix Seminary); Paul Copan, *Is God a Moral Monster? Making Sense of the Old Testament* God (Grand Rapids: Baker, 2011); Craig Blomberg, *Can We Still Believe the Bible? An Evangelical Engagement with Contemporary Questions? (Grand Rapids: Brazos, 2014);* Craig Blomberg, *The Historical Reliability of the New Testament: Countering the Challenges to Evangelical Christian Beliefs* (Nashville: B&H Academic, *2016);* D. A Carson and Douglas J. Moo, *Introduction to the New Testament* (Grand Rapids: Zondervan, 2005); Paul D. Wegner, *The Journey from Texts to Translations: The Origin and Development of the Bible* (Grand Rapids: Baker Academic, 1999).

Are Miracle Claims Scientific Nonsense?

Many thinkers in the past have attempted to discredit miracles and tried to show that miracles are impossible and they are scientific nonsense. One of the challenges came from Scottish skeptic philosopher David Hume, who argued, "A miracle is a violation of the laws of nature; …firm and unalterable experience has established these laws."[37] How do we deal with this challenge? A miracle is impossible and irrational if we presuppose naturalism. Naturalism is the belief that nothing exists beyond the natural world. However, a miracle is very likely if one admits the possibility of the existence of God. Miracles are possible in a theistic world. If one denies the possibility of miracles, one must disprove God's existence in the first place. Where does the evidence lead?

As I have argued earlier in part 2, there is much undeniable evidence for God's existence from modern scientific and philosophical points of view. All evidence points to a theistic world, which particularly points to the God of the Bible. If God exists, then miracles are possible. If God can create the universe out of nothing (*ex nihilo*), He can also intervene in creation. Christians do not believe God created a universe that is a closed system of cause and effect. God can continue to act in his creation whenever he wants. How do we deal with the miraculous resurrection of Christ and Hume's challenge to the miracle?

Hume's statement itself suggests a regularity in the natural law. If bodies rise from the dead frequently in the natural world, we cannot call it a miracle. The resurrection of Jesus Christ was a miracle. God did not change the natural law, but it was a special act of God in history. The natural laws were created by God, but he is free to supernaturally cause events that nature, on its own, could

---

[37]   David Hume, *Enquiries Concerning Human Understanding and Concerning the Principles of Morals.* 3rd ed. (Oxford: Claredon, 1975), 90.

not produce. Miracles are divine interventions into the natural world for distinctive purposes.[38] Theism makes miracles possible. If I put it into a logical syllogism:

Premise 1: If the universe is Theistic, then miracles are possible.

Premise 2: The universe is Theistic. (See part 2.)

Conclusion: Therefore, miracles are possible.

Philosophically, one can rationally believe--with confidence-- in the miracle claims in the Bible during an age of modern science. The only way to disprove miracles is to disprove God's existence. Given all philosophical and scientific reasons, the existence of God is undeniable. Therefore, miracles are possible. Along with this philosophical defense for the possibility of miracles, there are other abundant reasons, including the undeniable historical evidence for the resurrection of Jesus Christ since it was an event in human history.

Now, I will present the historical evidence surrounding the bodily resurrection of Jesus. I do not intend to give a detailed explanation of the events surrounding the resurrection because this topic has already been studied and critiqued by many prominent scholars. A short section is not sufficient to explain all the details. I refer to some of the scholarly comprehensive works if you are interested in exploring more.

Historical Evidence

In his book *Reasonable Faith*, philosopher Craig presents a detailed treatment of three independently established historical facts about the resurrection of Jesus Christ. They are:

---

[38]   See Chapter 3, Miracles: The Supernatural Precondition in Geisler, *Systematic Theology*, 38-39.

1) The discovery of Jesus' empty tomb.

2) The appearance of Jesus alive after his death, and

3) The origin of the Christian faith.[39]

Craig lists multiple lines of evidence for the empty tomb. There are several alternate explanations for the empty tomb offered by those who denied the resurrection. These are the conspiracy hypothesis, swoon or apparent death hypothesis, the wrong tomb hypothesis, the displaced body hypothesis, the disciples stole the body, the hallucination theory, the claim that a substitute took Jesus's place on the cross, the claim that the New Testament writers copied pagan resurrection myths, the disciples' faith led their belief in the resurrection, etc.[40] Many scholars have responded to the alternate explanations or theories for the empty tomb presented by those who deny the resurrection, and none of them are satisfactory, given the evidence. A New Testament critic Jacob Kremer writes, "By far most exegetes hold firmly to the reliability of the biblical statements about the empty tomb."[41]

Craig also examines the resurrection appearances by considering two major points: the fact of the postmortem appearances and explaining the resurrection of Jesus. Craig writes,

> ...it is well established that in multiple and varied circumstances, different individuals and groups saw Jesus physically and bodily alive from the dead. Furthermore, there is no good way to explain this away psychologically. So once again, if we reject the resurrection of Jesus as the only reasonable explanation of the resurrection appearances, we are left with an inexplicable mystery.[42]

The origin of the Christian faith is another fact surrounding the

---

[39] Craig, *Reasonable Faith,* 361.

[40] Craig, *Reasonable Faith,* 361-77; Norman L. Geisler and Frank Turek, *I Don't Have Enough Faith to Be an Atheist* (Wheaton: Illinois: Crossway, 2004), 301-315.

[41] Jacob Kremer, *Die Osterevangelien- Geschichten um Geschichte* (Stuttgart: Katholisches Bibelwerk, 1977), 49-50. as cited in Craig, *Reasonable Faith,* 370.

[42] Craig, *Reasonable Faith,* 387.

resurrection, as it depends on the belief that Jesus rose from the dead. All these three independently established facts point to God raising Jesus from the dead. Habermas did a comprehensive study of this topic and lists 12 facts that are agreed upon by critical scholars. They are:

1. Jesus died by crucifixion.

2. Jesus was buried.

3. Jesus' disciples were discouraged and lost hope.

4. The tomb was found empty soon.

5. The disciples believed that they later saw the literal appearance of the risen Jesus.

6. Disciples' lives were transformed thoroughly. They were willing to die for this belief.

7. The message of resurrection was the center of their early preaching.

8. Disciples preached the resurrection in the city of Jerusalem shortly after it happened.

9. The church was born and had rapid growth. The resurrection was the central message.

10. Sunday was the primary day of worship.

11. James, the brother of Jesus, was a skeptic who converted to belief in the resurrection of Jesus. He believed he saw the resurrected Jesus.

12. Saul of Tarsus (Paul) was converted and became a Christian believer and proclaimed that he saw the risen Jesus.[43]

---

[43]   Gary R. Habermas, *The Risen Jesus and Future Hope* (Lanham, Md.: Rowman & Littlefield, 2003), 9-10.; also see, Geisler, *Systematic Theology*, 361; Geisler and Frank Turek, *I Don't Have Enough Faith to Be an Atheist*, 299-300.

Groothuis treated the topic of resurrection by considering the four minimal facts that are broadly agreed upon by most New Testament scholars. (1) Jesus' death on the cross; (2) Jesus' burial in a known tomb; (3) the empty tomb; (4) Jesus' followers' experience of Jesus as resurrected. Groothuis writes, "a solid case for resurrection can be made from just these facts, as many have done."[44] In addition to the minimal facts, he also presents some other well-established evidence that supports the resurrection of Jesus, such as the transformation of the disciples, the early worship of Jesus, circumstantial evidence, spiritual experience in history and today, etc.[45] Resurrection is the best explanation of these facts.

In addition, the life, death, and resurrection of Christ were fulfillments of Jewish prophecies. Moreover, millions around the world testify to Christ's presence in their lives and the extraordinary transformation, including my own life. Indeed, Jesus rose from the dead physically. Any opposing claims are false claims. Now, let us move to the next chapter to evaluate the prophetic fulfillment and the divinity of Jesus.

---

[44]   Groothuis, *Christian Apologetics*, 550.
[45]   Ibid, 551-563.

CHAPTER 17

Prophetic Fulfillment and Jesus' Divinity

OLD TESTAMENT PROPHECIES
FULFILLED IN CHRIST

Blaise Pascal writes, "The most weighty proofs of Jesus are the prophecies."[1] The life and ministry of Jesus Christ were predicted in the Old Testament. Jesus' life and ministry fit the pattern of redemptive history. Messianic prophecies were fulfilled in Christ. Canon Liddon notes 332 distinct predictions that were literally fulfilled in Christ.[2] In the *Encyclopedia of Biblical Prophecy*, J. Barton Payne lists 191 predictions that were fulfilled in Christ.[3] House and Holden present a list of Messianic prophecies in the order of their fulfillment in Christ. Those are listed below (you may cross-reference all these details on your own):

1. Born of the seed of a woman (Genesis 3:15 – Galatians 4:4)

2. Born of the seed of Abraham (Genesis 12:2-3 – Matthew 1:1)

3. Born of the seed of Isaac (Genesis 17:19 – Matthew 1:2)

---

[1] Blaise Pascal, *Pensées,* Alban Krailsheimer, trans. (New York: Penguin, 1996), 102. Also see the book Douglas Groothuis, *Beyond the Wager: The Christian Brilliance of Blaise Pascal* (Downers Grove: IVP Academic, 2024)

[2] Cited in McDowell and McDowell, *Evidence That Demands A Verdict*, 229. See Floyd Hamilton, *The Basis of Christian Faith* (New York: George H. Doran, 1927), 160.

[3] Payne, J. Barton. *Encyclopedia of Biblical Prophecy* (London: Hodder and Stoughton, 1973), 665-670.

4. Born of the seed of Jacob (Numbers 24:17 – Matthew 1:2)

5. Descended from the tribe of Judah (Genesis 49:10 – Luke 3:33)

6. Heir to the throne of David (Isaiah 9:7 – Luke 1:32-33)

7. Times for Jesus' birth (Daniel 9:25 – Luke 2:1-2)

8. Born of a virgin (Isaiah 7:14 – Luke 1:26-27; 30-31)

9. Born in Bethlehem (Micah 5:2 – Luke 2:4-7)

10. Slaughter of the innocents (Jeremiah 31:15 – Matthew 2:16-18)

11. Flight to Egypt (Hosea 11:1 – Matthew 2:16-18)

12. Preceded by a forerunner (Isaiah 40:3-5; Malachi 3:1 – Luke 7:24-15)

13. Declared the Son of God (Psalm 2:7 – Matthew 3:16-17)

14. Galilean ministry (Isaiah 9:1-2 – Matthew 3:16-17)

15. The prophet to come (Deuteronomy 18:15 – Acts 3:20,22)

16. Came to heal the brokenhearted (Isaiah 61:1-2 – Luke 4:18-19)

17. Rejected by his own (the Jews) (Isaiah 53:3 – John 1:11)

18. A priest after the order of Melchizedek (Psalm 110:4 – Hebrews 5:5-6)

19. Triumphal entry (Zechariah 9:9 – Mark 11:7, 9, 11)

20. Betrayed by a friend (Psalm 41:9 – Luke 22:47-48)

21. Sold for thirty pieces of silver (Zechariah 11:12-13 – Matthew 26:15; 27:5-7)

22. Accused by false witness (Psalm 35:11 – Mark 14:57-58)

23. Silent to accusations (Isaiah 50:6 – Mark 15:4-6)

24. Spat upon and smitten (Isaiah 50:6 – Matthew 26:67)

25. Hated without reason (Psalm 35:19 – John 15:24-25)

26. Vicarious sacrifice (Isaiah 53:5 – Romans 5:6,8)

27. Crucified with transgressors (Isaiah 53:12 – Mark 15:27-28)

28. Body pierced (Zechariah 12:10 – John 20:27)

29. Scorned and mocked (Psalm 22:7-8 – Luke 23:35-36)

30. Given vinegar and gall (Psalm 69:21 – Matthew 27:35)

31. Prayer for his enemies (Psalm 109:4 – Luke 23:34)

32. Soldiers gambled for his coat (Psalm 22:18 – Matthew 27:35)

33. No bones broken (Psalm 34:20 – John 19:32-33, 36)

34. Side pierced (Zechariah 12:10 – John 19:34)

35. Buried with the rich (Isaiah 53:9 – Matthew 27:57-60)

36. Would rise from the dead (Psalm 16:10; 49:15 – Mark 16:6-7)

37. Would ascend to God's right hand (Psalm 68:18 – Mark 16:19)[4]

McDowell and McDowell present a detailed treatment of some of the Old Testament prophecies fulfilled in Christ. These are:

1. Christ our Passover lamb (Exodus 12:21 – 1 Corinthians 5:7)

2. Christ the Lord's provision (Genesis 22:1,2 – Hebrews 11:17-19)

3. Christ our High Priest and King (Psalm 110:4 – Hebrews 7:1-3)

4. The Angel of Yahweh (Exodus 3:2-5 – John 1:18)

5. The Bronze Serpent (Numbers 21: 8,9 – John 3:14,15)

---

[4]   H. Wayne House and Joseph M. Holden, Charts of Apologetics and Christian Evidences (Grand Rapids: Michigan: Zondervan, 2006), Chart 50.

6. The Son of Man (Daniel 7:13,14 – Mark 14:61, 62)

7. Pre-existent and Divine (Micah 5:2 – Colossians 1:17; Revelations 1:1,2; 1:17; 2:8; 8:58; 22:13)

8. A Prophet (Deuteronomy 18:18 – Matthew 21:11; Luke 7:16; John 4:19; 6:14; 7:40)

9. Of the line of Jesse and the House of David (Isaiah 11:1-3 – Romans 1:1-3)

10. Judge (Isaiah 33:22 – 2 Timothy 4:1)

11. King (Psalm 2:6; Jeremiah 23:5; Zechariah 9:9 – Matthew 27:37; Matthew 21:5; John 18:33-38)

12. Special presence of the Holy Spirit (Isaiah 11:2 – Matthew 3:16; Matthew 12:17-21; Mark 1:10; Luke 4:15-21, 43; John 1:32)

13. Preceded by Messenger (Isaiah 40:3 – Mark 1:1-3)

14. Ministry to begin in Galilea (Isaiah 9:1 – Matthew 4:12-14, 17)

15. Ministry of miracles (Isaiah 35:5,6 – Matthew 9:35)

16. Teacher of parables (Psalm 78:2 – Matthew 13:34, 35)

17. He was to enter the temple (Malachi 3:1 – Matthew 21:12)

18. He was to enter Jerusalem on a donkey (Zechariah 9:9 – Luke 19:35-37)

19. A "light" to the Gentiles (Isaiah 49: 5,6 – Acts 13:47, 48; Acts 26:23; 28:28)[5]

In addition to the above, the McDowells list Isaiah 52:13 – 53:12 (concerning the suffering and mission of the Messiah). They also list the prophecies regarding the time of the Messiah's coming. It

---

[5]   McDowell and McDowell, *Evidence That Demands A Verdict*, 205-231.

includes Genesis 49:10 (the removal of the Scepter or identity of Judah), Haggai 2:6-9 (the glory of the Lord filling the temple), and Malachi 3:1 (divine visitation at the temple before its destruction).

In his book *Science Speaks*, Professor of Mathematics and Astronomy, Peter Stoner of the American Scientific Affiliation examines the mathematical probabilities that apply to the fulfillment of the prophecies.[6] Just by considering eight prophecies (Messiah's birth in Bethlehem, preceded by a messenger, entry to Jerusalem on a donkey, betrayal by a friend, betrayer would receive thirty pieces of silver, the betrayal money would be used to buy a potter's field, silence before accuser, hands and feet would be pierced and would die accounted among criminals[7]), Stoner writes, "We find that the chance that any man might have lived down to the present time and fulfilled all eight prophecies is 1 in 10^{17}.[8] That would be 1 in 100 000 000 000 000 000 (17 zeroes after the one)." By considering 48 of the prophecies he writes, "We find the chance that any one man fulfilled all 48 prophecies to be 1 in 10.[157] This is really a large number and it represents an extremely small chance."[9] Pascal writes,

> If a single man had written a book foretelling the time and manner of Jesus's coming and Jesus had come in conformity with these prophecies, this would carry infinite weight. But there is much more here. There is a succession of men over a period of 4,000 years, coming consistently and invariably one after the other, to foretell the same coming; there is an entire people proclaiming it, existing for 4,000 years to testify in a body to the certainty they feel about it, from which they cannot be deflected by whatever threats and persecutions they may suffer. This is of a quite different order of importance.[10]

---

[6]   Peter Stoner, *Science Speaks: An Evaluation of Certain Christian Evidences* (Chicago: Moody Pub, 1958). Cited in McDowell and McDowell, *Evidence That Demands A Verdict*, 230-231.

[7]   Stone's work is summarized in McDowell and McDowell, *Evidence That Demands A Verdict*, 231.

[8]   Stoner, *Science Speaks*, 100-107.

[9]   Ibid, 109-110.

[10] Pascal, *Pensées*, 101.

In his book, *Beyond the Wager,* Groothuis writes,

> Strong arguments in favor of prophetic fulfillment are apologetically significant because they indicate a supernatural mind that predicts and coordinates events that are (1) antecedently unlikely and (2) which fit a recognizable pattern indicating intelligence. That pattern is God's redemptive action in the world. This is called a *design inference* and it is well established in science and elsewhere.[11]

All these fulfilled prophecies lent rational support for Jesus as Messiah. Let us now turn to the topic: the divinity of Jesus Christ.

THE DIVINITY OF JESUS CHRIST

There are many lines of evidence that prove the divinity of Jesus. Geisler lists many of them.[12] Here are some of them:

1.   *Jesus claims to be the Yahweh of the Old Testament*

Yahweh (YHWH) is the designation for God in the Old Testament. In English, this word for God is transliterated with an initial capital and then three small capitals-- LORD. This term refers to deity (Exodus 6:2-3; Isaiah 44:6; Isaiah 42:8; Isaiah 48.11 cf.). The name Yahweh was so sacred. Devout Jews would not even pronounce it. Jesus Christ claimed the very things that the Yahweh of the Old Testament claimed. The Jews understood the claims. Thus, Jesus was accused of blasphemy. The Jews also tried to stone Jesus (John 8:58 and 10:31-33).[13]

   a) Jesus claimed to be Shepherd (Psalm 23:1 – John 10:11)

   b) Jesus claimed to be the Judge of all humans and nations (Joel 3:12 – John 5:27-29; Matthew 25:31-46)

---

[11]   Groothuis, *Beyond the Wager,* "Chapter: Jesus Christ, Miracle and Prophecy."

[12]   Norman Geisler, *Christian Apologetics,* 2nd Ed. (Grand Rapids, Michigan: Baker Academic, 2013), 375- 418.

[13]   Geisler, *Christian Apologetics,* 375.

c)   Jesus claimed to be light (Isaiah 60:19; Psalm 27:1 – John 8:12)

d)   Jesus claimed to share eternal glory (Isaiah 42:8 – John 17:5)

e)   Jesus claimed to be the coming bridegroom (Isaiah 62:5 cf.; Hosea 2:16 - Matthew 25:1)

f)   Jesus claimed, "I am the first and the last" – quoted by John (Isaiah 44:6; - Revelation 1:17)

g)   Jesus claimed to be "I AM" (Exodus 3:14 - John 8:58)

2.   *Jesus claims equality with God.*
   a)   Jesus forgave sin (Matthew 26:28; Mark 2:5; Luke 7:48; John 8:1-11 cf.)

   b)   Jesus is the giver of life (Mark 5:41; Luke 23:42cf.; John 6:33; 14:6).

   c)   Jesus is the Judge (John 5:22; 8:15cf.)

   d)   Jesus received worship and did not refuse it (Matthew 2:2; 2:11 8:2; 9:18; 14:33; 28:9, 17; Mark 5:6; Luke 23:42; 24:52; John 9:38; 14:14).

   e)   Jesus claimed the power to raise and judge the dead (John 5:25, 29; 12:48; Matthew 25:34,41)

   f)   Jesus requests prayer in his name (John 14:13, 14; 15:7; 14:6).

   g)   Jesus demands honor equal to God (John 5:23)

   h)   Jesus placed his word on the same level as God's (Matthew 5:21,22; 28:18-19; John 13:34; Matthew 5:18; 24:35; John 12: 48)

3.   *Jesus claims to be the Messiah.*

Deity is attributed to the Messiah (Psalm 45:6; Psalm 110:1; Isaiah 40:9; Isaiah 9:6; Jeremiah 23:6; Daniel 7:13). Jesus applied Messianic predictions to himself (Matthew 22:43-44; Mark 14:61-64; John 4:25-26; Luke 24:27, 44; Matthew 26:54). High priest tore the garment and accused Jesus of blasphemy at his trial when Jesus cleared all the doubts directly (Mark 14:62).

4.   *Jesus claims to be God in parables, which are indirect claims to the deity.*[14]

Geisler writes the logic of this claim this way:

> (1) In the Old Testament God referred to himself by a certain image; (2) Jesus used this image to refer to himself; (3) therefore, Jesus used this image to claim that he was God.[15]

These images include,

a)   Sower (Luke 8:5-8 - Numbers 24:6-7 cf.; Psalm 80:8-15 cf.)

b)   Director of the Harvest (Matthew 13:24-30 – Isaiah 27:3-12; Jeremiah 51:22)

c)   Rock (Matthew 7:24-27 – Psalm 19:14; 28:1)

d)   Father (Luke 15:11-32 – Deuteronomy 32:6; 2 Samuel 7:14)

e)   Forgiver of Sins (Luke 7:41-50 – Exodus 32:32; 34:7)

f)   Vineyard Owner (Matthew 20:1-16 – Deauteronomy 8:8; Psalms 80:8-15)

g)   King (Luke 19:11-27 – 1 Samuel 12:12; Psalm 10:16)

---

[14]   Geisler, *Christian Apologetics,* 380; Also see Philip Payne, "Jesus' Implicit Claim to Deity in His Parables," Trinity Journal 1 (Spring, 1981): 2-23.

[15]   Geisler, *Christian Apologetics,* 380.

h) Shepherd (John 10:1-18 – Psalm 23; Ezekiel 34)

5.   *The earliest disciples claim that Jesus is God.*[16]

a) The writings of John (John 1:1;14; 1 John 1:1; Revelation 1:17; 2:8; 22:13; John 1:9)

b. The writings of Paul (Colossians 2:9; Titus 2:13; Romans 9: 5; Philippians 2:5-6; Galatians 1:3; Ephesians 1:2; Philippians 1:2; 2 Corinthians 13:14)

c) New Testament writers use the OT titles of deity for Jesus.

a. Rock (Psalm 18:2; 95:1 – 1 Corinthians 10:4; 1 Peter 2:6-8)

b. Husband or bridegroom (Hosea 2:16; Isaiah 62:5 – Ephesians 5:28-33; Revelation 21:2)

c. Shepherd (Psalm 23:1 – 1 Peter 5:4; Hebrews 13:20)

d. Forgiver of sins (Jeremiah 31:34; Psalm 130:4 – Acts 5:31; Colossians 3:13)

e. Redeemer (Hosea 13:14; Psalm 130:4 – Titus 2:14; Revelation 5:9)

f. Savior (Isaiah 43:3 – John 4:42)

g. Lord of glory (Isaiah 42:8 – 1 Corinthians 2:8)

h. Judge (Genesis 18:25; Psalm 94:2 – 2 Timothy 4:1)

i. The term Lord (*Kurios* (κύριος) in Greek) (John 6:68; 20:28; Acts 1:6; Romans 1:7)

d) Jesus as the Messiah God: The Messiah of the Old Testament is Yahweh (Zechariah 14:9; Isaiah 63:9; Psalm 118:22; Psalm

---

[16] Ibid., 385-390.

110:1; Isaiah 40:9; Isaiah 9:6; Zechariah 12:10; Isaiah 45:22-23;). The New Testament writers identify the Messiah of the Old Testament with Jesus (Acts 2:34-35; Matthew 1:23; John 19:37; Revelation 1:7; Philippians 2:10-11)

e) The disciples attributed the powers that only God possesses to Jesus:

   a. Raising the dead (1 Samuel 2:6; Deuteronomy 32:39 – John 5; 11)

   b. Creator (Isaiah 40:28; Jeremiah 10:16 – John 1:3; Colossians 1:16)

   c. Forgiver of sins (Jeremiah 31:34 – Mark 2:7; Acts 5:31; 13:38)

f) The association of Jesus' name with God: It is blasphemy to associate any name with God, but Jesus' name is associated with prayer and benedictions (1 Corinthians 5:4; Acts 7:59; Galatians 1:3; Ephesians 1: 2; Matthew 28: 19; 2 Corinthians 13:14)

g) Direct declaration of Jesus' Deity:

   a. "My Lord and my God" (John 20:28) This is the confession of Thomas, which Jesus accepted.

   b. "For in Christ all the fullness of Deity lives in bodily form" (Colossians 2:9);

   c. "Our great God and Savior" (Titus 2:13)

   d. "Your throne, O God, is forever and ever" (Hebrews 1:8)

   e. "Form of God" (Philippians 2:6-7)

f. "Reflects the glory of God" (Hebrews 1:3)

g. "The Word was God" (John 1:1)

h) The proclamation of Jesus' Deity by the "voice of God" (Matthew 3:17; Matthew 17:5; John 12:28; 31-36)

i) Angels proclaimed Jesus' Deity (Luke 1:32, 35; 2:11)

j) Demons acknowledged Jesus' Deity (James 2:19; Matthew 8:29).

6. *Historical Non-Christian writers of the early Christian era testify that Jesus' disciples believed that he was God:* This includes Josephus (ca. 37/38-100); Lucian (ca. 120-180); Suetonius (ca. AD 120); Pliny the Younger (ca. AD 112); Thallus (ca. AD 52); and, Letter of Mara Bar- Serapion (after AD 73).[17]

In addition to all these, Jesus Christ's sinless life, miracle-filled life, bodily resurrection from the dead, and fulfillment of Jewish prophecies confirm the deity of Christ. In *Mere Christianity*, Lewis formulated the "God or a bad man" argument.[18] He writes,

> A man who was merely a man and said the sort of things Jesus said would not be a great moral teacher. He would either be a lunatic—on the level with the man who says he is a poached egg—or else he would be the Devil of Hell. You must make your choice. Either this man was, and is, the Son of God, or else a madman or something worse. You can shut him up for a fool, you can spit at him and kill him as a demon or you can fall at his feet and call him Lord and God, but let us not come with any patronising nonsense about his being a great human teacher. He has not left that open to us. He did not intend to. . . . Now it seems to me obvious that He was neither a lunatic nor a fiend: and consequently, however strange or terrifying or unlikely it may seem, I have to accept the view that He was and is God.[19]

---

[17] Ibid, 390-391.

[18] Groothuis did a detailed treatment of this topic in *Christian Apologetics*, 507-526.

[19] C.S. Lewis, *Mere Christianity* (New York: Touchstone, 1996), 56.

Let us put Lewis's argument into a simple logical syllogism (*Disjunctive Syllogism*[20]):

Premise 1: Either Jesus is a liar or a lunatic, or Jesus is Lord.

Premise 2: Jesus was neither a liar nor a lunatic.

Conclusion: Therefore, Jesus is Lord.

Jesus is indeed God. Any claims opposing this must necessarily be false based on the given evidence. All false claims must be rejected. Let us use the rule of argumentation for clear thinking (*Modus Ponens*).[21]

Premise 1: If X is a worldview that denies the divinity of Jesus Christ, then X must be rejected or excluded.

Premise 2: X is a worldview that denies the divinity of Jesus Christ.

Conclusion: Therefore, X must be rejected or excluded. (You may fill in the X).

Now, let's move on to the next chapter to understand the Judeo-Christian worldview.

---

[20]   *Disjunctive Syllogism*: p or q; not p; therefore q.
[21]   *Modus Ponens*: If p, then q; p; therefore, q.

CHAPTER 18

The Judeo-Christian Worldview
in a Nutshell

Ultimate Authority

The study of God's revelation of himself to humanity has been classified in two ways: general revelation and special revelation.[1] I have presented enough evidence for the existence of the theistic God through general revelation (nature, history, conscience). This chapter focuses on special revelation. The Bible is God's special written revelation to humanity. It is the absolute credible authority to gain knowledge of God. The Bible is not one book but a collection of 66 books written over 1400 years by over 40 authors in different places with the Holy Spirit's guidance. There is a common thread passing through the entire book that reveals God's most excellent drama in human history that points to the Lord Jesus Christ--the only Savior. The Bible is an inspired, inerrant, and infallible word of God.[2] It is

---

[1] Millard J. Erickson, *Christian Theology*, 3rd ed. (Grand Rapids, Mich.: Baker Academic, 2013), 121.

[2] The Bible (original writing) is God's inspired, inerrant, infallible word of God. Since God exists and the Bible is divinely inspired, God knows how to reveal the truth without error. God cannot cause error. Let this philosophical foundation sink deep into your heart. Do not let others change this view on Scripture. Do not listen to any scholars who have different opinions about inspiration and inerrancy. Do not let the scholars decide what part of the Bible is inspired and inerrant. Let God decide it. See the book by Norman Geisler and William C. Roach, *Defending Inerrancy: Affirming the*

written to communicate to the people for their own good and God's honor and glory.[3] However, it is crucial to interpret the Scripture correctly. Misinterpretation can lead to a false conclusion about life and the world (2 Peter 3:16).

Those who are rebellious to the truth view the Bible as fiction that falsely satisfies the psychological needs of people. When an author writes fiction, the story comes out of his artistic imagination. Fiction writers can simply write fantasies or create an imaginary dream world. The contents do not necessarily have to be factual, historical, or correspond to reality. Fiction, as fiction, lacks those things. Earlier, I've presented evidence for the reliability of the Bible. Since we have good reasons to conclude that the Bible is a trustworthy source for gaining knowledge of God and his plan for the world and humanity, it is the ultimate authority (2 Timothy 3:15-17). What does it say about the ultimate reality?

Ultimate Reality: God

God is the first place to begin a theological inquiry once we consider the Bible as God's special revelation. The book of Genesis opens with the declaration, "In the beginning, God created the heavens and the earth" (Genesis 1:1). That means God was before the beginning of the natural world. He is outside of the space-time dimension. He did not begin to exist. God does not emerge over natural processes. He eternally existed (Isaiah 40:28; Acts 17:25). God is uncaused. He is distinct from creation.

Accuracy of Scripture for a New Generation (MI: Baker Publishing Group, 2011); R.C. Sproul and Norman Geisler, *Explaining Biblical Inerrancy: The Chicago Statements on Biblical Inerrancy, Hermeneutics, and Application with Official ICBI Commentary* (TX: Bastion Books, 2013); Hugh Ross, *Rescuing Inerrancy: A Scientific Defense* (CA: RTB Press, 2024).

[3] Groothuis, *Christian Apologetics*, 79.

God is personal. He is not a mere force, energy, or substance.[4] Two primary characteristics are required for personality: self-reflection and self-determination. God knows himself. He thinks and acts. God is like us in personality, but we are finite and limited. Scripture portrays God as hearing (Exodus 6:5), creating (Genesis 1:1), knowing all things (Psalms 147:5; John 3:20), seeing (Psalms 94:9), and having volition (1 John 2:17).[5] We can relate to God in a personal way.

God is a Trinity, which means one God eternally existing in three coequal persons: the Father, Son, and Holy Spirit. The Trinity is a mystery that is derived from the whole of Scripture. God has always been a Triune God–God who is three-in-one. Michael Bird states, "God's revelation of himself as triune unfolds progressively in the redemptive history and culminates in the incarnation of the Son and in the pouring out of the Holy Spirit."[6] There is a fourfold theological assumption for the doctrine of the Trinity.

1. God is One (Exodus 20:2-3; 3:13-15; Deuteronomy 6:4-5; 4:34,35)

2. The Father is God (Galatians 1:1; Ephesians 1:1-3; 3:15)

3. The Son is God (Philippians 2:5-11; Hebrews 1:1-3)

4. The Holy Spirit is God (Acts 5:3, 4);

Therefore, God is Triune. Father, Son, and Spirit are three persons in one God.

---

[4] Sire, *The Universe Next Door*, 28.
[5] Groothuis, *Christian Apologetics*, 83.
[6] Michael F. Bird, *Evangelical Theology: A Biblical and Systematic Introduction* (Grand Rapids, Michigan: Zondervan, 2013), 98.

Trinity highlights that God is intrinsically relational.[7] He was not alone before creation. He did not need to bring humans into existence to have relationships and communication. Trinity is not a contradiction but a mystery as I have argued earlier. Reason assists us in discussing that the Trinity is not a contradiction.[8] God's Triune nature is something that he revealed to us in the Scripture. Trinity is a vast topic to discuss because of all the controversies. I do not intend to give a philosophical defense of the Trinity in this book.

God is infinite, which means he is beyond scope and measure.[9] Nothing in the universe can challenge God in his nature. He spoke to Moses: "I AM WHO I AM" (Exodus 3:14). God is transcendent. That means God is separate from creation. He is independent of creation (Acts 17:15). He is superior to the creation. He is separate in terms of holiness, purity, and goodness (Isaiah 55:8-9; 6:1-5; 57:15; Psalms 113:5-6). God is immanent. That means God is with us. The Bible portrays God as involved in various ways within nature, history, and humanity.[10] God's activity is present in the universe (Jeremiah 23:24; Acts 17:27-28). God's activity is present in nature (Genesis 1:2; Matthew 5:45; 6:25-30; 10:29-30). God's activity is present in human beings (Genesis 2:7; Job 27:3; 33:4).

The goodness of God is expressed in two ways--through holiness and love. God's holiness involves an absolute personal standard of righteousness.[11] Righteousness involves perfect justice. God is separate from all that is evil. 1 John 1:5 says, "God is light; in him there is no darkness at all." God's goodness is also expressed as love.

---

7   Ibid.
8   See Millard J. Erickson, *God in Three Persons: A Contemporary Interpretation of the Trinity* (United States, Baker Books, 1995); "God's Unity and Triunity" in Norman Geisler, *Systematic Theology* in One Volume (Grand Rapids, Michigan: Bethany House Publishers, 2011), 537-564.
9   Sire, *The Universe Next Door*, 28.
10   Erickson, *Christian Theology*, 121.
11   Sire, *The Universe Next Door*, 31.

The Scripture says, "God is love" (1 John 4:16). Since God is love, there is hope for humanity because he will not abandon his creation. God is just and loving. Understanding God's goodness is important to make sense of the Christian worldview. Now, let us look at the grand story of the Bible.

Grand Narrative of the Bible

By taking the Bible as the ultimate authority for the Christian worldview, we can organize its grand narrative into four broad categories: *Creation, Fall, Redemption, and New Creation.*[12]

Creation

God created the material universe *ex nihilo* (out of nothing) (Genesis 1:1; John 1:1-3). God did not create the universe out of himself or from some preexistent chaos but out of nothing.[13] God spoke it into existence. There is only the triune God eternally existed before the beginning of the material universe. The origin of the universe is supernatural, not natural. It did not pop into existence without any cause or reason.[14] God can also intervene in this universe. In a theistic universe, miracles are possible, revelation is possible, and humans are not dehumanized as part of a mechanistic universe.

God did not create the world to be chaotic (Isaiah 45:18-19). The universe has orderliness and regularity. God is constantly involved in the operation of the universe. When God created the universe, he had a purpose to bring glory to his name. The earth was created to bring humans into existence for God's glory and honor. The Bible declares that human beings are made in God's "image and likeness"

---

[12]   Ibid, 39.

[13]   Ibid., 31.

[14]   Groothuis, *Christian Apologetics*, 81.

(Genesis 1:26-27) which is very different from all other creatures. What does it mean to be made in the "image of God?"

Image of God

The image of God (*Imago Dei*) is a unique claim of the Judeo-Christian worldview. The image of God is a theological notion that could change one's perspective and make one realize humanity's highest value if properly understood. God created both men and women in "His image," which gives every human being an intrinsic value. Christian worldview refuses to reduce human beings to a byproduct of unguided natural processes without value and meaning. Human beings are ordained to glorify God by cultivating creation through godly relationships.[15] It is vital to clearly understand the meaning of the key phrase "image of God."

The "image of God" does not mean humans physically look like God with hands and legs. God is not a physical being. Instead, the phrase image of God means humans are like God in personality in an analogous way but finite and limited in form. Humans are like God but not divine. Groothuis puts it, "Human beings share the attributes of personality--agency, intelligence, creativity, rationality, emotion, and relationality--but in a form forever finite, limited, and contingent."[16] This is the best status that humans can think of. No other worldview offers such an elevated status to human beings, and no other creature has such an elevated status. Human beings are unique. Let me try to unpack the attributes to have a profound understanding of the personalities unique to human beings.

1) *Creativity:* God is a creative being. Humans also share the attribute of creativity with God. God is the Creator of

---

[15]   Groothuis, *Christian Apologetics*, 81.

[16]   Ibid., 86.

everything, including humans. Since humans are made in God's creative image, they are also creators but in a finite and limited form. Human beings are little creators. An analogy by Don Payne helps us understand better. We can distinguish God, the Creator, with the capital letter "C" and humans, the little creators, with the small letter "c."[17] Human beings possess creativity – an ability to create simple to complex things. Humans have the capacity to plan, design, create art, paint, and draw. Human beings possess the power to discover and invent things. Humans can perform science and create new things (but not "out of nothing"). The creativity of human beings is distinct from the creativity of other living creatures. Human beings also appreciate the creativity of other humans. For example, that is why we have art museums. Humans have a unique creativity because they are made in God's creative image.

2) *Rationality:* God is a rational being. Humans also share the attribute of rationality with God. Humans possess the capacity for reason and knowledge because they are made in God's rational image.

3) *Morality:* God is a moral being. Humans also share the attribute of morality with God. Humans can recognize and understand good and evil because they are made in God's moral image. Human beings discuss moral philosophy. Humans make rational moral choices.

4) *Relation:* God is a relational being. Humans also share the attribute of relationality with God. Human beings value relationships with others. Humans are relational beings

---

[17] Don Payne. "*A Theological Framework of Calling and Vocation,*" Denver Seminary Lecture, SMMR 2017, accessed on October 18, 2018, link via TM500 Moodle.

because they are made in God's relational image. God created human beings to have a relationship with him and others.

5) *Intelligence:* God is an intelligent being. Humans also share the attribute of intelligence.

6) *Free-will:* God is free. Humans also have the power or capacity to make decisions freely.

7) Royal Function: God has given us a royal function. God ordained humans to have dominion over everything (Genesis 1:28). They are "rulers over the works of your hands" by exercising their power over the creation (Psalm 8:7-8). God wants us to be stewards and caretakers of creation. God created human beings in his image for the purpose of knowing God, filling the earth with humans, and governing and cultivating God's good earth (Genesis 1, 2).[18] We can simply observe this in reality. Are we not ruling all creatures? We make rules to care for plants and animals.

Every individual has a unique set of skills because they possess God's image. God distributed creativity to everyone in unique ways. The purpose is to bring glory to his name. All other living creatures cannot do things that human beings can do. Examples: Animals don't do science; animals don't use complex language; animals don't do philosophy; animals don't talk about moral or political or social justice issues; animals don't use symbols; animals don't practice religion, etc. Human beings are, in many ways, unique among all living beings.[19]

Even if most people do not believe or know this theological notion of the image of God, this claim corresponds well with reality.

---

[18] Groothuis, *Christian Apologetics*, 86.
[19] See the works of Reasons.org and Discovery.org.

A person does not have to become a Christian to possess God's image. All human beings, including those who deny God's existence, are made in God's image in essence. That is why they also have these attributes. For example, believers and non-believers in God can do good science, create things, and reason. However, non-believers will never realize the elevated status (intrinsic value) until they understand and connect with God. Some religions view human beings born in a particular category, tribe, or caste as inferior to them. In the Judeo-Christian worldview, all are equally made in the image of God with value and dignity. Human beings are dignified in Christian theism.

Genesis narrates that God breathed his Spirit upon mere dust to create living beings (Genesis 2:7).[20] They are not merely material parts but accompany an immaterial substance that interacts with the physical dimension. This aspect has profound implications for our understanding of human personhood, life after death, spirituality, and much more.[21] If God did not reveal this theological notion of being made in the "image of God," we would never find this out. Humans are made "a little lower than the heavenly beings" and have "crowned them with glory and honor" (Psalm 8:5). The dignity of a human being is derived from God. Helmut Thielicke says, "His humankind's greatness rests solely on the fact that God in his incomprehensible goodness has bestowed his love upon him. God does not love us because we are so valuable; we are valuable because God loves us."[22] We have meaning and value because we are made by God in his image.

Genesis records, "God saw all that he had made, and it was very good" (Genesis 1:31). Humans were once naturally in concord with

---

[20]　Groothuis, *Christian Apologetics*, 86.
[21]　Ibid.,87.
[22]　Helmut Thielicke, *Nihilism*, trans. John W. Doberstein (London: Routledge and Kegan Paul. 1962), 110.

themselves, others, nature, and God.[23] Everything was in harmony. When God created human beings, they were not designed as programmed machines. They were created with a capacity for self-determination.[24] Human beings were given the freedom to remain or not to remain in a close relationship with God.[25] What happened to the world and humanity that God created? Why is there a mess?

Fall

The doctrine of the Fall of humanity teaches that the original pair, Adam and Eve, chose to disobey their Creator. They were given one command—not to eat the forbidden fruit. That was the only limitation God put down in the Garden of Eden. For if they ate the fruit from the tree of the knowledge of good and evil, they would die (Genesis 2:17). However, they chose to become rebellious against God's command. They attempted to "become like God" (Genesis 3:5) by listening to Satan's[26] deceptive words. They ate the forbidden fruit. Everything changes at that point.

Humans were held responsible for their rebellion. Since they violated the command, they were subjected to divine punishment by being banished from the Garden of Eden. They were sent out into a now hostile, dangerous, and deadly world.[27] They lost the personal relationship they had with their Creator. Perhaps our first parents thought they would have a better life when they became independent of God.

---

[23] Groothuis, *Christian Apologetics*, 87.

[24] Sire, *The Universe Next Door*, 39.

[25] Ibid.

[26] Satan is a powerful fallen angel who gathered a group of angels to his force. Satan has access to the human realm until Christ returns. See the chapter "The Problem of Evil."

[27] Groothuis, *Christian Apologetics*, 87.

The result of the rebellion was death for Adam and Eve. Through moral transgression against God, constitutional corruption has been passed down to every human being (except Jesus Christ, who is sinless).[28] This has historically been called the doctrine of Original Sin. The image of God in humanity was defaced in all its aspects.[29] All humanity now experiences the same alienation from God. When Adam and Eve decided to turn away from God, God let them go.

The Bible accounts the human condition as "one of both war and peace, heroism and cowardice, love and lust, commitment and betrayal, love and hate, faith and unbelief."[30] The image of God in humanity is broken. In personality, we lost our capacity to know ourselves accurately; humanity became more servant to nature than to God and began to worship nature; we became less able to discern good and evil; we began to exploit other people socially; we created gods and idols in the image of creations; and we have a vacuum in the human soul. This is the essence of fallen humanity.[31]

When we analyze this with reality, we can identify the nature of fallen humanity in people. Due to sin and separation from God, human beings began to cause more problems in the world. Humanity is incapable of serving God properly, given its resources. We are under God's righteous condemnation and without hope in ourselves.[32] People try to find some satisfaction by engaging in different activities, but everything fails because these cannot give permanent satisfaction. There is a paraphrased statement by Blaise Pascal, "Everyone has a God-shaped vacuum that only God can fill."[33] Augustine prayed to

---

[28]   Ibid.

[29]   Sire, *The Universe Next Door*, 39.

[30]   Groothuis, *Christian Apologetics*, 87.

[31]   Sire, *The Universe Next Door*, 40.

[32]   Groothuis, *Christian Apologetics*, 81.

[33]   See Douglas R. Groothuis, *Philosophy in Seven Sentences: A Small Introduction to a Vast Topic* (Downers Grove: InterVarsity Press, 2016), 100.

God, "You have made us for yourself, and restless is our heart until it comes to rest in you."[34] Because of the alienation from God, we are prone to selfishness, obsession, addiction, idolatry, and false religion of all kinds.[35] The alienation from God is a big problem. No human attempts can bring us back to God. Our merits cannot save us.

Did God leave us alone? Is there hope for humankind? There is! God, the Creator himself, is the Redeemer. In the first three chapters of Genesis, the two parts of the grand story (Creation and Fall) are narrated. The rest of the Scripture talks about the story of redemption.

Redemption

It's fascinating to think about how God's plan for redemption was not a quick fix but rather a gradual process. Even after the Fall, God was there to provide for and care for Adam and Eve, as evidenced by how God immediately clothed them. Through his promise of a future liberator, God provided hope and assurance that he would ultimately undo the damage caused by the serpent (Genesis 3:15).[36] God held human beings accountable for their rebellion through the judgment at Babel and in the flood. Later, God selected Abraham to follow his guidelines and established a great people of God's own choosing for his redemptive purpose. God then delivered his people from the bondage of Egypt and put them in the promised land. God made several different covenants (Abrahamic, Mosaic, Davidic) with them.

Despite his people's forgetfulness and hardened heart, God sent prophets to warn them. Judgments have been made to the people to bring them back to their Creator and Redeemer. Through prophets, God intervened in history with the ultimate goal of revealing the

---

[34] Augustine, *The Confessions 1.1.1*, trans. Albert C. Outler (New York: Barnes & Noble, 2007), 3.

[35] Groothuis, *Christian Apologetics*, 81.

[36] Ibid., 81

divine Messiah who would rescue Israel and bring salvation to all people.[37] The Bible beautifully captures God's profound love for us in seeking us out even in our lost and alienated condition.[38] In the fullness of time, God sent his Son, Jesus Christ, the Second Person of the Trinity, into the world to culminate God's plan of redemption (Galatians 4:4; Hebrews 1:1-4). Through the Holy Spirit, he lived a perfect life, sacrificed his life to atone for human sin, and set us right with God. He was raised from the dead to defeat all the powers of death and darkness, sin, and Satan.[39] The resurrection of Jesus gives us true and guaranteed hope.

God's goodness is expressed clearly on the cross of Calvary. On the cross, Jesus Christ took the punishment we deserved for our sins and paid our debt (Isaiah 53; 1 Peter 3:18; 2 Corinthians 5:21; 1 Peter 2:24). On the cross, we can notice God's perfect unity of righteousness (justice) and love for humanity. God granted us the possibility of a new life in God's unmerited favor and great grace.[40] The new life involves substantial healing of our alienations and restoration to fellowship with God. John 3:16 says, "For God so loved the world that he gave his one and only Son, that whoever believes in him shall not perish but have eternal life."

God made the provision to come back to him, but he did not force anyone to accept him. We have to make a choice. Our role is to respond to God by repentance and accepting Christ as Lord and Savior. God forgives our sins and brings us into a relationship with him. Salvation is not based on our merits but on grace. There is substantial healing in every area of life for redeemed humanity. The new humanity is on the way to the restoration of the defaced

---

[37]   Ibid., 82.
[38]   Sire, *The Universe Next Door*, 40.
[39]   Groothuis, *Christian Apologetics*, 82.
[40]   Ibid., 40.

image of God.[41] The restoration here does not mean we will never face any suffering in this world anymore. We may still have to face many consequences of the fallen humanity. However, we can enjoy the relationship with our Creator and Redeemer. Our hearts can rest in our Maker. We enter into the Kingdom of God. Our eternity is safe in the arms of God. Jesus promised, "I am with you always, to the end of the age" (Matthew 28:20). Believers can experience the presence of the triune God all the time.

Is there any ultimate hope? Is there complete healing? Yes, there is! Let us look into the fourth category: The New Creation.

The New Creation

Jesus promised, "if I go and prepare a place for you, I will come back and take you to be with me that you also may be where I am" (John 14:3). Glorified humanity is humanity totally healed and at peace with God, and individuals at peace with others and themselves. This happens after Christ's return. Our physical death is not the end. As Dwight L. Moody preached, "There is a glorious inheritance beyond the grave."[42] We will forever be with God. He will make everything new – the new heaven and new earth (Revelation 21-22). There will be no more pain or suffering. There will be joy forever with God and God's people. We will be transformed into a purified personality. The fallen state will be fully restored to its original dignity.[43] This hope gives an eternal meaning and hope for our living.

The Christian worldview gives the greatest hope to humanity. The resurrection gives eternal hope to those who have accepted

---

[41]   Ibid., 41.

[42]   D.L. Moody, "Sermon on the Death of Mr. P.P. Bliss," *Wholesome Words Home*, December 31, 1876, accessed March 16, 2021. https://www.wholesomewords.org/etexts/moody/moodybliss.html.

[43]   Sire, *The Universe Next Door*, 41.

Christ as their Lord and Savior. The part of consummation is the Last Judgement (2 Cor. 5:10; 2 Peter 2:4; Acts 17:31; Matthew 12:36; Romans 2:16; Rev. 21:4; Rev. 20:11-15, etc). Those who are redeemed will be in heaven with God. Those who reject the offer of salvation will be given their choice of going to hell with Satan (the fallen angels), forever separated from God. Christianity teaches that those who are in Christ will live forever (John 11:25). This is the grand narrative of the Bible. Now, let me share a story.

Ever since I truly began to follow Jesus Christ, I always wondered why Jesus used the analogy of becoming like children (see Matthew 18:3; Luke 18:16). I thought if Jesus used this analogy, there must be some more profound insights that I may be able to learn from children. So, I began to observe the behavior of children whenever I got the chance. Here is what I observed and learned from a child.

JESUS AND THE CHILDREN

When I lived in Colorado at the Denver Seminary residence, my apartment was next to the children's play area. That was a blessing because, through my window, I could closely observe the little children playing. A new resident moved in with their little daughter, probably about a year old. There is a small circle-fenced area at the children's playground. The parents put their little child within the fence safely so that she could play with the mud and toys. It was beautiful to watch her playing in the mud. I observed that her face was filled with joy and innocence, and it was radiating out. Sometimes, I watched gestures of wonder and surprises on her face as she played with her little toys in the mud. I had no idea what she was thinking or the reasons for the wonders. Perhaps she was discovering something new in her little world. She always had joy on her face. In one sense, she was unaware of the pains and problems in a broken world as a child. She had her parents to care for her.

Sometimes, when I get out of my apartment, I walk on the pathway next to the ground where she plays. This is where I was so amazed at seeing this little child's contagious smile. She was radiating something that soothed my mind. As an adult, I might have been going through some difficult times in life. More often, her beautiful smile struck my mind. It also brought tears when I imagined the beauty of God's creation of children in His image and likeness. As a Christian, I had so much to learn from this little child.

Radiate Christlikeness

Just as her innocent and joy-filled life soothed my mind, my life must also radiate the same qualities when dealing with other people. As a Christian, I should radiate the character of Christ all the time. When I meet people, they should experience true love from me. My presence should bring peace to my neighbors. Perhaps all people are fighting some form of battle in this broken world. As a person carrying the image of Christ, I should soothe other people's minds.

To radiate Christlike character, we shall transform into the image of Christ. When we have a true Christ-like character, we will automatically radiate true love from the character we develop. This is what a Christian life should be like. This is what God expects from us. We may not always have to do great things for others. Sometimes, a pleasant smile or a good word could strengthen others. Eventually, others will love our character, and they may wonder why he or she is unique. And they will find out that he or she is a follower of Christ. Our hearts must have an innocence to radiate innocence just like that little child does.

Our hearts must be joyful to radiate joy. If not, we may have to fake before others to show that we are Christlike. Such a hypocritical character is not what God expects from us. As we get to know God deeper, we should feel wonders and surprises about God's greatness, just as when the little child expresses wonders and amazement when she (in my imagination) discovers new things. I also observed a few other important characteristics of that child after a few months when she began to walk. This observation benefits our individual lives.

The God Who Cares

As the child started to take steps, her parents used to leave her in the playground. They sat on a chair away from her, but they paid attention to her activities. Sometimes, she fell down when she tried to walk, but without much hurt. Her parents did not come to help her stand up because they knew that she was learning to take steps. In that instance, her parents' unresponsiveness was not a symbol of lack of love but because of their love. They wanted her to grow up. Little falls would make her grow stronger. However, whenever they noticed something serious, they immediately jumped off their chair and rescued her from danger. That is part of the love and caring of parents for their children. We could relate that to our Christian walk.

We are called the children of God (1 John 3:1). God, our Heavenly Father, wants us to grow up to maturity, and it requires training. We may feel that God is away when we face evil or go through suffering, but he is not actually away. He still watches over us. He wants us to be strong. When we go through extreme danger, God will rescue us according to His will. Perhaps we won't get complete healing in earthly life, but he gives us an abundance of grace to handle it. It is part of the love and care of our Heavenly Father for his children. Another lesson that I have learned from her life is when she learned to walk stronger without frequently falling.

A Secure Place to Trust

I assume that the little girl also started to get a sense of danger and fear when she noticed something strange in her life. For example, when she noticed something unusual that could scare her, she immediately ran to her father or mother and held tightly to their arms. This amazed me because that little child knew in her heart where the safest place for her to be was. Nobody taught that to her, but God has built such awareness within a human child. She gained her trust by experiencing the love of her parents. She had good reasons that she would be safe with her parents. Sometimes, when she got minor wounds and was intensely hurt, she cried immediately. But she was comforted when she went to her parents as they gave love to the little child. She then stopped crying.

When I related this to the Christian walk, I understood that it is often possible to get hurt in a broken world. We may even run into danger where we need help. At any moment, we have a Father in Heaven whom we can approach without any worries. He will comfort us. Our Father in Heaven knows what his children need. He cares for us just as the parents care for their children. From observing this child and her parents over many months, I have learned so deeply about how we should live as Christians and as children of the King of kings and the Lord of lords. Jesus does not want us to become childish but to become childlike. We have to develop an innocent character like a child. This is what the life of a Christian should be like. Now, let us move on to the next section, "scientific apologetics."

SECTION 3:

Scientific Apologetics

CHAPTER 19

Scientific Knowledge and Limits

Today, many people hold that science is the only way to know the truth and that science provides the only genuine knowledge of reality.[1] This is a view called scientism. According to this view, hard sciences--such as chemistry, physics, biology, and astronomy--alone have the intellectual authority to give us knowledge of reality. The only true knowledge is that which can be attained by testing in these fields of hard science. Those who hold to scientism think that all matters outside of science--for example, God and religious experiences--are not items of knowledge. Although religion and ethics are acceptable, they are subjective and regarded as private opinions. Therefore, the claims of the hard sciences are superior to all outside-of-science claims.

In the modern scientific era, we hear this from many people without realizing that they have fallen into this dangerous ideology called scientism. There is no doubt that science enables us to understand nature. Scientific progress has always helped to advance society in many ways. However, scientism is not a position in science; it is a position in philosophy, but a false philosophy. Most people do not realize it. Is science the only way to the truth? Is there a limit to science?

---

[1] J. P. Moreland, *Scientism and Secularism: Learning to Respond to a Dangerous Ideology* (Wheaton, Illinois: Crossway, 2018), 26.

Different Sources of Knowledge and the Limits of Science

The basic strategy of this section is 'refutation by counter-example.' Scientism restricts knowledge to science. If we presuppose that 'only science can deliver truth,' schools and universities should eliminate all other disciplines, such as philosophy, literature, art, music, etc. There are many sorts of truths that we rationally accept that cannot be scientifically proven—mathematical truths, logical truths, metaphysical truths, ethical truths, and aesthetic truths. Non-scientific knowledge permeates science. To do science, one needs to believe in the laws of logic, basic mathematics, personal conscious states, some moral values, and much more.

There are true and rational beliefs and propositions outside of science. For example, 'red is a color' and 'torturing innocent babies for fun is wrong' are truths outside the disciplines of hard sciences. While many scientific theories held as truth for many years were later refuted, many truths outside of science have never changed. The history of science presents many successful theories-- that explained facts, guided much research, passed tests, and predicted accurate data-- later proved false.[2] Examples include Ptolemaic astronomy, Newtonian mechanics, classical thermodynamics, wave optics, etc. The current theories and findings of science may be replaced at a later time when scientists attain more knowledge. Scientific claims are always inductive and hence probabilistic, while some claims in other areas (e.g., logic, mathematics, certain ethical principles) are deductive and hence certain.

Science has limitations. There is no way that science can tell whether a poem is a bad poem or a work of a genius. Yet these judgments can be rightly made. There is no way science can find out an artist's character by scientifically testing one of their artworks.

---

[2]   Moreland, *Christianity and the Nature of Science*, 154-55.

Science cannot tell that we should be moral people. Science cannot tell if a husband loves his wife. Natural science can explain the structure and function of nature. But natural science cannot explain the purpose—why is there nature at all in the first place? Nobel Prize winner Sir Peter Medawar wrote,

> The existence of a limit of science is, however, made clear by its inability to answer childlike elementary questions having to do with first and last things – questions such as "How did everything begin?"; What are we all here for"; "What is the point of living?"[3]

Scientism is Self-Refuting and an Enemy of Science

The people who defend scientism often fail to realize the basic logical problem with the definition of this view. A statement such as 'the only true knowledge is that which can be attained by testing scientifically' is self-refuting because it is a philosophical statement about science that cannot itself be tested scientifically. Moreover, scientism is an enemy of science. To do science, many presuppositions are necessary. Scientism does not adequately allow for the task of stating and defending the necessary presuppositions to practice science.[4]

Moreland and Craig list a few philosophical presuppositions of science : (1) The existence of an external world independent of mind, language, or theory; (2) The orderly nature of the world; (3) the knowability of the external world; (3) the existence of objective truth; (5) the existence of the laws of logic and mathematics; (6) the reliability of our sensory and cognitive faculties to gain truth and knowledge of the world and to justify beliefs; (7) the existence of various types of values and moral oughts.[5] Now, do you see why scientism doesn't make sense? When scientists criticize or defend any assumptions, they are using non-scientific knowledge.

---

[3]   Peter Medawar, *Advice to a Young Scientist* (New York: Harper and Row, 1979), 31.
[4]   Moreland, and Craig, *Philosophical Foundations for a Christian Worldview*, 2nd ed., 372.
[5]   Ibid.

Things Science Cannot Explain in Principle
(But Theism Can)

Scientism is a conviction that science can explain virtually everything.[6] Chemist Peter Atkins expressed the essence of scientism by writing, "There is no reason to suppose that science cannot deal with every aspect of existence."[7] It is important to realize that there are so many areas that science cannot explain. First, scientists can tell us that the universe had a beginning, but they cannot explain how the universe began to exist in the first place. Second, science cannot explain the origin of the fundamental laws of nature. Third, science cannot explain why the universe is fine-tuned. But scientists can tell us that fine-tuning exists.

Fourth, science cannot explain the origin of consciousness, the existence of moral, rational, and aesthetic objective laws and intrinsically valuable properties. Science cannot, in principle, explain any of these phenomena. These issues are in a different category. Science has nothing to say about them philosophically. However, theism can persuasively explain all of them. Philosophers who are committed to studying both science and theology can integrate the knowledge from both these fields to present a well-articulated true worldview. Earlier, I have presented several arguments for theism using scientific knowledge and philosophical reasoning.

In conclusion, we can say that the ideology called scientism is a false philosophy. Science, as it progresses, can offer excellent knowledge of reality, but truth claims are not limited to the discipline of science. Science has limits to what it can do. It cannot explain everything now or in the future. Many other fields give unchangeable truths that are more reliable than many progressing scientific

---

[6]   Moreland, *Scientism and Secularism*, 135-57.

[7]   Cited in John Cornwell, *Nature's Imagination: The Frontiers of Scientific Vision*, (Oxford, Oxford University Press, 1995), 125.

knowledge of reality. Science is great, but scientism is a dangerous and foolish ideology. Many scientists often make big philosophical blunders. Unfortunately, many people fell into scientism without realizing its philosophical problem.

This is an important matter in apologetics today because many people have been deceived into a belief that science is the only way to know the truth, that science can explain everything, and that science has authority over every topic. The proponents of scientism convinced many young people to leave religious beliefs as irrational. In fact, philosophy has authority over every topic, and philosophers have more to say about life and the world than scientists. In pursuit of truth, philosophers have more to bring to the discussion table than scientists.

CHAPTER 20

God and Science: Conflict?

Are God and science in conflict? 'God and Science' is a widely debated topic in the age of modern science. There is a popular belief that God and science do not get along. Atheist scientists always want to expel God from the premise and popularize that those who believe in God are ignorant and fools. Is there an actual conflict between God and science? If we look at the list of Nobel Prize winners between 1901 and 2000, over 60% were Christians, and over 20% were Jewish.[1] If God and science conflict, it would be unlikely that Nobel Prize winners were believers in God. So, we need to find out where the actual conflict lies. I aim to point out that the real conflict does not lie between God and science but between the two worldviews- *Naturalism* and *Theism*.

Naturalism is the belief that nothing exists beyond the natural world. A naturalistic worldview is equivalent to atheism. In the scientific naturalistic worldview, the universe gives no evidence of God, and one should only believe what can be scientifically proven. On the contrary, theism holds that there is an infinite, personal God who is the creator and sustainer of the universe. He can also supernaturally act within the universe. Where does the evidence lead? Does science lead us to naturalism or theism?

---

[1]   Baruch Aba Shalev, *100 Years of Nobel Prizes* (India: Atlantic Publishers & Distributors (P) Limited, 2003), 57-59.

Science clearly leads us to theism. The popular idea that God and science do not get along is false. Such a false idea results from some misunderstanding. Let me begin by demonstrating the nature of the actual job of scientists using an illustration by Lewis. He writes,

> Science works by experiments. It watches how things behave… it really means something like, 'I pointed the telescope to such and such a part of the sky at 2.20 a.m. on January 15th and saw so-and-so,' or, 'I put some of this stuff in a pot and heated it to such-and-such a temperature, and it did so-and-so.[2]

Geisler and Kerby Anderson make a distinction between *origin science* and *operation science*.[3] The examples used by Lewis are the experimental science of regularly occurring events. Geisler calls it *operation science*. In addition to operation science, there is another science called *origin science*. Events such as the Big Bang and the Cambrian explosion are origin science. These are not regularly occurring events and cannot be repeated. These cannot be tested in laboratories since they are historical data from the natural world. Both origin science and operation science give us knowledge of the natural world. Lewis is trying to demonstrate that a scientist's primary task is not to gain knowledge of God but to gain knowledge of a particular field of study or object in the natural world. For example, biological cells, gravity, chemical reactions, star formation, etc. After studying the material world, when a scientist makes authoritative statements such as "God does not exist" or "the natural world is all that exists," they are going outside their field of study. This is one main problem with scientific naturalists.

People often say, "Since we cannot prove God scientifically, we should not believe in God." This statement is irrational because if God created this natural world, he must be outside of material creation. Then, we will never be able to test him in laboratories as we do with

---

[2]   C. S. Lewis, *Mere Christianity,* (San Francisco: HarperCollins, 2001), 22.

[3]   Norman Geisler and Kerby Anderson, *Origin Science* (Grand Rapids: Baker, 1987); also see Groothuis, *Christian Apologetics,* 299-300.

blood and tissues. A person only needs common sense to understand this. Lewis uses an illustration, "if there was a controlling power outside the universe, it could not show itself to us as one of the facts inside the universe – no more than the architect of a house could actually be a wall or staircase or fireplace in that house."[4]

Lewis means that when we notice a house's complexity, specificity, and design, we can conclude that it has an architect. Similarly, much data from the natural world (such as the information in DNA, fine-tuning parameters of the universe, the absolute beginning of the universe, and many other scientific findings) undeniably points to an outside causal agent or intelligent designer. At this point, it is the job of a philosopher to demonstrate the causal agent and designer further. Let the philosopher do the rest of the work by integrating it with theology. However, many scientists who are not generally trained in philosophy and theology go outside their field of study and enter into fields in which they are untrained as if they know how to deal with them. This often results in big mistakes. Most of them do not realize their folly.

The Different Levels of Rational Explanation

Oxford mathematician and philosopher of science John Lennox looks at the 'God and science' topic in the levels of explanation. Lennox illustrates the different levels of rational explanation using the example of an electric kettle that boils water.[5] Suppose you ask, "Why is this water boiling?" The scientific explanation is that the water is boiling in a kettle due to heat energy's conduction through the copper kettle, and making changes to the molecules results in boiling. This is a correct explanation. However, the scientific

---

4   Ibid., 24.
5   John C. Lennox, *Can Science Explain Everything?* (United Kingdom: The Good Book Company, 2019), 35-36.

explanation is not the only explanation. There is another one, which is an agent explanation, that is, "water is boiling because I would like a cup of tea." Agent explanation tells the purpose. Both these explanations are not in conflict. Both levels of rational explanations are necessary for a comprehensive understanding. It is irrational to say that "only the scientific explanation is true, but the agent explanation is false." Both explanations are reasonable. The same is true about the material universe.

Scientists can tell us the structure and function of the universe, but they cannot explain 'why there is a universe at all in the first place.' It requires a theistic explanation. God is an agent-creator explanation of the universe. The scientific explanation is not a complete explanation of the universe. For a comprehensive understanding of the universe, a theistic explanation is also necessary. Theism can persuasively reveal who the designer of the universe is and his purpose for creation. Now, do you see a conflict between the scientific explanation of the universe and the theistic explanation of why there is a universe?

Natural science cannot directly study the character of God, as we can in theology in reliance on special revelation. Science, as it examines nature, finds God's handiwork. The universe is an effect that needs a cause. By studying the effect, a philosopher can reason back to the necessary causal agent. When there is abundant scientific evidence of design, the only way naturalists could hold that a designer doesn't exist is by blind baseless faith. The theological concept of God as Creator is studied as a philosophical concept. The integration of science and theology is under the domain of philosophy. Many top-level scientists make authoritative statements and make big philosophical mistakes.

Many people tend to give authority to the statements made by scientists without even trying to understand the basic logic of their statements. One of the most excellent examples is the famous brilliant physicist Stephen Hawking's statement in his book, *The Grand Design*. In the opening chapter, Hawking writes, "philosophy is dead… Scientists have become the bearers of the torch of discovery in our quest for knowledge."[6] However, the main topic of his book itself is the philosophy of science. He contradicts himself since he is giving a philosophy of science.

In the same book, Hawking claimed that God is not necessary to explain the beginning of the universe. He writes, "Because there is a law like gravity, the universe can and will create itself from nothing."[7] Since the writer is a scientist, the statement looks scientific to people. However, the statement is neither scientific nor rational. Lennox notes three major flaws in this statement.[8]

First, the statement is self-contradictory. When Hawking says, "Because there is a law like gravity," he presupposes the existence of the law of gravity. That means he presupposes "something." His statement follows, "the universe can and will create itself from nothing." How can "nothing" be "something?" Nothing is "no thing." Nothing has no causal power or properties. He presupposes "something" and "nothing" at the same time. His statement is a flat contradiction. The second flaw is that the law itself cannot create anything. Theories or laws do not bring matter or energy into existence. It is irrational to believe that.

The third flaw is that self-creation is incoherent. "The universe can and will create itself from nothing" is a meaningless statement. If one says, "X creates Y," it presupposes the existence of X in the first place to bring Y into existence. If one says, "X creates X," it presupposes the existence of X in order to account for the existence

---

6   Stephen Hawking and Leonard Mlodinow, *The Grand Design* (New York: Bantam Books, 2010), 5.
7   Hawking and Mlodinow, *The Grand Design, 180.*
8   Lennox, *Can Science Explain Everything?* 37.

of X. It is logically incoherent to presuppose the existence of the universe to account for its own coming into existence.[9] According to Hawking the universe created the universe, which is incoherent.

The British Astronomer Royal, Martin Rees of Ludlow, a friend of Hawking, was once asked by the *Guardian* newspaper about Hawking's pronouncement that God is not required to explain the beginning of the universe. Rees' response was, "I know Stephen Hawking well enough to know that he has read little philosophy and less theology, so I don't think his views should be taken with any special weight."[10] From Hawking's flawed statements themselves, one can understand his poor philosophical skill. He was indeed a great scientist, but a poor philosopher.

In one sense, these atheist scientists don't want to accept God. For intellectual satisfaction, they appeal to science. They simply want to justify their naturalistic worldview by appealing to science. A careful thinker realizes what scientists can and cannot explain. We can make a general conclusion that God and science get along very well. When the confusion is cleared, we can conclude that the real conflict is between the two worldviews-- naturalism and theism. Naturalists hold that the universe is all that exists, while theism holds that the universe is not all that exists. Naturalists hold that the ultimate reality is mass/energy, but theism holds that the ultimate reality is God. Science is wonderful as it helps to increase our knowledge of the natural world, but we should not fall into the philosophical mistakes of atheist scientists! Now, let's move on to discuss the general Christian view of science.

---

[9]   Lennox, *Can Science Explain Everything?* 37-40.
[10] Martin Rees, cited in Lennox, *Can Science Explain Everything?* 27.

CHAPTER 21

General Christian View of Science

The Judeo-Christian Origin of Modern Science

Many people opposed to Christianity charge that the Christian faith is inherently anti-science. The works of the 'new atheists,' such as Richard Dawkins, Christopher Hitchens, Bill Nye, Neil deGrasse Tyson, and many others around the world, popularized the idea that Christianity has historically remained a force to slow down scientific progress. Is it true or false? How do we know it? If Christianity can be proven as not anti-science, their accusations will fall short. In this chapter, I aim to show that Christianity was not anti-science and gave birth to modern science in the 16th century. This task is simple as it only needs some basic understanding of the history of science. Let us begin with the origin of modern science.

Modern science has its roots in the Judeo-Christian worldview. The early pioneers of modern science were believers in God. Some of them were: Francis Bacon (1561-1626), Galilei Galileo (1564-1642), Johannes Kepler (1571-1630), Blaise Pascal (1623-1662), Robert Boyle (1627-1691), Isaac Newton (1642-1727), Michael Faraday (1791-1867), Charles Babbage (1791-1871), Gregor Mendel (1822-84), Louis Pasteur (1822-95), Baron Kelvin (1824-1907), and James Clerk Maxwell (1831-1879). Most of the pioneers of modern science were Christians, and all were theists. They had a conviction about the orderliness and regularity of the universe because they believed in a personal God who created it. This was the initial motivation behind all the further discoveries. Nobel Prize winner in biochemistry Melvin Calvin wrote,

> The fundamental conviction that the universe is ordered is the first and strongest tenet [of scientists]. As I try to discern the origin of that conviction, I seem to find it in a basic notion discovered 2000 or 3000 years ago, and enunciated first in the Western world by the ancient Hebrews: namely that the universe is governed by a single God, and is not the product of the whims of many gods, each governing his own province according to his own laws. This monotheistic view seems to be the historical foundation for modern science.[1]

The Judeo-Christian worldview encouraged scientific discovery and was hopeful that nature would reveal her secrets to good scientists. These were not predictions of the naturalistic atheistic worldview. Without certain beliefs, science would have never started. Kepler (1571-1630) expressed it this way:

> The chief aim of all investigations of the external world should be to discover the rational order which has been imposed on it by God and which he revealed to us in the language of mathematics.[2]

Irish natural philosopher and chemist Robert Boyle (1627-1691) -- one of the founders of modern chemistry-- sent a message in his last will to scientific colleagues in the Royal Society, in these words,

> Wishing them also a happy success in their laudable attempts, to discover the true nature of the works of God; and praying that they, and all other searchers into physical truths may cordially refer their attainments to the glory of the great Author of nature and the comfort of mankind.[3]

Astronomer and mathematician Nicolaus Copernicus (1473-1543) said, "To know the mighty works of God, to comprehend His

---

[1] Melinda Baldwin, *Making "Nature": The History of a Scientific Journal* (United Kingdom: University of Chicago Press, 2015), 5.

[2] Cited in Morris Kline, Mathematics: The Loss of Certainty (Oxford University Press, New York, 1980), 31.

[3] Quoted in Gilbert, Lord Bishop of Sarum, *A Sermon preached at the Funeral of the Hon. Robert Boyle* (London, 1692), 25. Also see John Hayward, *A Dictionary of the Principle Religious Sects in the World* (N.P: Delmarva Publications, Inc, 2015).

wisdom and majesty and power... surely all this must be a pleasing and acceptable mode of worship to the Most High.[4]

From history, it is clear that Christianity gave birth to modern science and was not at all against scientific advancement. Christians were contributors in all fields of development, not only science. The new atheists' accusations are false. They have continued to spread many myths to suppress the truth of Christianity to promote a view that modern science is inherently atheistic. Many myths confuse our understanding of science and religion (Christianity in particular). A historian of science, Michael Keas, presents seven myths about the history of science and religion in his book *Unbelievable: 7 Myths About the History and Future of Science and Religion*,[5] which I highly recommend. I will briefly present two of the myths, "Galileo's Arrest" and "Dark Ages". Why was Galileo arrested? There is a popular accusation that the Catholic church persecuted Galileo to stop the growth of science. In fact, it is a myth.

Galileo's Arrest

It is important to note that Galileo was a firm believer in God. Aristotelianism was the prominent view at that time. Early Christianity preserved Greek science. The Aristotelian paradigm had a geocentric cosmology (the Earth is in the center of the solar system). The Catholic church sided with the geocentric view. When Galileo advocated the Copernican heliocentric (Sun-centered) theory of the solar system, the scientific concensus (Indeed, the available observational evidence to that point supported geocentrism) was powerfully against it. There were many scientists and theologians who sided with Galileo, and

---

[4]   Quoted in Francis Collins, *The Language of God: A Scientist Presents Evidence for Belief* (New York: Free Press, 2006), 230-231.

[5]   Michael Newton Keas, *Unbelievable: 7 Myths About the History and Future of Science and Religion* (Wilmington, DE: ISI Books, 2019), 3-4.

there were many scientists and theologians who were against Galileo. The majority of scientists and theologians were against him. The real conflict was not between science and religion, but it was between the Greek classical Aristotelian paradigm and the new Copernican paradigm. The Catholic church affirmed the scientific consensus of that time because the majority of scientific opinion was against Galileo.

Galileo held that the Bible was free of error and that science could find the truth by reading nature. However, Galileo disagreed with some of the interpretations. He was trying to educate the church about its false interpretations of the Scripture and false interpretations of nature. He was not against the church but was helping them understand the truth clearly. When the Aristotelianism of the Academy was threatened, the secular philosophers did not like that move. They were enraged at Galileo's criticism of Aristotelianism. Galileo claimed that the academic professors influenced the church to speak against him. The opposition was purely intellectual and political. Moreover, additional factors contributed to the opposition.

Galileo was not a diplomatic person. For instance, he irritated the elite of his day by publishing in Italian instead of Latin. Galileo wanted to give some intellectual empowerment to ordinary people. In addition to that, the protestant reformation was also challenging Rome at that time. The protestant reformation enabled others to interpret Scripture for themselves. There was an increasing threat to religious security because of the protestant reformation. When Galileo advocated his view, the church also thought Galileo was trying to interpret the Scripture for himself. Church wanted to side with the Aristotelian view of that time and wanted to protect that view because the secular philosophers wanted to keep that view. The church authorities overreacted to Galileo's book. The Catholic church charged Galileo with heresy. He was placed under house arrest but was never thrown into prison or tortured. He enjoyed all luxuries. It was later that the church realized its false interpretation of the Scripture when the Copernican view was proven. In short, the accusation that the Catholic church persecuted Galileo to stop the growth of science is a myth.[6]

The "Dark Ages" Myth

Another myth is that the medieval Catholic Church suppressed the growth of science, causing Europe to descend into the Dark Ages.[7] There is a claim that Christianity caused horrific and science-killing cultural damage.[8] Atheist biologist Jerry Coyne wrote, "Had there been no Christianity, if after the fall of Rome atheism had pervaded the Western world, science would have developed earlier and be far more advanced than it is now."[9] According to Carl Sagan, Christianity ushered in the "Dark Ages" because Christianity is a treacherous, superstitious science stopper in his version of history.[10] Some see the Dark Ages as only the early Middle Ages. Keas argues that the medieval Catholics positively influenced science and other intellectual pursuits. There were no Dark Ages.[11] We can identify several lines of evidence that Christians were contributors in all fields of development. Some of them are:

Saint Augustine (354-430) wrote the "two books" metaphor, the Bible and the Cosmos, to affirm the harmony of Christianity and science.[12] Alongside Augustine, the records indicate that a highly educated Christian, the Roman senator and intellectual Anicius Manlius Severinus Boethius (475-524), supported scientific

---

6　See Lennox, *Can Science Explain Everything?* 21-23; also see Keas, *Unbelievable.*
7　Keas, *Unbelievable*, 3.
8　Ibid., 26.
9　Quoted in Keas, *Unbelievable*, 27.
10　Ibid., 28.
11　Ibid., 3.
12　Ibid., 34.

developments.[13] The English monk Bede (673-735) addressed astronomical and cosmological theory in the Ptolemy and Augustine's traditions. His Christian worldview was compatible with the analysis of the natural world.[14] From later history, it is clear that Christians were not anti-science; instead, they gave birth to modern science and continuously contributed to science.

Even before modern science, the first universities in Europe itself were Christian contributions.[15] The invention of the university had much to do with the rise of intellectual giants in the Middle Ages, beginning with the University of Bologna (11th century), University of Paris (12th century), and University of Oxford (12th century), and more than fifty others by 1450.[16] According to an estimate, science education held 30 percent of the academic curriculum.[17] Between 1200 and 1450, thousands of students studied science, medicine, and mathematics. It was improved by generations of European faculty. Many works were translated and transmitted to the next generation. The translated previous works have been transmitted to others through the universities, including the key figure, Johannes Kepler. A historian of science Michael Shank wrote,

> If the medieval church had intended to discourage or suppress science, it certainly made a colossal mistake in tolerating--to say nothing of supporting–the university. In this new institution, Greco-Arabic science and medicine for the first time found a permanent home, one that–with various ups and downs--science has retained to this day. Dozens of universities introduced large numbers of students to Euclidean geometry, optics, the problems of generation and reproduction, the rudiments of astronomy, and arguments for the sphericity of the earth.[18]

---

[13]　Ibid.

[14]　Ibid., 35.

[15]　Moreland and Craig, *Philosophical Foundations for a Christian Worldview*, 16.

[16]　Keas, *Unbelievable*, 36.

[17]　Ibid., 37.

[18]　Michael H. Shank, "Myth 2: That the Medieval Christian Church Suppressed the Growth of Science," in *Galileo Goes to Jail*, 21. Quoted in Ronald L. Numbers, *Galileo Goes to Jail: And Other Myths About Science and Religion* (Cambridge, MA: Harvard University Press, 2009), 22.

Keas reports that the earliest "Dark Age" myth he found was published in 1809, and it was based on lectures that began in the 1780s. During the Enlightenment in the eighteenth century, this myth pops into existence to discredit religion, particularly the Roman Catholic Church.[19] Such a move was necessary to deny the credit to religion for the rise of science.[20] It was merely an anti-Christian agenda. Sociologist Rodney Stark writes, "…not only that there is no inherent conflict between religion and science, but that Christian theology was essential for the rise of science."[21] Historian of medieval science Edward Grant argues,

> The three pre-conditions just discussed—the translations, the universities, and the theologian-natural philosophers—laid a foundation for the emergence of modern science because they provided an environment that was conducive to the study of science. . . . And without the support of the theologians and the Church, the medieval universities would have been unable to institute the science-logic-natural philosophy curriculum that began Western Europe's long, uninterrupted involvement with scientific thought and problems.[22]

History shows that the Christian church never opposed scientific endeavors, either in the Middle Ages or during the Renaissance and Enlightenment. Why do atheists lie about Christianity and history then? The Scripture (the Bible) claims that Satan is a deceiver and the father of lies (John 8:43-45; Revelation 12:9). Satan only wants people to believe in a lie. His job is to suppress the truth so that people will not follow it. One of the best ways atheists can suppress the Christian truth is by presenting false stories and myths that may sound plausible to many. Satan continues to lead people to believe

---

[19] Rodney Stark, *For the Glory of God: How Monotheism Led to Reformations, Science, Witch-Hunts, and the End of Slavery* (Princeton, N.J.: Princeton University Press, 2003), 166.

[20] Stark, *For the Glory of God*, 166.

[21] Ibid, *123*.

[22] Edward Grant, *The Foundations of Modern Science in the Middle Ages: Their Religious, Institutional, and Intellectual Contexts* (Cambridge: Cambridge University Press, 1996), 176.

in false worldviews. When atheists lie, they are representing their father, Satan.

Science is a system of knowledge about the world and its behavior. Christianity teaches about the One who created the world, morality, and the afterlife. It teaches the value, meaning, and purpose of human life. Christians celebrate when people make discoveries that reveal the glory of God. Christians from the past held a high view of science, and they were in harmony with faith in God. Scripture is very clear about knowing God through nature (Psalm 19:1-6; Romans 1:18-20). When Christians attempt science, they are trying to understand God's handiwork. Both Christians and people of other faiths can do good science because all are made in God's image and capable of doing it. Christian scientists see objective meaning in their scientific endeavors. They worship and bring glory to God through their discovery.

We can learn that modern science has its roots in the biblical worldview. Lewis sums it up, "Men became scientific because they expected law in nature and they expected law in nature because they believed in a Legislator."[23] Science and Christianity--when both are properly understood-- are never in conflict but instead support each other. Francis Schaeffer wrote,

> It was because the infinite-personal God who exists—not just an abstraction—made things together, that the early scientists had courage to expect to find out the explanation of the universe. The God who is there made the universe, with things together, in relationships. Indeed, the whole area of science turns upon the fact that he has made a world in which things are made to stand together, that there are relationships between things. So God made the external universe, which makes true science possible, but he has also made man and made him to live in that universe. He has not made man to live somewhere else. So we have three things coming together: God, the infinite-personal God, who made the universe; and man, whom he made to live in that universe; and the Bible, which he has given us to tell us about that universe.[24]

---

[23]   C.S. Lewis, *Miracles* (New York: Simon and Schuster, 1996), 140.
[24]   Francis Schaeffer, *He is There and He is Not Silent* (United States: Tyndale House Publishers, 1972), 59.

The Two Books Written by God

Many Christian thinkers from the early times onwards expressed in a metaphor that God has given us two books: *the Book of Nature* and *the Book of Scripture*. Both books contribute to our knowledge of the existence of God, who he is, and his plan for humanity. The Book of Nature is the natural world we experience, which scientists and philosophers attempt to read and interpret. The data we have from reading the Book of Nature undeniably reveals the existence of God as the Creator and sustainer of the universe. The Book of Nature is considered a general revelation that is accessible to all people (Romans 1:18-20; Psalm 19:1-6) regardless of their understanding of who God is. (General revelation about God's existence comes not only from our knowledge of the natural world but also from history and human nature.)

Natural science is a discipline that helps to unpack the mystery of physical reality by reading the Book of Nature with several scientific sub-disciplines. The Book of Nature explains many things about the natural world, but not everything. God also revealed himself in the Book of Scripture (the Bible) to make him known to us personally. How do the two books interact?

Interaction Between the Two Books

Many people promote that scientific understanding of the physical universe and the Bible are in conflict. This is a false claim out of ignorance. It is important to note that if both books are written by the same author, these cannot conflict. Both books reveal God's truth. A systematic thinker should organize all truth about God and his plan for humanity revealed through both books. We must always remember that our interpretations of both books can be wrong sometimes. Misinterpretation can lead to a false conclusion about life and the world. It is crucial to interpret the Scripture correctly.

The word of God revealed in the Book of Scripture is infallible, but all our interpretations are not. The same applies to the Book of Nature. We know from the Book of Nature the current understanding of the natural world. Our current interpretation of the natural world may change as scientific study progresses. We can learn many examples in the history of science where many understandings and theories were later replaced. There are also many features of the universe that we can believe with certainty from our scientific knowledge of the world.

Whenever it appears there is a conflict, it is due to human misinterpretations of the Book of Scripture or, human misinterpretation of the Book of Nature, or both. The author of both books never made an error because God cannot make an error. God, who is all-powerful and all-knowing, cannot make an error. We finite human beings keep making errors. Many people make some mistakes by interpreting many biblical texts in a strictly literal sense. It is important to note that the Bible uses many literary devices to communicate with people. There are proper and improper ways to interpret both books. One should follow the basic principles inherent to each. Sometimes, both books support each other to avoid incorrect interpretations and for an accurate understanding of reality. One who has a deep interest in this topic should study it with a lot of humility, patience, and research. One should not draw a quick, wrong conclusion by listening to some ignorant critiques, but find the right resources and evaluate the evidence for himself.[25]

When both books are properly interpreted, they provide sufficient reasons and evidence to put all our trust in the God of the Bible. Together, they reveal the existence of God, who he is, and his plan for humanity. The book of nature declares the handiwork and glory

---

[25]   See Moreland, *Scientism and Secularism.*

of God; the book of Scripture reveals why the natural world exists in the first place, who God is, and his great plan of salvation through Jesus Christ. While the Bible is scientifically accurate upon proper interpretation, it is not a science textbook. The central message in the Bible is God's plan of salvation. An honest study continues to reveal very clearly that the author of the Book of Nature and the Book of Scripture is the God of the Bible.

The Undeniable Scientific Claims in The Bible

The Bible made many clear claims about the universe's origin, history, and properties 2000-3500 years ago, which modern science tested. It turns out that the Bible got them right and before modern science. Modern science only discovered these recently and found the biblical claims to be true. Someone couldn't write those details such a long time ago unless God specially revealed them to the authors. I will present a few of those undeniable claims.

For many centuries, philosophers wondered whether the universe had a beginning. Without any modern scientific evidence, the Bible claimed that the universe had a finite beginning, and God brought it into existence. Theologians always held a view that the universe had a finite beginning because that is what the Bible teaches (Gen 1:1; 2:3; 2:4; Ps 148:5; Is 40:46; 42:5; 45:18; John 1:3; Col 1:15WHeb 11:3; 2 Tim1:9). The Bible not only claims that matter and energy had a beginning but also space and time. If the universe had a beginning, then it requires a beginner who can operate beyond the space-time dimension. Therefore, a creator-explanation was necessary to bring the universe into existence. On the contrary, for so many reasons, naturalists (who believe that the universe is all that exists) denied a beginning and held that the material universe is eternal and self-existent. Therefore, a creator-explanation was unnecessary because there is no need for a beginner when there is no beginning to the universe.

While both these views are in place, modern science made an unexpected discovery that the universe had an absolute beginning of time, space, matter, and energy. Physicist Alexander Vilenkin wrote, "With the proof now in place, cosmologists can no longer hide behind the possibility of a past eternal universe. There is no escape, they have to face the problem of a cosmic beginning."[26]Astronomer Robert Jastrow wrote,

> This is an exceedingly strange development, unexpected by all but the theologians. They have always accepted the word of the Bible: In the beginning God created heaven and Earth... For the scientist who has lived by his faith in the power of reason, the story ends like a bad dream. He has scaled the mountains of ignorance; he is about to conquer the highest peak; as he pulls himself over the final rock, he is greeted by a band of theologians who have been sitting there for centuries.[27]

The Bible not only makes scientific claims about the finite beginning of the universe but also explains many important features of the universe that scientists have discovered. The biblical description was accurate thousands of years before modern science discovered them. In his book, *Why the Universe Is the Way It Is*, Astronomer and Theologian Hugh Ross presents several scientific claims in the Bible that have been proven true by modern science.[28] I will address a few claims here. The Bible claims that the universe has been continuously expanding since the moment of beginning (Job 9:8; Is 40:22; 42:5; 44:24; 45:12; 48:13; 51:15; Zech 12:1; Ps 104:2; Jer 51:15; 10:12). The Scripture (Ps 104:2, Is 40:22) describes the continuous expansion of the universe as the "stretching out" of the heavens. Until the twentieth century, no one had a clue that the universe continued to expand. Today, we have abundant scientific reasons that confirm this claim of the Bible.

---

26   Alexander Vilenkin, *Many Worlds in One* (New York: Hill & Wang, 2006), 176.
27   Robert Jastrow, *God and the Astronomers* (New York: Norton, 1978), 116.
28   Ross, *Why the Universe Is the Way It Is*, 125-145.

In addition, the Bible also claims many important details about the laws of physics. It claims the physical laws are fixed (Gen 1-2; 3:17; Eccl 1:4-10; 3:11-15; Jer 33:25; Rom 8:18-23; Rev 20:7-22:5). This explains that the universe is fine-tuned. Moreover, the Bible (Rom 8:20-22) claims that the entire creation is subject to the law of decay, which is the second law of thermodynamics. In his book, *The Nature of the Universe*, scientific materialist Astronomer Sir Fred Hoyle writes, "There is a good deal of cosmology in the Bible... It is a remarkable conception."[29] I recommend the work of Ross, who further demonstrates several Biblical claims regarding the Earth's features, history of life, the role of advanced animals, the uniqueness of human beings, and many more.[30] Then, you can evaluate the case for yourself based on evidence and reason.

I conclude this portion by pointing out that we have good reasons to trust the Bible as the cosmic Creator's manual. If the biblical authors can write such accurate scientific details 2000-3500 years before modern science discovered them, the writers must be inspired by the author of the Book of Nature. At least the Bible got them right and said them first, which is undeniable. The author of the Book of Nature must be the author of the Book of Scripture. One should consider reading the Bible seriously, which not only contains these accurate scientific claims but, most importantly, God reveals himself and describes his plan for humanity and an unimaginable realm beyond the cosmos. The Bible gives you the highest knowledge and wisdom possible as it is revealed by the Creator of the universe, who is the source of all truth.

---

[29]   Hoyle, Fred. *The Nature of the Universe*, 2nd ed. (Oxford: Basil Blackwell, 1952), 109.
[30]   See Hugh Ross, *The Creator and the Cosmos* (CA: RTB Press, 2018).

CHAPTER 22

The Great Debate on Biblical Creation

How old is the universe? Is it about 14 billion years or 6000 years old? Doesn't the Bible say God created everything about 6000 years ago in the six literal 24-hour periods? Is this not scientifically incorrect? How do we deal with this issue? This is a widely disputed topic famously called '*Young-Earth Creationism (YEC)* vs. *Old-Earth Creationism (OEC) Debate.*' The challenging questions are: are the days in the book of Genesis literal 24-hour periods, and did the creation take place about 6000 years ago? This subject needs to be discussed with a lot of humility and respect because there are different views on Genesis' creation days. This topic is unique, complex, and important to understand as you are on an intellectual journey.

In this chapter, I will present the different views on the biblical creation days, the rules for interpretation, and the view of creation by *Reasons to Believe* (RTB). Please note that my goal is not to discredit any opposing views but to encourage truth seekers to maintain a charitable approach to this discussion, even within the Christian community. I also aim to equip you with important information and resources to answer honest skeptics and biblical critiques on this hot topic. What are the different views on Genesis creation days?

The Different Views of the Creation 'Days' in the Book of Genesis[1]

1. **Fiat Creation**: This view, widely known as Young-Earth Creationism, holds that the 'days' are literal 24-hour solar days, and it is a 144-hour creation week. According to this view, the Earth was created between 6000 and 15000 years ago.

2. **Progressive Creation**: This view, widely known as Old-Earth Progressive Creationism, holds that the 'days' are long, finite periods. According to this view, the Earth was created about 1.5-4.6 billion years ago. The universe's age is about 14 billion years.

3. **Gap Theories**: This view holds a long gap between Genesis's first two verses (1:1 and 1:2), into which all the geological ages fit. However, this view holds a 24-hour day from verse 2 of Genesis. This way, the 'day' could be 24 hours, but the world could be millions/billions of years old.

4. **The Revelatory-Day view**: This view holds that the 'days' may be 24-hour days of revelation but not days of creation. This view proposes that it took God a literal solar week to reveal to Adam (or Moses) what God had done in the long ages before humans were created.

5. **Alternate-Day-Age view**: This view holds that the days are 24 hours, but the days are separated by long periods in between.

6. **Relative Time view**: This view holds that the universe is billions of years old, measured from the standpoint of humans. But the

---

[1] I took much of this information from a lecture slide by Professor of Philosophy Dr. J. T Bridges. Also see Geisler, *Systematic Theology, 1531-33.*

creation only took six literal days when measured from God's standpoint.[2]

7. **Ideal-Time view**: This view holds that all things were created with the appearance of age. That means these were created mature. So, for example, Adam may have looked 21 years old a minute after he was created, but he was really only a minute old. Therefore, according to this view, the world can be actually young and only apparently old.

8. **Literary- Framework view**: This view holds that the terminologies and phrases such as 'days,' 'evening and morning' are used as ancient literary devices to cover certain periods.

9. **Religious Myth view**: This view holds that the Genesis account is purely religious or mythical. Recently, some view Genesis as a mytho-history. Theistic Evolution (or some use the terminology "Evolutionary Creationism") comes under this view.

Interpretation

Earlier, I addressed the two books metaphor, the Book of Scripture and the Book of Nature, which are given by God. There is no conflict between the Bible and the scientific facts. The actual conflict is between some interpretations of the Scripture and some scientific theories. Both biblical and scientific interpretations are not free from error. It is important to understand that the Bible does not say how old the Earth or universe is. Since the Bible does not say it, the age of the world is not a test for orthodoxy. It doesn't matter what view one holds, but it must preserve

(a) The historical-grammatical interpretation,

---

[2] See Geisler, *Systematic Theology, 1533.*

(b) The historicity and context of Genesis 1-2, and

(c) The inerrancy and infallibility of the Scripture.

It is important to respect all views that can preserve the above points. Everybody should treat each other's views with a lot of gentleness and respect instead of trying to attack opposing views arrogantly. People on all sides present good reasons to support their claims. Defenders on all sides are honest conservative Christians. Defenders include intelligent academic theologians, philosophers, and scientists with great credibility. They all commonly believe that God created everything out of nothing (creation *ex nihilo*). Everyone believes that we all need Jesus Christ for salvation, which is the central point. For biblical orthodoxy, it is acceptable to believe in an old earth or young Earth as long as the central salvation message of the Bible is not neglected. It is fine to kindly disagree with each other's view on how God created the world.

The central debate is between Young-Earth creationists and Old-Earth creationists. Young-Earth creationists claim that the Young-Earth model (six literal 24-hour days and about 6000 years old) is the only accurate interpretation of the Genesis creation account. The Old-Earth creationists refuse the Young-Earth interpretation, claiming that the Genesis account indicates a longer period. Therefore, believing that the world was created billions of years ago and siding with the scientific consensus is legitimate. As far as I understood this topic, the proper exegesis of the Scripture refutes Young-Earth Creationism. Now, I will present some biblical reasons why the Genesis creation days are longer than 24-hour periods and my personal view, which I find reasonable in this debate. You do not have to agree with me on this. You can evaluate the creation model I present here.

The View of Creation by RTB

I hold the Old-Earth Progressive Creationism that the organization *Reasons to Believe* (RTB) promotes. RTB holds that the days in Genesis are 'literal long finite periods.' RTB contains a scholarly community of scientists, theologians, biblical scholars, and philosophers. RTB's position is that we should take the creation accounts in the Bible literally and consistently. This view interprets Genesis's days as literal long periods while maintaining consistency with other texts in the Bible. RTB demonstrates a bigger-picture understanding of the universe and God's redemptive plan. I will present three biblical reasons why the 'days' in Genesis are not literal 24-hour periods by referring to the book *Navigating Genesis: A Scientist's Journey through Genesis 1-11* by astronomer and theologian Hugh Ross.[3] You may evaluate the reasons for yourself.

Biblical Reasons

The Hebrew word *Yôm* (יוֹם) for Day has four literal definitions.

The four definitions are:

a) 24-hour period.

b) A portion of the daylight hour or all of the daylight hour.

c) A week (Genesis 2:4 summarizes the entire creation week and calls it 'day').

d) A long but finite period of time. ("the day of the Lord" (Joel 2:31); "A Day is as thousand years" (Psalm 90:4)).[4]

---

[3] Hugh Ross, *Navigating Genesis: A Scientist's Journey Through Genesis 1-11* (CA: RTB Press, 2014). Dr. Ross was one of my professors of physics and astronomy. Some of the information came from his presentation slides. For more details, see his books or the RTB website (www.reasons.org).

[4] Ibid, 35.

It is important to note that Genesis is written in the ancient Hebrew language. I am a student of the Hebrew language. In biblical Hebrew, many nouns do multiple duties. The only word to describe 'A long but finite period' is '*Yôm*.' It is important to understand the context to determine the meaning of the word 'day.' What about the days in the book of Genesis?

Day Seven is Longer than 24 Hours

Genesis 2:2-3 says God rested on the *Seventh Day* after his acts of creation. Other biblical texts (Psalm 95:11; Hebrews 4:3-5) declare we are still on God's Seventh Day. That means the Seventh Day continues till today. Although the Seventh Day had a beginning, it has yet to finish. The Seventh Day will only end when the humans are redeemed (Romans 8:22-25) and when God creates again in the new Creation (Revelation 21). The end of *day 'Seven'* will mark the beginning of the New Creation.

Moreover, we can see the phrase *'evening and the morning'* for the first six days. This phrase is absent on *Day Seven*. This also indicates that the Seventh Day was not yet complete in Moses' time frame. Therefore, even if we take the shortest of all chronologies of humankind, the Seventh Day has been at least six thousand years long. The phrase *"evening and morning"* may be a figure of speech indicating a *beginning* and *ending* to a definite period of time. Often, the phrase is used as a figure of speech in the Old Testament with the meaning *"continually"* (Exodus 18:13; 27:21; Leviticus 24:3; Job 4:20.) The phrase minimally would be bracketing a beginning (morning) and an ending (evening) of each creation day.

[Day 1 beginning....... Day 1 ending]

[Day 2 beginning....... Day 2 ending]

[Day 3 beginning....... Day 3 ending]

[Day 4 beginning....... Day 5 ending]

[Day 5 beginning...... Day 5 ending]

[Day 6 beginning...... Day 6 ending]

Day 7 continues till now...............

Even if we take the phrase "evening and the morning" in Genesis 1 literally, it does not encompass all of a 24-hour day, but only the afternoon of one Day and the early morning of another, which also rules out the possibility of a literal 24-hour period. The Bible clearly states that Day Seven is a long period that has not yet finished. Therefore, when Day Seven is a long period, the Genesis 1 grammatical structure requires the first six creation days to be long. Let's narrow our focus to Day Six. What can we learn from the Sixth Day?

Day Six is longer than 24 hours

In Genesis 1, in terms of the creation of human beings, both male and female were created on creation *Day Six*. Genesis 2 (second account of creation) further unpacks the creation of Adam and several events in more detail (before Eve came on the scene).

Adam was created first outside of the Garden of Eden, and God placed him in the Garden of Eden. Then, God had him work the garden and guard it. God told Adam to name all the creatures. Adam couldn't find a suitable helper and companion among other creatures. The narrative suggests that Adam had sufficient interaction with the plants and animals to realize something was missing from his life. God put Adam to sleep and did the surgery. When Adam woke up, he was introduced to a brand-new creature (Eve) like him. When Adam saw Eve, he exclaimed *hap.pā.ʿam* (הַפַּעַם) (Genesis 2: 23). This is translated as "at last" or "now at length."[5] The expression also appears in Genesis 30:20, which is translated as "now at last."[6] The same appears again in Genesis 46:30 as "now finally." This indicates that Adam has been longing/searching for his companion for a reasonable amount of time. Moreover, in Genesis 1, we can see Adam and Eve receiving instructions from God (still on *Day Six*).

All the events indicate that creation Day Six is longer than 24 hours. If creation Day Six is longer than 24 hours, then the Genesis 1 grammatical structure requires all creation days to be much longer than 24 hours. There are also reasons for other days to be longer, but I recommend the works of *Reasons to Believe* for a more comprehensive understanding of this topic. From all these reasons, it is clear that Genesis creation days are longer than 24-hour periods. In addition to the biblical reasons, there are plenty of scientific reasons for the age of the universe (in billions). Here are some reasons the scientists at the RTB present why the universe is old.[7]

Scientific Reasons[8]

1) The universe is filled with burnt-out stars (white dwarfs, neutron stars, black holes). For white dwarfs, the burnout times are in the billions of years. Cooling sequences for white dwarfs establish that many of them have been cooling for billions of years.

---

5   See R. Laird Harris, Gleason L. Archer, and Bruce K. Waltke, *Theological Wordbook of the Old Testament* (Chicago: Moody, 1989), 2:730; and Francis Brown, S. R. Driver, and Charles A. Briggs, *The Brown-Driver-Briggs Hebrew and English Lexicon* (MA: Hendrickson, 1997), 822. Cited in Hugh Ross, *A Matter of Days*: Resolving a Creation Controversy, 2nd ed. (CA: RTB Press, 2015),72.

6   Ross, *A Matter of Days, 72.*

7   Ross, *Why the Universe Is the Way It Is.* Also see *The Creator and the Cosmos* (CA: RTB Press, 2018).

8   Quoted from a lecture by Dr. Ross. See his books for more details.

2) The discovery of ice cores. The ice core layers must be annual. These reveal known volcanic eruptions and eight cycles of Earth's orbital eccentricity variation. The core shows a continuous record of 800,000 annual layers. All six deep ice cores yield the identical result: Earth is more than 100,000 years old.

3) The speed of light and the distance of the stars.

4) The rate of expansion of the universe.

5) The Big-Bang cosmology is the best-tested model, which goes hand in hand with the biblical creation account. Astronomers can measure the physical and chemical properties of the universe, galaxies, stars, and planets. Those methods are reliable and trustworthy. It is important to note that Christians should avoid protesting against the Big Bang theory and should consider how these theories relate to Christian theism. The Big-Bang Cosmology is the philosophical route to Genesis's account of creation out of nothing (creation *ex nihilo*). The Big Bang is a label that explains there was a beginning. A philosopher or theologian can further argue that the God of the Bible caused the Big Bang.

6) The majority who deny the reliability and trustworthiness of scientific discoveries are the young-earth creationists. For example, the discovery of 'Dark Energy' does not fit the YEC model. Dark energy indicates an aged universe. The 'Dark Energy' is confirmed by independent measuring techniques - galaxy cluster x-rays, WMAP of CMB, ground-based CMB, type Ia supernovae, gravitational lenses, radio galaxy distributions, Sloan Digital Sky Survey, Two-Degree Field Survey, and velocity distributions.[9]

---

[9] Quoted from Ross' lecture slide. See his books.

Ross writes, "With no exceptions, all reliable scientific age-measuring tools confirm that the universe and Earth are billions of years old."[10] There are many independent measurements that support the age of the universe to approximately 13.73 billion years ago. The scientific data accurately supports the biblical scientific claims but not the interpretation of the young-earth 24-hour period. As I have presented earlier, the Bible makes accurate scientific claims such as the finite beginning of the universe, fixed laws, fine-tuning, expansion of the universe, etc.

Question 1: What about those scientists who claim the universe is less than 10,000 years old?

Ross comments, "Only a dogmatic insistence on a peculiar interpretation of a few Bible passages would even cause any scientist to claim the universe is less than 10,000 years old."[11]

On *KKLA* Radio Los Angeles live with Dr. John Morris (President of the *Institute for Creation Research* (YEC)), John Stewart asked Morris if he knew any scientist who agreed, apart from a particular Bible interpretation, that the universe or Earth is young. Morris's answer was "no." Later, the Radio program host asked Dr. Duane Gish (ICR) the same question, and he also said, "No."[12]

There are many arguments that YEC brings forward to show that the Young-Earth model is the only accurate interpretation of the Bible, but a proper interpretation rules out that possibility. For instance, YEC claims that God radically altered the laws and constants of physics at the Fall or Flood. But the Bible rules out this young-

---

[10]   Ibid.

[11]   Ibid.

[12]   "The John Ankerberg Show," 2009, *ICR*, Accessed 8 January 2022 https://www.icr. org/i/articles/news/The-John-Ankerberg-Show-January-2009(1).pdf.

earth teaching. The Bible talks about the fixed physical laws in many verses (Gen. 1-2; 3:17; Eccl. 1:4-10; 3:11-15; Jer. 33:25; Rom.8:18-23; Rev.20:7-22:5). There was no change in the laws and constants of physics according to the Bible. There are also other arguments offered by YEC, but I do not want to take space to address and respond to all of them.[13] RTB has good responses to all of them.

Question 2: Isn't the Old-Earth view a modern idea?

The longer days interpretation of Genesis is not a modern idea. Here are two quotes from early times. Early Church Father St. Augustine wrote in *The City of God*, "What kind of days these are is difficult or even impossible for us to imagine, to say nothing of describing them."[14] In his letter to Thomas Burnet, Isaac Newton wrote, "Now for the number and length of the six days by what is said above you may make the first day as long as you please, and the second day too."[15]

Points to Note

1) God has written two books: The Book of Scripture and The Book of Nature. Since the same author writes both books, both cannot conflict.

2) The Bible is the inspired, inerrant, and infallible word of God.

3) However, our interpretations of either book may be wrong.

4) Both books can contribute to avoiding major errors in interpretation. Sometimes, even science can help correct wrong interpretations of the Scripture. For example, there was a time

---

[13] See Geisler, *Systematic Theology*, 1526-31; also see Reasons.org.

[14] St. Augustine, *City of God* (New York: Penguin, 1984), 436.

[15] Isaac Newton, "Copy Letter from Isaac Newton to Thomas Burnet," *The Newton Project*, published online in August 2007, Accessed 15 December 2022 https://www.newtonproject.ox.ac.uk/view/texts/normalized/THEM00253.

when some held that the Earth was flat based on a particular interpretation of some verses. But later, when we got great scientific evidence against the flat earth view, such an interpretation of the Scripture became invalid.

5) There is no doubt that we should trust the Bible more than science because it comes from God, and we have good reasons to support that. But if the Bible rules out the possibility of literal 24-hour interpretation, then it is valid to hold other views that make sense when interpreted by considering all the biblical texts and a bigger picture.

RTB dedicates its ministry to showing that the proper interpretation of the Scripture and nature shows no conflict. For example, "God's rest" answers the enigma of the fossil record. Before humanity came on the scene, there was abundant scientific evidence of speciation. After humanity, we do not see any. We don't see anything happening now because God stopped creating. RTB does not hold macro-evolution for scientific and Biblical reasons.

As far as I understand, the Bible is an old-Earth book when we look at it from a bigger picture and if we give particular attention to the days in Genesis. The old-Earth view has more explanatory power than YEC. If the Bible allows a longer period for the days of Genesis and scientific data supports it, then I think there is nothing wrong with holding the Old-Earth Progressive Creationism. However, I absolutely respect those who believe in Young-Earth Creationism. I avoid unnecessary debates to make a division. Since the age of the earth/universe should not be a test for orthodoxy, we should not make a division based on our views of Genesis days.

RTB dedicates its ministry to showing that the Bible and science are not in conflict when the Book of Scripture and the Book of Nature are correctly interpreted. I encourage you to explore this topic and evaluate the evidence for yourself. As scientists continue to study the natural world, we will have more clarity in our understanding. We should keep an open mind, respect all other views, and engage in charitable discussion. We should be faithful to the Scripture and proper interpretation of it. In the next chapter, I will introduce you to the Scientific Theory of Intelligent Design (ID) and the *Discovery Institute*'s Centre for Science and Culture.

CHAPTER 23

The Scientific Theory of Intelligent Design

Ancient Greek and Roman sources show a conception of nature as teleological, that is, nature exists for a purpose. The works *Philebus* by Plato[1] and *On the Nature of the Gods* by Cicero[2] testify that teleology is evident in nature. However, the rise of scientific naturalism by the end of the nineteenth century destroyed the teleological view of nature by attempting to explain everything in terms of matter, energy, and blind natural processes.[3] Paleontologist Stephen J. Gould writes, "We are here because one odd group of fishes had a peculiar fin anatomy that could transform into legs for terrestrial creatures;… We may yearn for a 'higher' answer—but none exists."[4] Joy Davidman summarized the creed of scientific naturalism this way: "Men… are only apes. Virtue is only custom. Life is only an electrochemical reaction. Mind is only a set of conditioned reflexes…

---

[1] Linda Zagzebski, *The Philosophy of Religion: An Historical Introduction* (United Kingdom: Wiley, 2007), 31.

[2] Cicero, *The Nature of the Gods*, trans. P.G. Walsh (Oxford: Oxford University Press, 2008); Plato, *The Great Books of the Western World 7. Plato*, ed. Robert M. Hutchins, (Chicago: Encyclopedia Britannica, 1952), 609-639.

[3] John G. West, *Darwin Day in America*, (Wilmington: Delaware, ISI Books, 2007), 23-42.

[4] Gould interview, *Life Magazine* (December 1988); See Carl Gaither, Alma Gaither, *Gaither's Dictionary of Scientific Quotations* (Netherlands: Springer New York, 2008.), 464.

Love, art, and altruism are only sex. The universe is only matter."[5]

Intelligent Design (ID) is a scientific theory of design detection. ID is a scientific research program with a community of scientists, philosophers, and other scholars who seek evidence for design in nature.[6] The *New World Encyclopedia* defines Intelligent Design as

> the view that it is possible to infer from empirical evidence that certain features of the universe and of living things are best explained by an intelligent cause, not an undirected process such as natural selection. . . ID relies on scientific evidence rather than on Scripture or religious doctrines. ID makes no claims about biblical chronology, and technically, a person does not have to believe in God to infer intelligent design in nature.[7]

ID is a scientific theory that seeks to demonstrate design through the scientific method. The intelligent design theorist can determine whether certain features discovered from empirical evidence are the product of chance, necessity (natural law), design, or a combination thereof. The initial goal of ID was design detection. But now, ID also attempts to resurrect teleology within science by going a step further.

The Scientific Method

The scientific method is commonly described as a four-step process involving *observation*, *hypothesis*, *experiments*, and *conclusion*.[8]

Step 1 (observation): ID begins with observing that intelligent agents produce Complex Specified Information (CSI). For example, if we see some random letters, "hdfmoSsDsxtYcbxpLQq," it looks complex

---

[5]   David W. Soper, *These Found the Way: Thirteen Converts to Protestant Christianity*, (United States: Westminster Press, 1951), 16.

[6]   "What is Intelligent Design?" *Intelligent Design.* Accessed September 05, 2022. https://intelligentdesign.org/whatisid/.

[7]   "Intelligent Design." *New World Encyclopedia.* Accessed September 06, 2022, https://www.newworldencyclopedia.org/entry/Intelligent_design.

[8]   The Center for Science and Culture, "What is the Science Behind Intelligent Design," *Discovery*, May 01, 2009, Accessed September 06, 2022, https://www.discovery.org/a/9761/.

but not specified. If we see the information "1212121212121212," it looks specified but not complex. However, if we see the writing, "TRUTH IS THE MOST VALUABLE THING IN THE WORLD," it is complex and specified.

Step 2 (hypothesis): The ID theorists hypothesize that if a natural object was designed it will contain CSI.

Step 3 (experiment): ID theorists perform experiments and make observations to see if they can find CSI. Examples of CSI include irreducible complexity (a purposeful arrangement of parts), fine-tuning parameters of the universe, DNA codes, etc.

Step 4 (conclusion): When scientists find CSI through experiments and observations, they conclude that such features were not the product of chance or natural law but were designed.[9]

How to Detect Design?

There are multiple methods to detect design. This includes William Dembski's "Explanatory Filter", Michael Behe's "Purposeful Arrangement", Stephen Meyer's "Inference to the Best Explanation" and Casey Luskin's Positive Case." Mathematician and philosopher William Dembski developed a method to detect design in nature by using an "Explanatory Filter."[10] There are three broad modes of explanation when trying to explain something: *natural law, chance,* and *design.*[11] The explanatory filter asks the following three questions

---

[9]   Casey Luskin, "Intelligent Design (ID) Has Scientific Merit Because it Uses the Scientific Method to Make its Claims and Infers Design by Testing its Positive Predictions," *Discovery Institute*, September 8, 2008, Accessed September 06, 2022, https://www.discovery.org/a/7051/.

[10] See William Dembski, *The Design Inference: Eliminating Chance Through Small Probabilities* (NY: Cambridge University Press, 1998). Cited in Groothuis, *Christian Apologetics*, 244.

[11] William A. Dembski, *The Design Revolution: Answering the Toughest Questions About Intelligent Design* (Downers Grove, Ill.: InterVarsity Press, 2004), 87.

about the thing one tries to explain: Is it *contingent*? Is it *complex*? Is it *specified*?

If something is contingent but not complex, we may ascribe it to natural law. If something is contingent and complex, we may ascribe it to chance. But if something is contingent, complex, and specified, we must ascribe it to design. If three questions can answer "yes," it filters out *natural law* and *chance* and infers *design* as the best explanation.

Dembski's explanatory filter attempts to locate specified complexities in the natural world, pointing to intelligent design. Groothuis presents the structure of the design filter this way:

1. X is either designed, or the result of chance, or the result of natural law, or the combination of chance and natural law.

2. X is not the result of chance or natural law or the combination of both.

3. Therefore: X is the result of design.[12]

The evidence for intelligent design comes from many areas of science, including physics, cosmology, paleontology, information theory, animal biology, systematics, genetics, cell biology, biochemistry, and many more. The ID movement has a growing number of new examples of design from different scientific fields. The major discoveries come from physics and cosmology, the origin of life, and biological complexity.

---

[12]   Groothuis, *Christian Apologetics*, 246.

Is ID the Same as Creationism?

As soon as the label "Intelligent Design or ID" is noticed, scientific naturalists reject it by claiming it is a different version of creationism. Honest critics of ID can easily identify the difference between creationism and intelligent design. Creationism starts with religious texts, but ID starts with empirical evidence and infers design based on the findings. Why do some critics give the creationist label to ID? A historian of science, Ronald Numbers, a critic of ID, agrees that "the creationist label is inaccurate when it comes to the ID movement."[13] Numbers also says giving such a label is "the easiest way to discredit intelligent design."[14]

If something is designed, obviously, there is a theistic/philosophical implication to it since a designing agent is implied. However, the scientific method does not help us to find who that agent is. It is the job of philosophers and theologians to take the argument further. ID theorists include skeptics and people from various religious affiliations. Dean H. Kenyon and Percival Davis wrote,

> The idea that life had an intelligent source is hardly unique to Christian fundamentalism. Advocates of design have included not only Christians and other religious theists but pantheists, Greek and Enlightenment philosophers, and now include many modern scientists who describe themselves as religiously agnostic. Moreover, the concept of design implies absolutely nothing about beliefs normally associated with Christian fundamentalism, such as young Earth, a global flood, or even the existence of the Christian God. All it implies is that life had an intelligent source.[15]

Historian of the ID movement Thomas Woodward puts it:

> There is no "Made by Yahweh" engraved on the side of the bacterial rotary motor—the flagellum. In order to find out what or who its designer is, one

---

[13] Ibid.

[14] John G. West, "Intelligent Design and Creationism Just Aren't the Same." *Discovery Institute*. December 01, 2002). Accessed 02, April, 2021, https://www.discovery.org/a/1329/.

[15] Dean H. Kenyon and Percival Davis, *Of Pandas and People: The Central Question of Biological Origins*, (United States: Haughton Publishing Company, 1993), 161.

must go outside the narrow discipline of biology. Cross-disciplinary dialogue must begin with the fields of philosophy, sociology, history, anthropology, and theology. The design itself, however, is a direct scientific inference; it does not depend on a single religious premise for its conclusions.[16]

Philosopher of science Stephen Meyer wrote,

The theory of intelligent design does not claim to be able to determine the identity or any other attributes of that intelligence, even if philosophical deliberation or additional evidence from other disciplines may provide reasons to consider, for example, a specifically theistic design hypothesis.[17]

Biochemist Michael Behe puts it,

ID is not an argument for the existence of a benevolent God… I recognize that philosophy and theology may be able to extend the argument. But a scientific argument for design in biology does not reach that far.[18]

Mathematician and philosopher William Dembski wrote,

Intelligent design is modest in what it attributes to the designing intelligence responsible for the specified complexity in nature. For instance, design theorists recognize that the nature, moral character, and purposes of this intelligence lie beyond the competence of science and must be left to religion and philosophy.[19]

It is clear for honest thinkers that ID is not creationism. While there are plentiful reasons to consider design hypothesis, many people refuse to consider it "on the grounds that it does not qualify as 'scientific.'"[20] It is due to their commitment to methodological naturalism (or materialism).

---

[16]   Thomas Woodward, *Darwin Strikes Back: Defending the Science of Intelligent Design* (Grand Rapids, Mich.: Baker Books, 2006), 15.

[17]   Stephen C. Meyer, *Signature in the Cell: DNA and the Evidence for Intelligent Design*, (United Kingdom: HarperCollins, 2009), 429.

[18]   Michael Behe, "The Modern Intelligent Design Hypothesis," *Philosophia Christi*, Series 2, Vol. 3, No.1 (2001), 165.

[19]   William A. Dembski, *The Design Revolution: Answering the Toughest Questions About Intelligent Design* (Downers Grove, Ill.: InterVarsity Press, 2004), 42.

[20]   Stephen C. Meyer, "A Scientific History and Philosophical Defense of the Theory of Intelligent Design," *Discovery Institute*, 07, October, 2008, Accessed March 01, 2021. https://www.discovery.org/a/7471/.

Methodological Naturalism

Methodological naturalism asserts that in order for a hypothesis or theory to qualify as scientific, it must invoke only natural explanations.[21] According to methodological naturalism, ID theory does not qualify. Design theorists argue that, whatever its classification, the design hypothesis constitutes a better explanation for many structures and functions in nature than a naturalistic explanation.[22] "Simply classifying an argument as 'non-scientific' does not refute it."[23] "If the mandate of science is to follow the evidence wherever it leads," methodological naturalism restricts intellectual freedom to select the best hypothesis.[24] It restricts people from pursuing the truth. Methodological naturalism doesn't stop ID theorists or proponents from seeking truth. Now, let us look into some examples of design detection from various scientific disciplines. Let's begin with the origin of life and biological complexity.

Design in the Origin of Life and Biological Complexity

When we think about the origin of life, the first thing that comes to our mind may be Charles Darwin's theory of evolution---the work is well known as *On the Origin of Species*.[25] Many people believe that Darwin has explained everything related to the origin of life; therefore, God is not necessary to explain life's origin. It is important to note that Darwinism doesn't say anything about the origin of life from non-life; it only tries to explain the evolution of life since the

---

[21]   Groothuis, *Christian Apologetics*, 278.

[22]   Stephen C. Meyer, "A Scientific History and Philosophical Defense of the Theory of Intelligent Design," *Discovery Institute*, 07, October, 2008, Accessed March 01, 2021. https://www.discovery.org/a/7471/.

[23]   Ibid.

[24]   Groothuis, *Christian Apologetics*, 279.

[25]   Charles Darwin, *On the Origin of Species by Means of Natural Selection*, (New York: The Heritage Press, 1963).

first life emerged. Darwinism requires replicating organisms for its explanation of life. It does not say how replicating organisms got there.

Prominent atheist and evolutionary biologist Richard Dawkins thinks Darwin's theory gives intellectual fulfillment to atheists since God is no longer required for the explanation.[26] On a side note, even if macro-evolution turns out to be true (so far, the evidence is against it), it still cannot eliminate a causal agent from the scene because something has to start the process in the first place. Apart from how life came about, fine-tuning is a necessary condition for life but not sufficient for ID theorists). Darwin proposed a mechanism called natural selection, which is an unguided natural process without a purpose. This slow process could develop new species over plenty of time.

When Darwin proposed the theory, he knew nothing about the molecular level of the cell. He simply used some observations to conclude his theory. Upon genetic discoveries by Gregor Mendel (father of genetics), Darwinists claimed that the changes in species take place through random genetic mutations[27] and natural selection. This is the dominant model in the biological world, and it is called "the neo-Darwinian synthesis."[28] Neo-Darwinists think that an intelligent agent is not involved in these processes. This theory influenced many Western scientific intellectuals to keep religion away from the scientific commitment to methodological naturalism.

Many Christian Darwinists hold that God created the universe and left it to evolve by chance and necessity (natural law); therefore, it is impossible to detect design in biology.[29] This is a false claim because the evidence for intelligent design is clearly observable in

---

[26]   Richard Dawkins, *The Blind Watchmaker,* (England: Penguin Books, 2006), 06.
[27]   Groothuis, *Christian Apologetics,* 276.
[28]   Ibid.
[29]   Ibid., 277.

biology. The scientific evidence for Darwinism only explains small changes (microevolution) within the species; it does not support a total change (macroevolution) from one species to another.[30] It might explain minor speciation, but not all of biology.

It is extremely unpopular among biologists to criticize Darwinian evolution because they may be persecuted by their colleagues if they do so.[31] However, there are many scientists and philosophers of science boldly working in ID research and challenging evolution scientifically. The prominent among them are Michael Behe (biochemist), Jonathan Wells (molecular and cell biologist), Douglas Axe (molecular biologist), James Tour (synthetic organic chemist), Richard Sternberg (evolutionary biologist), Michael Denton (geneticist), Stephen Meyer (philosopher of science), Ann Gauger (biologist), Paul Nelson (philosopher of biology and evolutionary theory), Casey Luskin (Geologist), Gunter Bechly (Paleontologist), Brian Miller (Physicist), Stuart Burgess (Biomechanics), Marcos Eberlin (Chemist) and many others working in this area of research.

Darwinists think that all the criticisms of Neo-Darwinism come from religious people. Therefore, those criticisms should not be considered scientific criticism.[32] It is an invalid claim because scientific criticisms were present in the following years after Darwin published his book.[33] There has been a growing number of criticisms of Darwinism from various thinkers since Darwin's time. One of the greatest examples we can observe today is "the scientific dissent from Darwinism." That is, during recent decades, over a thousand scientists (from different scientific disciplines) began to question

---

[30] Ibid., 271.

[31] Jonathan Wells, *Icons of Evolution: Science or Myth?* (Washington, DC: Regnery Pub., 2000), 8. Also, see the film, "*Expelled*" (2008), and Bergman, J., Wirth, K. H. (2021). *Slaughter of the Dissidents* Vol. I 3rd ed. (NP: Primedia eLaunch LLC, 2021).

[32] Groothuis, *Christian Apologetics*, 268.

[33] Ibid.

Darwinism's central tenet of natural selection when they discovered new evidence that does not work well with Darwinism. They hold various worldviews. They publicly signed the statement:

> We are skeptical of claims for the ability of random mutation and natural selection to account for the complexity of life. Careful examination of the evidence for Darwinian theory should be encouraged.[34]

In his book *Icons of Evolution*, molecular and cell biologist Jonathan Wells argues that "much of what we teach about evolution is wrong."[35] He argues that these are not science but myths. Examples include the Miller-Urey experiment, Darwin's tree of life, homology in vertebrate limbs, Haeckel's embryos, archaeopteryx, peppered moths, Darwin's finches, four-winged fruit flies, fossil horses, and the ultimate icon depicting apes evolving into humans. Wells follows this up in his book *Zombie Science*.[36] Wells argues that the list of evidence (he calls "icons" of evolution) that supports Darwin's theory is, in one way or another, misrepresents the truth.[37] James M. Tour, a synthetic organist chemist,[38] listed in "The World's Most Influential Scientific Minds" by Thomson Reuters in 2014, holds over 130 patents and is an origin of life researcher who says scientists are "still clueless about the origin of life."[39] There is no empirical evidence for how the first life originated. What about Darwin's tree of life? Darwin's tree of life is a well-known diagram. Do fossil records show any evidence for Darwin's tree of life?

---

[34] "A Scientific Dissent from Darwinism," Discovery Institute, Accessed June 05, 2023. https://www.discovery.org/m/securepdfs/2023/05/Scientific-Dissent-List-05012023-2.pdf.

[35] Wells, *Icons of Evolution*, 08.

[36] Jonathan Wells, *Zombie Science: More Icons of Evolution* (Seattle, WA: Discovery Institute Press, 2017).

[37] Wells, *Icons of Evolution*, 08.

[38] Charles Thaxton et al., *The Mystery of Life's Origin: The Continuing Controversy* (Seattle: Discovery Institute Press, 2020), 473.

[39] Thaxton et al., *The Mystery of Life's Origin*, 323.

Fossil Evidence

The truth must correspond to reality. According to what is illustrated in Darwin's tree of life, paleontologists should find simple to complex organisms in the fossil records. Moreover, "there should be a substantial record of transitions between species" because evolution proceeds by many small changes from one species to another.[40] However, the fossil records do not show the patterns depicted in the tree of life. Therefore, Darwin's tree of life is very misleading.

Another important discovery in the fossil record is the event known as "the Cambrian explosion," which shows the sudden appearance of numerous new animal forms, dated 530 million years ago.[41] It contradicts the neo-Darwinian expectations. According to Darwinism, these increases in new animal forms should show gradual appearance, over long periods of time, in the fossil record. Wells writes, "The fossil record, however, shows that almost all of the animal phyla appear at about the same time in the Cambrian explosion, with the number declining slightly thereafter due to extinction."[42]

In his book *Darwin's Doubt: The Explosive Origin of Animal Life and the Case for Intelligent Design*, philosopher of science Stephen Meyer offers a detailed explanation of the Cambrian explosion event. Meyer presents a list of many leading biologists and paleontologists who have raised questions about the adequacy of the standard neo-Darwinian mechanism. This includes Gerry Webster and Brian Goodwin, Günter Theissen, Marc Kirschner, and John Gerhart, Jeffrey Schwartz, Douglas Erwin, Eric Davidson, Eugene Koonin, Simon Conway Morris, Robert Carroll, Gunter Wagner, Heinz-Albert Becker and Wolf-Eckhart Lönnig, Stuart Newman and Gerd Müller, Stuart

---

[40] Groothuis, *Christian Apologetics*, 286.

[41] Stephen C. Meyer, *Darwin's Doubt: The Explosive Origin of Animal Life and the Case for Intelligent Design* (New York: Harper One, 2013), back cover.

[42] Wells, *Icons of Evolution*, 43.

Kauffman, Peter Stadler, Heinz Saedler, James Valentine, Giuseppe Sermonti, James Shapiro and Michael Lynch, and others.[43]

Darwin's tree of life does not correspond to fossil data. There are many areas in the origin of life research that Neo-Darwinism fails to explain, but an intelligent design can explain sufficiently. Let us look at a few pieces of evidence from DNA information.

DNA Information: Indicating Design

In his book *Information and the Origin of Life*, biophysicist Bernd-Olaf Kuppers pointed out that "the problem of the origin of life is clearly basically equivalent to the problem of the origin of biological information."[44] Since the late 1950s and 1960s, researchers studying the origin of life have discovered that DNA contains large amounts of genetic information in the form of language. Francis Crick, the co-discover of DNA structure, proposed that the chemical constituents in DNA function like letters in a written language or digital symbols in a computer code. Software developer Bill Gates said, "DNA is like a computer program but far, far more advanced than any software ever created."[45]

The living cell contains organic molecules, including "proteins, DNA, RNA, lipids, and complex carbohydrates."[46] DNA contains the information necessary to specify the sequence of the proteins. The "letters" (the nucleotides) code for proteins, and the correct sequence of the letters is necessary to translate molecules into specific proteins. In his book *Signature in the Cell*, Meyer points out three

---

[43]   See Meyer, *Darwin's Doubt.*

[44]   Bernd-Olaf Küppers, *Information and the Origin of Life* (Cambridge: MIT Press, 1990), 170-72.

[45]   Bill Gates, *The Road Ahead*, rev.ed. (New York: Viking, Penguin Group, 1996), 188.

[46]   Jonathan Wells, *The Politically Incorrect Guide to Darwinism and Intelligent Design,* (Washington, DC: Regnery Publishing, 2006), 96.

important properties that enable DNA to carry information.[47] First, the subunits of DNA are like a four-letter alphabet (A, T, G, C) arranged like meaningful sentences that convey a particular message. Second, the information in DNA is thus extremely complex. Third, the information in DNA is specified.[48] The information contents in the DNA are complex and specified. Dawkins writes, "Biology is the study of complicated things that give the appearance of having been designed for a purpose."[49] As I have presented earlier, specified complexity cannot be formed by chance or necessity (natural law). Therefore, the best explanation for the origin of specified complexity in DNA is intelligent design.[50] Let us now look into the irreducible complexity which indicates design.

Irreducible Complexity: Indicating Design

In his book, *On the Origin of Species*, Darwin wrote, "If it could be demonstrated that any complex organ existed, which could not possibly have been formed by numerous, successive, slight modifications, my theory would absolutely break down. But I can find out no such case."[51] Biochemist Michael Behe, in his book *Darwin's Black Box*,[52] scientifically demonstrates what Darwin did not know, namely DNA, the presence of genetic information, which breaks down his theory just as he wrote. In this book, Behe sparked a revolution against Neo-Darwinism. Moreover, he demonstrates that intelligent design is the best explanation for his scientific findings.

---

[47] Wells, *The Politically Incorrect Guide to Darwinism and Intelligent Design*, 96.

[48] Ibid.

[49] Dawkins, *The Blind Watchmaker*, 06.

[50] Groothuis, *Christian Apologetics*, 312.

[51] Darwin, *On the Origin of Species*, 189.

[52] Michael Behe, *Darwin's Black Box*. (New York: Free Press, 1996).

To every contemporary scientist of Darwin's time, the cell was a black box (as Behe puts it).[53] They knew nothing about the complex inner workings of the cell. They thought those were simple mechanisms. Since the mid-1950s, biochemistry has been able to discover the workings of life at the molecular level. Thanks to scientific advancements, the invention of the electron microscope, and well-established molecular biology.[54] In Behe's language, scientists were able to open the "black box." He argues that Darwinian evolution cannot account for the molecular structure of life.[55]

Behe argues that the molecular machines could not have originated through undirected natural processes. For molecular machines to function as they are intended to, all part necessary must be present at the same time. Behe calls it "irreducible complexity." He demonstrates this using the illustration of a mousetrap. A simple mousetrap to function properly requires all the parts (platform, spring, hammer, holding bar, and catch).[56] If any of the parts are not present, or placed correctly, it will not catch a mouse. By irreducible complexity, Behe means "a single system composed of several well-matched, interacting parts that contribute to the basic function, wherein the removal of any one of the parts causes the system to effectively cease functioning."[57] He also notes that,

> An irreducibly complex system cannot be produced directly (that is, by continuously improving the initial function, which continues to work by the same mechanism) by slight, successive modifications of a precursor system because any precursor to an irreducibly complex system that is missing a part is by definition nonfunctional. An irreducibly complex biological system, if there is such a thing, would be a powerful challenge to Darwinian Evolution.[58]

---

[53]   Behe, *Darwin's Black Box*, 09.
[54]   Ibid., 33.
[55]   Ibid.
[56]   Ibid., 66.
[57]   Ibid., 39.
[58]   Ibid.

Behe presents many examples of molecular machines that are irreducibly complex and cannot be formed by slight, successive modification. Examples include the blood clotting system, the cilium, and the bacterial flagellum. He also claims that we can find examples of irreducibly complex molecular machines on every page of the biochemistry textbook.[59] Behe demonstrates that irreducible complexity is present in the molecular structure of life, which is evidence for specified complexity. Specified complexity cannot be formed by chance, necessity (natural law), or the combination of the two.[60] Therefore, the best explanation for the origin of the specified complexity of molecular machines is intelligent design.

Darwinists raised many critiques against Behe's irreducible complexity. One of the objections is made by Kenneth Miller.[61] He points out that it is possible to use individual parts of the irreducible structure for other purposes. This is often called the co-option theory. Miller finds that a part of the bacterial flagellum is found in another organism outside of the flagellum.[62] This objection is a straw man fallacy because Behe never claimed that a part of an irreducibly complex system must have no other function outside that system. For example, a part (a spring) in a mousetrap could be used for something else. He only claimed that a flagellum by itself could not have directly evolved to the present irreducibly complex structure.[63] Behe refutes all of his critics in his book, *A Mousetrap for Darwin*.[64]

---

[59] Michael Behe, "Design in the Details: The Origins of Biomolecular Machines," in *Darwinism, Design, and Public Education*, ed. John Angus Campbell and Stephen C. Meyer (East Lansing: Michigan State University Press, 2003), 298. Cited in Groothuis, *Christian Apologetics*, 307.

[60] Groothuis, *Christian Apologetics*, 305.

[61] Ibid., 311.

[62] Ibid.

[63] Ibid.

[64] Michael J. Behe, *A Mousetrap for Darwin: Michael J. Behe Answers His Critics* (Seattle: Discovery Institute Press, 2020).

Due to their commitment to methodological naturalism, many people were outraged by Behe and pointed out that he was breaking this principle of modern science..[65] As I have presented earlier, methodological naturalism doesn't stop ID theorists from inferring design from empirical observation. Behe puts it, "We are not inferring design from what we do not know but from what we do know. We are not inferring design to account for some black box but to account for an open box."[66]

Design in Human Life

Biology of Human Uniqueness

Technological innovation during the past century has enabled scientists to discover and bring into light many mysteries of the natural world that were unknown to human beings earlier. I have presented some of them in the previous sections, including the structure and function of the cosmos, DNA, and molecular machines. Using light and radio telescopes, scientists were able to discover many astonishing facts about the sky. Using the electron microscope, scientists discovered what is happening inside a cell. All new inventions help scientists study more deeply. However, it is important to understand that it was discovering one primal thing (which we do not think often) that opened a path toward the modern technological advancement we experience today. What is that one primal thing? The discovery of Fire! Geneticist Michael Denton wrote,

> Of all the discoveries made in the course of mankind's long march to civilization, there was one primal discovery that made the realization of all this possible. It's a discovery we use every day and take completely for granted. But this discovery changed everything. Humankind discovered how to make and tame *fire*.[67]

---

[65] Groothuis, *Christian Apologetics*, 312.
[66] Behe, "Design in the Details," 301.
[67] Michael Denton, *Fire-Maker: How Humans Were Designed to Harness Fire and Transform Our Planet*, (WA: Discovery Institute Press, Kindle Edition, 2016), 9-10.

Denton argues that humans were designed to harness fire and transform our planet. He points out many facts about fire and its relation to human beings and planet Earth. I will summarize a few points here.

There are many elements of fitness in nature that help humans to harness fire. Denton points out that the atmosphere on Earth has the right properties for fire-making and the fire-maker. There are no other known planets that have these unique features of the Earth. Our ancestors must have conceived the idea of fire from natural causes (lightning or volcanoes). It was the ability to tame fire that led to the art of cooking. It then led to the transformation of clay into hard stone or molded pottery to store food. The mastery of fire also led to the discovery and manufacture of charcoal by burning wood in an oxygen-depleted environment.[68]

When charcoal was discovered, people realized that it could generate greater heat than an ordinary wood fire. It then eventually led to the discovery of metallurgy. Although no one knows the sequence of events, there is little doubt that metallurgy comes second to the mastery of fire.[69] Metallurgy opened possibilities for many other future inventions. If we look around today, we can see the usage of metal in most areas (automobiles, computer chips, mobile phones, to name a few). Copper smelting requires a 1,150-degree temperature, which mankind mastered as early as 7,000 years ago. Iron smelting requires an even higher temperature, which was only mastered around 1200 BC,[70] which initiated the Iron Age.

Another element of fitness in nature crucial to the development of metallurgy is the existence of woody plants, which are the right fuel

---

[68]   Denton, *Fire-Maker*, 10.
[69]   Ibid.
[70]   Ibid., 11.

for the fire and the raw material to manufacture charcoal. Burning small plants does not help to obtain high temperatures. It requires hardwoods. To grow tall and woody trees, an essential component of the plant cell, known as *lignin*, is necessary.[71] Trees were designed to contain *lignin* molecules. As we study deeper, we can find many elements that are designed and linked to one another to harness fire. There are more remarkable examples of fitness in nature (which I did not cover here) for the harnessing of fire and developing metallurgy. Other fire-enabled technologies, such as glassmaking and chemistry, opened a path to invent microscopes and telescopes, which led scientists to unlock the mysteries in nature.

Above all, in order to unlock the potential of metals that led to modern technological inventions, there must also be a creature capable of maintaining and controlling fire. Denton points out that our own species, *Homo sapiens*, is the only creature with unique physical attributes (along with high intelligence) to perform the task.[72] An elephant, rat, dolphin, or monkey cannot maintain and control fire. For Homo sapiens to perform the task, they require a unique physical design (along with high intelligence). The physical conditions required are the right size, the right strength, and finely controlled muscular activity.[73]

In short, humans were designed to harness fire and transform our planet through scientific discoveries and inventions. The technological world we see today would not exist without human beings learning how to harness fire. To harness fire, we have the right planet, the right fuel, and the right fire-maker. Many elements of fitness in nature and the unique design of human beings point to an Intelligent Design. Astronomer Fred Hoyle puts it,

---

[71]   Ibid., 38.
[72]   Ibid., 48.
[73]   Ibid., 47-61.

> A commonsense interpretation of the facts suggests that a super-intellect has monkeyed with physics, as well as with chemistry and biology, and that there are no blind forces worth speaking about in nature... The numbers one calculates
>
> from the facts seem to me so overwhelming as to put this conclusion almost beyond question.[74]

The scientific theory of Intelligent Design has philosophical implications.

Philosophical Implication: The Existence of God

Design points to a Designer. Obviously, if something is designed, it has a theological implication and leads us to try to find out the designing agent. This requires further philosophical reasoning. The one who is committed to the discipline of philosophy takes the scientific data and uses reason to make a further argument for the designing agent. From multiple points of view, we have good reasons to conclude that the God of the Bible is the designing agent. This fits well with the biblical claim that God is the creator and designer of the universe.

I have only covered some basic information on Intelligent Design theory. This field of study is vast. If you are interested in scientific research in the field of ID, I recommend keeping up to date with **Discovery Institute's Centre for Science and Culture**, which is based in Seattle, Washington.[75] The ID movement has been growing globally over the past several years.

□□□

---

[74] Fred Hoyle, "The Universe: Past and Present Reflections," *Annual Reviews*, September 20, 1982. 20. 1-36.

[75] See Discovery Institute: www.discovery.org ; www.evolutionnews.org.

SECTION 4:

The Existential Quests

CHAPTER 24

The Problem of Evil

The problem of evil is widely debated in the philosophy of religion because we deal with evil every day in our lives. We cannot avoid the reality of evil. Every worldview has to answer the question, "Why is there evil in the world?" If the Christian worldview is true, it must sufficiently and satisfactorily answer this question. In this chapter, I aim to give a very short response to the problem of evil from a Christian perspective.[1] As I have mentioned earlier, there are two categories of evil. They are:

1. Moral evil (moral evil is something that is caused by rational individuals.)

2. Natural evil (natural disasters.)

The problem of evil has always been an argument against the existence of a theistic God, particularly the God of the Bible. The God of the Bible is defined as Omnipotent (all-powerful), Omniscient (all-knowing), and Omnibenevolent (all-good). I will use "3-O God" to represent the God of the Bible in the rest of this chapter. There are three major problems of evil. They are:

---

[1]   A lot of insights come from the slides and lectures by Professor of Philosophy Dr. Garry DeWeese. I sat in his Apologetics and Ethics class at Denver Seminary in 2018. I also give credit to the lectures by Professor of Philosophy Dr. Timothy Brown. I sat in his Philosophy of Religion class at Southern Evangelical Seminary in 2022.

1) The Logical Problem of Evil.

2) The Evidential Problem of Evil.

3) The Existential Problem of Evil.

The Logical Problem of Evil

The logical (also called deductive) problem of evil is an attempt to prove that God (specifically the 3-O God of the Bible) and evil cannot exist at the same time. The existence of God and the existence of evil are logically incompatible according to the logical problem of evil. This will be an issue for Christianity if the argument is successful because the deductive argument claims to give certainty. The argument assumes that a God who is all-powerful, all-knowing, and all-good would eliminate evil. The logical problem of evil can be reduced to a syllogism (*Modus Tollens*[2]):

Premise 1: If 3-O God exists, then evil cannot exist.

Premise 2: Evil exists.

Conclusion: Therefore, 3-O God does not exist.

The alleged logical contradiction is that

1) 3-O God exists.

2) Evil exists.

According to the logical problem of evil, both (1) and (2) cannot be true. I will respond to this after stating the other two problems.

---

[2] Modus Tollens: *If P then q; not q; therefore, not p.* In Premise 2, when we negate "q" (i.e., "evil cannot exist") = evil exists.

The Evidential Problem of Evil

The evidential problem of evil rests on the belief that the presence of evil in the world makes the existence of God improbable or less likely. This is called an inductive problem because inductive reasoning generally only claims to yield probability, not certainty. The evidential problem of evil only claims a probability that God may not exist. It does not claim logical incompatibility between the existence of God & the existence of evil. These two are the arguments that atheists raise against the existence of 3-O God. Let's look at the existential problem of evil.

The Existential Problem of Evil

We are human beings. We personally deal with many problems of evil sometimes in our lives. We ask questions such as, "Why is this happening to me in this way and at this time?" "Why did God allow this horrific evil in my life? These questions need to be addressed adequately. If not, it can bring great damage to one's life and faith. While it is important that we need intellectual satisfaction, we also need experiential and emotional satisfaction. We need love, care, and empathy. We may need someone to listen, guide, and encourage us. Giving lectures on philosophy or theology may not help when one goes through intense suffering. At this point, a pastoral response is needed. The Christian worldview must sufficiently deal with the existential problem of evil. Now, let's evaluate the logical and evidential problem.

Evaluation of the Logical and Evidential Problem

The logical problem of evil assumes that it is logically impossible that 3-O God and evil can coexist. How do we refute this argument? Philosophers in the past have been able to show that both are not logically inconsistent by showing a possible solution. If I put it into a syllogism (*Modus Ponens*[3]):

Premise 1: If 3-O God and evil coexist, then it is possible that God has morally sufficient reason for allowing evil.

Premise 2: 3-O God and evil coexist.

Premise 3: Therefore, it is possible that God has a morally sufficient reason for allowing evil.

On purely logical grounds, 3-O God and evil can coexist if there is a sufficient reason for God to allow evil. It is the goal of a Christian philosopher or apologist to explain God's morally sufficient reason for allowing evil. In short, the logical problem of evil is not a problem at all for theists, as philosophers have defeated this argument. Australian atheist philosopher J.L Mackie shows that the logical problem of evil has failed. Mackie writes, "We can concede that the problem of evil does not, after all, show that the central doctrines of theism are logically inconsistent with one another."[4] American atheist philosopher Michael Martin states, "Because of the failure of deductive arguments from evil, atheologians have developed inductive or probabilistic arguments from evil for the nonexistence of God."[5] Since the logical problem of evil has failed, we only have to deal with the evidential problem of evil. The evidential problem of evil only claims to have a probability that God may not exist. This is still a problem that requires explanation from theists.

---

[3]　Modus Ponens: *If p then q; p; therefore q.*

[4]　J. L. Mackie, *The Miracle of Theism* (Oxford: Clarendon Press, 1982), 154.

[5]　Michael Martin, *Atheism: A Philosophical Justification* (Philadelphia: Temple University Press, 1990), 335.

The Articulation of the Problem of Evil

The problem of evil is classically stated by Epicurus in early times,

> God either wished to take away evil, and is unable, or He is able, and unwilling;
> or He is neither willing nor able, or He is both willing and able. If He is willing
> and unable, He is feeble, which is not in accordance with the character of God;
> if He is able and unwilling, He is envious, which is equally at variance with God;
> if he is neither willing nor able, He is both envious and feeble, and therefore not
> God; if He is both willing and able, which is alone suitable to God, from what
> source then are evils? Or why does He not remove them?[6]

Scottish skeptic philosopher David Hume picks up Epicurus's question and writes, "Epicurus' old questions are yet unanswered. Is he willing to prevent evil, but not able? Then is he impotent. Is he able, but not willing? Then is he malevolent. Is he both able and willing? Whence then is evil?"[7] Groothuis writes, "The problem of evil is a heavy weight for Christianity (and for any worldview…), but a strong constitution can bear a heavy load."[8] Christian thinkers in the past have taken the challenge and responded to the problem of evil.

Analysis and Response

From the method I used to construct the case so far, I do not intend to write about how other worldviews answer this issue of evil, although it is good to understand the arguments offered by other worldviews (I refer to the work by Groothuis on it[9]). Instead, I will address the problem of evil from a Christian perspective.

We have already established the existence of a theistic God using undeniable reasons and evidence. God's existence is a metaphysical necessity. The presence of evil cannot count against God's existence

---

[6]   Epicurus quoted in William Dyrness, *Christian Apologetics in a World Community* (Downers Grove.Ill.: InterVarsity Press, 1983), 153.

[7]   David Hume, *Dialogues Concerning Natural Religion* (Amherst: Prometheus Books, 1989), 84.

[8]   Groothuis, *Christian Apologetics,* 617.

[9]   Groothuis, *Christian Apologetics,* 617-625.

at all. When I think about the problem of evil, the very first thing that comes to my mind is that if God can create this universe out of nothing, we can presuppose that he also knows how to operate the world he created. God knows how to do his job. Therefore, all we need is a clear understanding of the presence of evil.

We know without doubt that God exists, and evil exists. The existence of God is the foundation from which I will try to show that the 3-O God has morally sufficient reasons for allowing evil. I will also try to show that God has a solution to the problem of evil by considering the bigger picture of the biblical worldview. What can God do about the world and humanity? Why did God create the world the way it is? We can think of a few options.

1) God could have not created at all.

2) God could have created robot-like creatures without free will.

3) God could have created a world without an evarlasting plan where humans could exercise free will and where Satan had access. In this case, physical death is the end.

4) God could have created a world without an everlasting plan where humans could exercise free will and where Satan had no access. In this case physical death is the end.

5) Our current world with free creatures, with the possibility of evil for a destined period, but with a higher eternal purpose for allowing evil. In this case, God has an eternal plan for humanity that has not yet been fulfilled.

The first four options do not make sense. Option five is possible, and that is my defense. The eternal plan may be that God could create an everlasting world where there is no possibility of evil. Humans could freely choose to accept or reject the offer to enter into this everlasting world. In such an everlasting world, Satan must have no access. Such an everlasting world could be a possible future destiny. This is the grand narrative of the Bible, and it makes sense. God has such a redemptive plan for humanity where human beings could freely choose to go to that possible world by trusting Jesus Christ. As part of the bigger redemptive plan of God, he could create our current temporary world, to which Satan had access, where humans could exercise maximum free will and choose to go to their destinies freely. In the Christian worldview, along with the choice of a world where there is no possibility of evil, there is another world with the possibility of evil destined for those who reject God's offer of salvation; thus, their choice is free.

General Christian Response to the Problem of Evil

It is important to note that if God can create this vast, magnificent, and complex universe out of nothing, we have to assume that God knows not only how to operate this world but also its destiny. So, we have to keep a great humility before this undeniable truth so that reasonable answers can be brought forth by relying on God's revelation.

Generally, the problem of evil is answered within the framework of the Christian worldview--Creation, Fall, Redemption, and New Creation. God created this world and called it good. Everything was in harmony. God created human beings with free will for a purpose of keeping their relationship with God. God gave them a command they should not violate. However, the Fall of the first parents (Adam and Eve), by listening to the deceiving words of Satan, brought all problems since human beings were separated from the Holy God due to sin. The image becomes broken once human beings become separated from God. Christians point to the doctrine of Fall as the reason for all evil.

The Christians call this world a fallen world. This includes humans' rebellion in following the commands of God. However, the great act of God in human history, the redemptive work on the cross, allowed human beings to regain the relationship with God that had been lost. Salvation is a free gift of God for those who choose. Finally, in the New Creation, humanity will be redeemed. God also allows free creatures their choice of destiny. Those who reject the gift of salvation shall be given their choice of staying forever separated from God.

In the New Creation, human beings will come to a glorified state and live forever with God. Satan has no access to that realm. God will put Satan in Hell along with the human beings who rejected the free gift of salvation. The problem of evil is temporary. It has a higher purpose. Those who have accepted Jesus as Lord and Savior can live with an eternal hope that the current pain is temporary and there is an everlasting life awaiting them, where they no longer have to face the problem of evil and the pain and suffering that comes with it. We may not receive full healing in this world, but God's presence shall be with one who trusts the Lord.

In this world, God wants people to love God and love neighbors. God does not want his people to do evil for evil but to practice love and forgiveness. God desires everyone to come to him through Christ and follow in his footsteps. Human beings can always rely on God for help and become more like Christ each day by spending time with God (Scripture, prayer, devotion, worship, study, and church). Most Christians generally point to the doctrine of Fall as the reason for both moral and natural evil.

The general Christian response to the problem of evil is a fine explanation according to the overall biblical framework. In addition to this general Christian response, I would also like to include some insights from the works of the organization *Reasons to Believe*. Their response to the problem of evil comes from God's two books, the Book of Nature and the Book of Scripture. This helps to understand the problem of evil with better clarity. Ross gives a more detailed treatment of this topic in his book, *Why the Universe Is The Way It Is*.[10] I will present some of them below.[11]

God's Two Books

There are insights and hints we can glean from both books: the Book of Nature and the Book of Scripture. From the Book of Nature, it is clear that the universe has order and regularity. The laws of physics are extremely fine-tuned. The universe is operated by the second law of thermodynamics (in simple terms, "the law of decay"). It "has to do with the heat transfer from hot bodies to cold."[12] We experience the law of decay every day in living and nonliving things. Everything that we see in this world decays. If we do not maintain our belongings properly, they get decayed. For example, if you do not maintain the roof of your house or paint things once in a while, it starts to decay. If you do not give coating to iron materials, it starts to rust and breaks down eventually. It is interesting to know that the second law of thermodynamics is extra-ordinarily fine-tuned so that life is possible here. This rate of the law of decay is optimal for our lives. If the rate of decay is lower or higher, life is not possible.

The Bible claims, "The whole creation has been groaning"... [under] "its bondage to decay" (Rom 8:21-22). The same physical laws have been in operation since the beginning of the universe. In Genesis, God called his creation "very good" (Genesis 1: 31). That means the laws of physics itself are good.

---

[10]   Ross, *Why the Universe Is the Way It Is.*

[11]   I had the privilege of having several classes with Dr. Ross. I will be using some insights he shared in the presentations. For more detailed information on each issue, see his book.

[12]   Ross, *Why the Universe Is the Way It Is,* 95.

Did the Sin (the Fall) of human beings in the Garden bring all the decays and natural disasters we experience? Some Christians believe that the Fall made God curse the Earth, pointing to Genesis 3:17, "Cursed is the ground because of you." They claim the Fall brought radical alterations to the laws and constants of physics. Some also point to Noah's flood to make this claim. However, this isn't the case when we carefully study the Scripture. The Scripture itself gives us clear hints about the laws of physics. The Bible clearly states that the laws of physics are fixed (Gen 1-2; 3:17; Eccl 1:4-10; 3:11-15; Jer 33:25; Rom 8:18-23; Rev 20:7-22:5). There is no change in the laws of physics according to the Book of Scripture, before or after the Fall. The Book of Nature also confirms the biblical claim because the universe has order and regularity. If the Bible clearly makes a statement about the fixed laws of physics, then a claim that contradicts the Bible does not stand.

What we can understand by considering the laws of physics (that we know from the Book of Nature) and Genesis 3:17, "Cursed is the ground because of *you*" (from the Book of Scripture), is that because of the laws of physics, sin, leads to more pain, more work, and more wasted time.[13] Because of sin, we often fail to keep things maintained and in order. For example, if there is a fix needed to our house, when we delay it, it can create more work and wasted time. Our evil practices, laziness, selfishness, and greed can create more pain. If the authorities of a society do not restrain sin, the whole people will suffer more pain, work, and wasted time. For example, if the roads are not maintained properly, it can cause more problems. The more we delay maintenance, the more damage it will bring. Therefore, we have to keep good discipline to avoid more pain, work, and wasted time. In one sense, the laws of physics teach us to maintain better discipline.

---

[13] Ibid, 168.

The physical constants are finely-tuned for restraining evil. For instance, if the rate of decay is so high, it will discourage our productivity of work. If the decay rate is too low, human sin goes uncontrolled. The finely-tuned physical constants have the purpose of encouraging avoiding sin. It is our sin that causes us to improperly manage our things. The laws of physics that God designed are perfect to keep us disciplined. What about other natural disasters such as hurricanes, earthquakes, tsunamis, wildfires, tornados, volcanos, and floods? Is the Fall of human beings the root of all-natural disasters?

As I have mentioned earlier, the laws of physics have never changed according to the Book of Nature and the Book of Scripture. All the constants of physics are designed for the significant benefit of humanity. If the universe is operated by these physical laws, then natural disasters are guaranteed. Natural disasters are not intrinsically evil, but they have a greater purpose for the existence of human life on Earth and for their benefit. We can think about some examples.

Volcanos deposit several minerals necessary for life. Therefore, volcanoes cannot be removed. Hurricanes have a role in inputting sea salt aerosols and bacterial and viral particles into the atmosphere. If hurricanes are removed, it will reduce the input, thus resulting in reduced rainfall. It also creates irregularities in tropical ocean temperatures. The frequency and average intensity of hurricanes are set to maximally benefit humanity.[14] Just like that, all other natural activities are set for the maximal benefit of human civilization. In the universe, with the current laws of physics, these natural activities are necessary for humans to flourish, and these must be optimal. We can also think that the sin of human beings has also perhaps intensified the pain we experience through these natural disasters. Perhaps God allows more natural disasters to occur due to human

---

[14]   Ibid., 171.

sin. But such natural activities are not intrinsically evil but necessary for the greater good.

We have the responsibility to be wise in our actions. In some places, people construct tall buildings without following the codes and rules. When natural disasters strike, it breaks down easily. In some places, even if people are aware of the potential natural disasters in that area, they do not take the needed precautions earlier. These are unwise actions that people do. Some people build houses near water where there is always a possibility that water may overflow. Others make poor town planning about directing water flows. Society authorities have the responsibility to plan things well so that it will reduce the effect of natural activities. Often, the authorities fail to plan and act wisely.

In one sense, our own irresponsibility intensifies the problem. Sin is the root cause of all irresponsibility in people's lives. We need a solution to the problem of sin in the first place. But God has made a solution through Jesus Christ. We also have to walk in the ways of the Lord as it helps us to make better decisions and maintain better lives according to God's word. Wise people stay closer to the Lord in obedience and restrain sin. This, in turn, reduces pain. Some people say, "Why is God letting good people suffer?"

Biblically, nobody is innocent before God in an absolute sense. All have sinned (Rom 3:9-12) and need redemption. There is another way to look at sickness. For instance, a rare sickness one experiences today may help some people research that issue and develop a cure for it. In return, when more people face the same issue, the solution is already there. A greater number of people benefit from it because somebody previously suffered earlier, which caused others to research it for the greater good. In this world, we have the responsibility to exercise love, care, and compassion for those struggling. We have the opportunity to express the image of God in those who suffer. We can use our God-given intelligence and creativity to help those who are facing problems. We are called to love our neighbors.

Moreover, this Earth wasn't our intended permanent home. Even the pre-fallen state wasn't intended to be permanent. This world is temporary. We are awaiting everlasting life with the Lord Jesus Christ in the New Creation. Whenever I hear about or experience natural evil, it reminds me over and over that there is nothing that is guaranteed in this world. The only thing that is guaranteed is God's promise of eternal life through Jesus. As Jesus warns, "Do not store up for yourselves treasures on Earth, where moths and vermin destroy, and where thieves break in and steal. But store up for yourselves treasures in heaven, where moths and vermin do not destroy, and where thieves do not break in and steal" (Matt 6:19-20).

God has morally sufficient reasons to allow evil in this world. Even in the Garden of Eden, God could have never allowed Satan. In a limited sense, we can say a world where Satan has access is not the best world. But we know that God allowed Satan to test human beings. If God allowed it, it is definitely for a good purpose. That is all we can conclude. While allowing Satan to test human beings, God has also given a command. The human beings failed the test. They used their freedom of choice to disobey God's command.

In the Garden of Eden, everything was in harmony. Human beings experienced a beautiful and comfortable life in the Garden. However, they were not made to sit back and relax (like many lazy people do today). They were also assigned duties to work in the Garden. It is also important to realize that "work" was not a post-fall idea but a pre-fall duty. However, they likely experienced pleasure and satisfaction in work before the Fall. However, the Fall of human beings brought a curse and alteration to the fulfillment they experienced with work in the Garden of Eden.[15] God informed the first parents that they would experience more pain and more work. In the post-fallen state, they began to experience more pain. Due to the consequences of sin, they experience less satisfaction and pleasure. God said to Eve,

> "I will greatly increase your pains in childbearing;
> with pain you will give birth to children.
> Your desire will be for your husband,
> and he will rule over you" (Gen. 3:16).

God said to Adam,

> "Cursed is the ground because of you;
> Through painful toil you will eat of it
> All the days of your life.
> It will produce thorns and thistles for you,
> And you will eat the plants of the field.
> By the sweat of your brow
> You will eat your food
> Until you return to the ground" (Gen. 3:17-19).

From Scripture, we can understand that sin intensified the pain. But pain and suffering are not forever. God has the solution. We have to constantly remind ourselves that this is not our permanent home. The perfect is yet to come. God's plan is to remove evil permanently. But it only happens when life on Earth comes to an end, which is under God's authority. God designed the universe with the present laws of physics for a redemptive purpose. In the New Creation, Satan has no access to the redeemed because Satan will be thrown into its destined place (Hell). When we read the Book of Nature and the Book of Scripture together, we can understand that the current world is very good for God's great purpose of redeeming human beings.

Human beings are responsible for living a disciplined life by submitting lives to Christ. The better we discipline, the lesser the pain we will be experiencing. God has a greater purpose for

---

[15]   Ibid, 168.

designing nature the way it is. We do not have to view everything that is happening in this world as evil, but it has purposes. Ross states, "God designed the universe for the redemption of billions of humans and the permanent eradication of evil…God designed the laws of physics for the removal of evil and for willing humans to receive redemption and enhanced free wills."[16] Ross gives a more detailed treatment of the purpose of the universe with the redemptive purpose of God in mind.

The Two-Creation Model

The Book of Scripture reveals a two-creation model.[17] The first creation (our current world) is temporal, and the second creation (the New Creation) is everlasting. To understand God's plan, we have to look at the bigger picture. We should not limit our thoughts to what has been happening since the creation of human beings, but we have to step back further and try to understand what was happening prior to human beings, the angelic realm. A lot of valuable insight about evil could be drawn from the angelic realm because God had to do something with the fallen angels as well.

Archangel Lucifer (Satan) was the most powerful being God created. He rebelled against God and had one-third of the angelic host join the rebellion (Rev 12:1-9). It is also important to note that human beings were not the first fallen creatures (Isaiah 14:12-14; Jude 1:6; 2 Peter 2:4; Rev 12:9, etc). Angels were fallen before human beings. God's big plan of salvation includes the angelic realm. Therefore, we should have a bigger picture understanding of the Scripture. However, the fallen angels do not have the possibility of redemption. Hell is a place destined for those rebelled angels, but humans who choose to reject the gift of salvation can also freely go there.

---

16   Lecture slide by Ross.
17   Insights from the lecture slides by Ross; see Ross, *Why the Universe Is the Way It Is*, *186*.

In this world, Satan had access to the human realm but within God's higher purpose of a redemptive plan. The higher purpose was not intended by Satan or demons. The laws of physics of this universe have a great role in making redemption in the best way. In this world, humans can exercise free will maximally with the current laws of physics in operation. Through it, humans can freely choose to obey or disobey God; humans can also freely choose to listen to Satan by rejecting the perfect commands of God. Ultimately, God would redeem humanity from all evil and place human beings either with God or apart from God. Eternal destiny is based on the free choice of human beings. They can either accept or reject the free gift of salvation.

In the New Creation, Satan no longer has access to the redeemed. This is God's great plan of redemption through Jesus Christ. The New Creation will be an unimaginable realm where the laws of physics are not the same. There will be no death, decay, disease, or disability. The redeemed human beings will dwell with God forever with maximum fulfillment. This life on Earth is a temporary platform where human beings can make a choice to enter into such an everlasting world where there is no evil. The present effect of evil is for the greater good. The current world is a training ground that prepares us for an unimaginable eternal destiny totally free of Satan's power.

With God's help, we will be able to make the right moral choice in the present world. God will help us to make true and perfect moral choices. With God's help, it is possible to overcome the Satanic temptations of this world. But we have to remain closer to God and increase our faith in God. Our flesh is weak. But the indwelling Holy Spirit helps us overcome our weaknesses. With God's help, it is possible to suffer meaningfully because we know who is watching over us. We can always look at the cross for what Jesus did for us to save us from everlasting separation from the Holy God. In this world, we may face the problem of evil in many ways, but Christ has overcome the world. The pain and suffering of this world are temporary. They are for the greater good. In many cases, we don't know the answer to why certain things are happening in such ways. An illustration might help.

When a child is born, that baby will be given several vaccination shots for various reasons. That baby has no idea why those long needles are injected into their tiny arms. It is a great problem of evil for that baby because of the great pain it has to go through. But adults who know the consequences of not having the shots force it into the baby. It comes out of love for the safety of the child. Once the child grows up, he realizes why the shot was necessary. Likewise, sometimes we do not know what the higher purpose behind all pain is, but we can put all our trust in the Lord throughout the process because he has a better picture of the end.

Maybe we don't find exact answers in this life. Maybe we will. But no matter what, God will carry us through. An eternity is waiting for those who trust the Lord. The Christian worldview is built on reason and evidence, not blind opinions of people. Having said all this, one should expect the greatest tests and trials during this life on Earth. But one can choose whether to trust God throughout it. We always have to make sure to stay closer to the Lord. He will carry us through. Suffering is real and inevitable, but wise people suffer well with God aside. The Scripture says, "I consider that our present sufferings are not worth comparing with the glory that will be revealed in us" (Romans 8:18).

We Are Not Alone

The problem of evil is real. We face it. There is no escape from it. But we have the assurance that God has a purpose for allowing evil. As long as we trust the process, we can live with great comfort even in the midst of suffering. We are not alone. God is with us. We have good reasons to trust. All sufferings are not because we have done something terribly wrong but to mold us into better people in Christ. This may also prepare us for greater roles in the New Creation. Perhaps there are also times when God wants to teach us something because of a lack of discernment and wisdom about something. If one doesn't go through a difficult situation, he will not learn something great. God has the best plan for an individual's life as long as one trusts Christ. Christians should also radiate Christlikeness as they grow in the knowledge of God. This can soothe others who are going through pain and suffering in life.

A Glimpse of Heaven and Hell on Earth

We have a glimpse of Heaven and Hell on Earth. With a relationship with God, we can experience a glimpse of heaven on Earth. The more we come closer to the Lord, the more wonderful the experience will be. A life with God is filled with hope, love, wisdom, meaning, purpose, and tears of joy. Even in the midst of suffering, God's presence is guaranteed. There is no friendship or relationship which is greater than what we can have with the almighty God. The resurrection of Christ offers us guaranteed hope. He is preparing an everlasting place for those who trust the Lord Jesus Christ. The New Heaven and New Earth are free from all evil that we experience here on Earth. It is an unimaginable realm.

On the other side, we also experience a glimpse of Hell on Earth. In this life, we may face injustices, betrayal, sickness, pain, torture, and all kinds of immoral behaviors from people. But even in the midst of all evil, we have provisions to experience some goodness on Earth. But have you ever imagined what Hell will be like? The intensity of evil will be far greater than what we experience on Earth. It is a place where one can no longer experience anything good, and there is no escape from that realm (Isaiah 66:24; Daniel 12:1-2; Matthew 18: 6-9, 25: 31-46; Mark 9: 42-48; 2 Thessalonians 1:5-10; Jude 7; Jude 13; Revelation 14: 9-11, 20:10-15). Can you imagine living in such a realm where pain is the only thing you experience and that lasts forever? This is not the place one wants to go, but God will grant one's choice. If God paid the price by letting his Son face the most excruciating death on the cross to save us from Hell, then God will not show any mercy to those who intentionally reject his free gift of salvation. It is the justice of the Holy God.

No other worldview satisfactorily and sufficiently answers the problem of evil, pain, and suffering. The Christian worldview explains it well, and it makes sense. The Christian worldview is true, rational, and important to whole life. Since the Christian worldview is true, we also have good reasons to believe in the existence of Heaven and Hell. The word of God says,

> So we must listen very carefully to the truth we have heard, or we may drift away from it. For the message God delivered through angels has always stood firm, and every violation of the law and every act of disobedience was punished. So what makes us think we can escape if we ignore this great salvation that was first announced by the Lord Jesus himself and then delivered to us by those who heard him speak? (Hebrews 2:1-4)

In the next chapter, I will give short answers to the existential questions we raised at the beginning of the book.

CHAPTER 25

Answers to the Existential Quests

Initially, we raised several problems that human beings face in life. We raised the problem of heart's desire, the problem of evil, pain, and suffering, the problem of guilt, the problem of long delays, and the problem of the brevity of life. Moreover, we also looked into the questions of the meaning and purpose of life. Our goal was to arrive at the objective truth. In our journey, we came to the conclusion that the Judeo-Christian worldview is objectively true, reasonable, and important to life. Sufficient and satisfactory answers can only be found in the Christian worldview. How do we answer all the existential questions? I will make this section short because I have already given related explanations in all the previous chapters. The answers below cover all the existential questions raised earlier.

God Fills Vacuum of Heart

The God-shaped vacuum can only be filled by God. When you invite Christ into your life, God fills the vacuum within your heart by filling it with the Holy Spirit. You will experience the presence of the Triune God. He will lead you to an everlasting life. He will guide your life and carry you through. This world will never satisfy you permanently. The presence of the Triune God in your life satisfies you sufficiently. His love has no limits or measures. Everything in this world will perish, but the Word of God remains forever and ever and ever.

No More Guilt and Shame

You may be the most wretched and worst person in society. Maybe you are hated by many people. But God loves you! He wants to save you and clean your heart. He will give you a new life. The old will be gone. Christ forgives sinners. Once God forgives your sin, that is all you need. You will receive freedom from guilt and shame. You may not receive forgiveness from society or a person. But you can trust the word of God. The blood of Christ is sufficient to wipe away your sins. You no longer have to live with guilt. You have to accept forgiveness by faith. Once you become a Christian, you should also learn to forgive others. All Christians should practice forgiveness.

The Meaning of Life

The meaning of life is knowing that you are made in the image of God with intrinsic value and dignity. This is the utmost value you can have. God loves and cares for you. The ignorant world may consider you less valuable. But to God, you are precious. Every human being from every people group is equally valuable. Everyone needs Jesus Christ. If one people group views another people group as inferior to them, the problem is with their heart, which is sinful. They need to repent and turn to Christ because the Creator of the universe gives equal value to everyone.

The Purpose of Life

We are made for a relationship with the highest being, the Triune God. The higher purpose of life is to enjoy an everlasting relationship with the Triune God-- God the Father through God the Son by the power of God the Holy Spirit. He will give joy, peace, and strength. Moreover, we received this life to glorify God throughout our lives on Earth. God has brought you into existence for a unique purpose for the glory of God. We all have the purpose of bringing the message of salvation to those who are lost. You may discern that unique purpose in your relationship with God. You may not waste your life by spending time on things that do not do any good to your life. Use your time wisely. Do not forget to spend time with God and Scripture.

Suffering has Purpose

You may face trials in this life, but God knows it. He will carry you through. His grace will be sufficient to move forward. Stay closer to the Lord. Learn to suffer well by trusting the process. God has a higher purpose for allowing suffering. Always remember that Jesus suffered for us on the cross so that we can have life. Pain and suffering can mold you to become a better person. Always think about our future life with the Lord in the New Creation, when God will conquer Satan. We will no longer face the suffering. We will have everlasting joy. The suffering of this world may prepare you for an eternal crown. In this life, God offers his grace and strength.

Annie Johnson Flint was a great hymn writer who was an orphan and suffered from a chronic, incurable illness in her life. In the midst of the horrendous suffering, she wrote,

> He giveth more grace when the burdens grow greater,
> He sendeth more strength when the labors increase,
> To added affliction He addeth His mercy,
> To multiplied trials, His multiplied peace.
>
> When we have exhausted our store of endurance,
> When our strength has failed ere the day is half done,

When we reach the end of our hoarded resources
Our Father's full giving is only begun.

Fear not that thy need shall exceed His provision,
Our God ever yearns His resources to share;
Lean hard on the arm everlasting, availing;
The Father both thee and thy load will upbear.

His love has no limit, His grace has no measure,
His power no boundary known unto men,
For out of His infinite riches in Jesus,
He giveth and giveth and giveth again.[1]

Christians can also lament meaningfully in this broken world. We have Psalms of Lament (Psalms 22, 39, 88, 90, etc.) and the Book of Lamentations. Even Jesus lamented on the cross, "My God, my God. Why have you forsaken me?" (Matt. 27:46; Psalm 22:1 cf.) The lament shouldn't be grumbling (Phil. 2:14). God counts all our tears (Psalm 56.8). One day, God will wipe away all our tears (Revelation 21:4). Christians should learn to lament well. I recommend the book *Walking Through Twilight: A Wife's Illness--a Philosopher's Lament* [2] by Groothuis who went through several years of suffering. He gives us the wisdom to lament meaningfully as Christians.

Delay is not Denial

Maybe many things in our lives are delayed. We may be losing all hope. But remember, the delay is not a denial from God. God knows what we are going through. He has a higher purpose for our lives.

---

[1] Annie Johnson Flint, "He Giveth More Grace" *Hymnary*, Accessed February 10, 2024, https://hymnary.org/text/he_giveth_more_grace_as_our_burdens.

[2] Douglas R. Groothuis, *Walking through Twilight: A Wife's Illness--a Philosopher's Lament* (Downers Grove: InterVarsity Press, 2017). Also see chapter "Lament as Apologetic for Christianity" in Groothuis, *Christian Apologetics* 2nd ed.

We have to learn to be patient with God's perfect timing. Maybe what we have already planned or desired is not what God wants in our lives. Maybe God wants us to get a little closer to Him. Maybe God wants us to repent in some sinful ways. No matter what, we have good reasons to trust Christ. God has an everlasting purpose for our lives (Romans 8:28).

Physical Death and the Brevity of Life: A Blessing

People strive their best to protect their own lives from death, no matter how costly it is. Death is the greatest fear of most people in the end. We should always keep in mind that physical death is not the end. It is simply a change of location. In one sense, physical death is a blessing for those who die in the Lord. Why? They no longer have to suffer in this world. They are in a better place-- with Jesus. If God did not introduce physical death into the fallen world, we would have suffered more in a fallen world. For instance, if we have a severe health issue that has no potential cure but every moment is in deep pain. We may cry with great agony in this situation. What if we remain like that forever until God makes everything new? Isn't it better to be with the Lord at that time instead of deep pain for such a long time? In that sense, a shorter life and death is a blessing. This is how a true Christian should view the brevity of life and death because we have an assurance that we will be with the Lord.

The greatest fear one can have is the fear of death. But if one does not have a fear of death, they no longer have to be fearful in life. Those who die without the Lord, even if they do not have a fear of death, have made the dumbest decision ever in life. How beautiful it is to die with the hope that physical death is not the end. In that sense, physical death is the greatest blessing one should enjoy. We will be with the Lord Jesus Christ when we die. The resurrection of Christ gives us the greatest hope. When the time comes, our bodies will be resurrected, and God will make everything new. He will transform us into the glorified state. The Scripture says, "Since the children have flesh and blood, he too shared in their humanity so that by his death he might break the power of him who holds the power of death—that is, the devil— and free those who all their lives were held in slavery by their fear of death" (Hebrews 2: 14-15).

Hope from Fine-Tuning

When things get delayed, we think it is unjust and unloving. It is important to know that we don't know the end, but God knows. He knows what will result from it if things do not get delayed. We have good reasons to trust the Lord because he is the Creator. In some cases, God delays things so that we will repent of sins. We should try to recognize sin and worldliness in our lives. God listens to the prayers of his people. In the end, we will realize that all delays happen for a good reason.

Earlier, we learned that the physical laws in the universe are extra-ordinarily fine-tuned so that life is possible on Earth. If there is a slight change in any of the physical laws and constants, life will be impossible. Just like that, those who have committed their lives to Jesus Christ are born again as children of God. God takes over the life of individuals. God will also fine-tune their lives for the best. It ultimately brings glory to God. God knows how to do his job. He knows what we need and what we do not need. God wants people to stay closer to him. He wants to train and test those who are his.

Sometimes, people get the toughest test possible. However, throughout that rough journey, God will never forsake that person. God knows to what extent the suffering is bearable to an individual. Oftentimes, when we go through suffering, we tend to raise our voices against God for allowing it. We may lose hope. But it is important to remember that God loves us. He wants to fine-tune us for a greater purpose. God, who is all perfect, who fine-tuned the universe the way it is, who claims to love us being made in his image, knows how to fine-tune our individual lives.

Oftentimes, God will only work things out at the very last moment. Sometimes it is to test our faith. God allows suffering for a greater purpose. In some cases, God delivers us from evil. In some cases, we don't see deliverance, and we don't know why. But God gives us the grace to handle it. We can still trust God because God is the truth. It is written in the Scripture, "And we know that all things work together for good to those who love God, to those who are the called according to His purpose" (Romans 8:28).

A Word of Wisdom from G. K. Chesterton

When life gets tough, many tend to turn away from God. Christian philosopher and apologist G. K. Chesterton writes, "When belief in God becomes difficult, the tendency is to turn away from Him; but in heaven's name to what?" [3] This is a powerful statement that you may ponder for some moments. By turning away from God, what is the next option? There is no better solution. Therefore, all we can do is trust the Lord. If Christianity is not true, there is no other hope in this world. No other worldview explains life and the world better than Christianity.

There is no other place we can turn to that offers a permanent solution to any suffering. We know that this world is temporary. Christ has also suffered the worst. In the end, God will make everything new. Until that, we have to trust the Lord, who is all-knowing, all-

---

[3]   Quoted in Ravi Zacharias, *Cries of the Heart* (Nashville, TN: Thomas Nelson, 2002), 65.

powerful, and all-loving. There is nowhere else I can turn to. As Jesus' disciple Simon Peter said to Jesus, "Lord, to whom shall we go? You have the words of eternal life?" (John 6:68).

Let's turn to the final chapter.

SECTION 5:

Conclusion

CHAPTER 26

Who is Wise Enough to Understand This?

God is not a fairy tale. The idea of Heaven is not a wish fulfillment. The idea of Hell is not a human construct. All religious ideologies, except the Christian worldview, teach about human attempts to reach out to God. God's drama in human history is a love story. The Judeo-Christian worldview is a grand love story of God's sacrificial action in human history to reach out to the human beings made in God's image. This is a unique claim. We can experience the love of God through Christ. The most tremendous confidence about the Judeo-Christian worldview is that it is an evidence based and reasonable faith. There is no blind faith required. I have presented a case for the Christian faith. Although my book is not comprehensive, I believe I have included enough details in this book. One can further explore different topics. What have we learned so far?

1. Truth is valuable.

2. The laws of Logic are undeniable.

3. Objective, absolute, universal truth exists; truth is knowable; truth is narrow; truth excludes its opposite.

4. God exists.

5. All religions cannot be true.

6. Theism (Monotheism) is true.

7. Any claims opposite to Theism must be false.

8. All theistic religions cannot be true at the same time.

9. Miracles are possible in a theistic universe.

10. The Bible is historically, archaeologically, and scientifically reliable (upon proper interpretations).

11. Jesus Christ lived, died, and was resurrected from the dead historically.

12. Jesus claimed to be God.

13. Any claims opposite to points 11 & 12 must be false.

14. Jesus claimed, "I am the Way, the Truth, and Life."

15. Each individual must repent of their sins and invite Jesus Christ as his or her Lord and Savior.

16. Life has intrinsic value and meaning because we are made in the image of God.

17. Human beings are made for a relationship with God.

18. The major purpose of life is to enjoy and glorify God.

19. The Bible answers the big questions sufficiently and satisfactorily.

20. God allows evil for a purpose.

21. The physical Law is designed the way it is for a purpose.

22. God's bigger plan is to eliminate evil and create an unimaginable new realm.

23. Physical death is not the end.

24. Those who are saved by the blood of Christ will live forever with God.

25. Science and faith are not in conflict.

26. God expects his people to walk in His ways by following his words.

27. Heaven and Hell are real.

28. The Christ will return. Jesus Christ is our hope.

29. The Christian worldview is a system of objective truth.

30. All reasons and evidence prove that the Judeo-Christian Worldview is objectively true, rational, and important in every aspect of life.

Pascal's Wager

Human beings are sinful and need deliverance. Sin is a major human illness that needs deliverance. The only way to cure human illness is through the grace of God through Jesus Christ. He will deliver one from the bondage of sin and bring one into a personal relationship with the triune God. Blomberg summarized Blaise Pascal's famous wager:

> If atheism is right and Christianity wrong, all Christians can lose are their physical lives, whereas if atheism is wrong and Christianity right, atheists can suffer horribly, banished from the presence of God and all things good forever. If some other world religion is right and Christianity wrong, most Christians still stand a reasonable chance at a good afterlife, because all other religions at one level or another boil down to salvation by works. And true Christians demonstrate many good works as their lives are increasingly conformed to the image of Christ. But if it all depends on grace through faith, then people of all other religions or ideologies must renounce any attempt to merit God's favor and must throw themselves entirely on his mercy, believing that he alone can save them, uniquely through the cross of Christ. Believers likewise triumph not in life but in death. Their subsequent victory over death makes everything in this life pale in comparison.[1]

---

[1]   Craig L. Blomberg. *From Pentecost to Patmos: An Introduction to Acts through Revelation* (Nashville: Broadman & Holman, 2006), 557.

Christianity is a system of objective truth. Christianity is an intellectual option. However, Jesus did not force anybody to follow him. You have to make a rational choice whether to accept the truth. It takes courage to pursue truth. What is your rational choice after analyzing the evidence? You can have a lot of knowledge of God, but faith is action based on true knowledge gained. Though not comprehensive, I believe I introduced some major reasons to put all your trust in the Lord Jesus Christ as Savior. Our good works do not save us, but the grace of God will. You must be born again (spiritually) through faith and repentance of sin. You have to make an individual decision freely. At this point, if you are convinced of the truth, you may repent of your sins and invite Christ into your life as Lord and Savior.

Call to Repentance: Choose Freely

Romans 3:23 *"For everyone has sinned; we all fall short of God's glorious standard." Yet God, in his grace, freely makes us right in his sight. He did this through Christ Jesus when he freed us from the penalty for our sins."*

Mark 11:28-30 *"Jesus said, "Come to me, all of you who are weary and carry heavy burdens, and I will give you rest. Take my yoke upon you. Let me teach you, because I am humble and gentle at heart, and you will find rest for your souls. For my yoke is easy to bear, and the burden I give you is light."*

John 3:16 *"For God so loved the world that he gave his one and only Son, that whoever believes in him shall not perish but have eternal life. For God did not send his Son into the world to condemn the world, but to save the world through him."*

John 14:6 *"I am the way, the truth, and the life. No one can come to the Father except through me."*

The evangelist Reinhard Bonnke often uses an analogy in his sermons: Soap does not do its work if you simply have the knowledge that soap can clean you. You have to pick it up and apply it to your body to get cleaned. Just like that, the knowledge of God's truth is not enough for your heart to get cleaned. It needs to be applied in your life with a step of faith. God loves you. But if you do not want to choose God freely, he will grant your desire to stay separated from God forever. God does not want to force anyone to love Him. However, if you are convinced of the truth, would you say this prayer from your heart?

Dear Lord Jesus Christ:

I realize that I am a sinner. Please forgive my sins. I believe you died for my sins and rose from the dead so that I can have eternal life. I invite you to be the Lord and Savior of my life. Please transform my life and lead me in all truth. I surrender my life to you with all my heart. Amen!

You are no longer dead and separated from God. You have been given the free gift of everlasting life through Christ by the power of the Holy Spirit. You are now born again into the Kingdom of God. You have begun a relationship with God. Enjoy the true freedom in Christ. What next?

Find a church

We need a good Bible-teaching church community to grow in the knowledge of God and for spiritual guidance. It is important not to become part of a liberal church that compromises on the word of God. Such a church can lead you astray. God is Holy. Holiness is God's standard. Be part of a church that stands for biblical truths. A good church will guide you to the next step in the faith journey. As Scripture teaches:

"Let us think of ways to motivate one another to acts of love and good works. And let us not neglect our meeting together, as some people do, but encourage one another, especially now that the day of his return is drawing near" (Hebrews 10:24-25).

Grow in the Knowledge of God

As you continue this faith journey, you should grow in the knowledge and wisdom of God by spending time with the Word of God and spending time in prayer. You will be conformed to the image of Christ as you continue your spiritual journey. Set your appointment with God on a regular basis intentionally. You should remain humble before the Lord so that God will teach and guide you.

Turn Away from Sinful ways

Flee from temptations that may lead you to sin. Continue to repent of your sins that may try to overtake you. Always stay closer to the Lord so that you will be able to overcome struggles with sin. Always ask for help from God. In this life, we may face all kinds of temptations. Discipline your life with wisdom. Do not allow things that may lead you to temptation. The only way to fight this battle is to stay closer to the Lord. Always walk in the way of the Lord, which is true, good, and beautiful. Follow the footsteps of Christ and imitate him.

Christ is the Perfect Point of Reference

An analogy may help. After replacing a dead battery of a watch, we need a point of reference of the accurate time by which one can set the watch to the correct time. Jesus Christ is the point of reference that we can use to correct ourselves. We should become more like Christ each day. Our focus should not be on becoming like some other person but on Christ. Human beings may fail at some point.

But Christ never. He is the point of reference we can always trust. The Bible is the manual where we can listen to the instructions of God. We must dig deeper into the Scripture. We should never follow the opinions of other people on all matters. If opinions conflict with Scripture, we should reject opinions and accept God's word.

Potential Biblical Difficulties

I have given enough evidence to the truth of the entire Bible as the word of God. The Bible is our credible authority. You may come up with some biblical difficulties. It is important to note that the Bible has been attacked more than any other book. It has been misinterpreted by many people, both at the lay level and highly academic-level individuals. There are many attacks raised against many events in the Old Testament as if God is cruel. In fact, that is not the case. Such attacks are due to misinterpretations by taking the word of God out of context and without trying to understand the background. We should not interpret the Bible without understanding the context. Some of the issues may require some extra help. Many good thinkers have already worked through all those issues and provided reasonable answers to difficult passages. Understanding the context is the most important thing. When you come across difficulties with biblical passages, note the question down and find the right resources. You will never find any new difficulties other than those issues many good thinkers have already dealt with (See footnote).[2] Be a good and mature student with humility and patience.

---

[2] Here are some recommendations: Gleason L. Archer, *Encyclopedia of Bible Difficulties* (Grand Rapids, Michigan, 1982); Normal Geisler and Thomas Howe, *The Big Book of Bible Difficulties: Clear and Concise Answers from Genesis to Revelation* (Grand Rapids, Michigan: Baker Books, 1992); Bernard James Mauser, *Reading to Grow: A Field Guide to the Bible* (Eugene, OR: Wipf & Stock, 2017); Paul Copan, *Is God a Moral Monster? Making Sense of the Old Testament* God (Grand Rapids: Baker, 2011).

Now let us think about two approaches to God: rational and non-rational approaches to God. Philosophers Ed Miller and Jon Jensen demonstrate the distinction between rational and non-rational approaches to God.[3]

RATIONAL AND NON-RATIONAL APPROACHES TO GOD

The *rational* approach to God includes natural theology, comparative religion, and systematic theology (to some extent). In part two, we have used natural theology to demonstrate the existence of God. We also evaluated worldview which includes religion. We used ordinary reasoning in that. The *non-rational* approach to God includes religious experience. Religious experience includes mystical experiences. Those are not directly rationally demonstrable. By *non-rational*, Miller and Jensen do not mean *irrational*. They clearly distinguish *nonrational* and *irrational* by writing,

> That which is irrational is that which is in some way contrary to or incompatible with reason. Certainly this is not intended by those who press for a nonrational approach to God. On the contrary, they intend a knowledge of God that is *other* than rational, and, indeed, they usually mean a knowledge that is higher than, or *superior* to, what is knowable through ordinary reason and experience.[4]

Now we know the difference between *irrational* and *non-rational*. Let's get into our topic then. There are people holding two extremes. On the one side, oftentimes, when someone has too much knowledge about God, they often neglect the non-rational (experiential or mystical) elements. Instead, they try to reason everything using their theological knowledge. Their approach is always intellectualistic and rationalistic. I am not saying that it is intrinsically bad. However,

---

[3]   I owe credit to the lectures by professor of philosophy Dr. J. T. Bridges for sharing this thought in the class at Southern Evangelical Seminary.

[4]   Ed. Miller and Jon Jensen, *Questions that Matter: An Invitation to Philosophy* (United States: McGraw-Hill Education, 2008), 257.

many knowledgeable people have widely rejected the element of true Godly religious experiences. The religious experience may include the exercise of emotions or some unique spiritual experiences-- an endowment of extraordinary power given by the Holy Spirit. Some people think such experiences are irrational, delusional, fantasies, or demonic. But what if God has given some individuals some special experiences?

I think Christian intellectuals should not outrightly reject the non-rational elements of Christian life. On the other side, many believers who had some special religious experience reject theological knowledge and wisdom (doctrine, dogmas, etc.). Such people think that theological wisdom is not important but stresses more towards religious experiences. Both sides have problems because both are important for a balanced Christian living. That is my point here.

Religious experiences are possible in Christian life. Religious experiences are non-rational elements. The religious experiences must be part of the Christian life. German philosopher Rudolf Otto writes, "...orthodox Christianity manifestly failed to recognize its [nonrational element's] values, and this failure gave to the idea of God a one-sidedly intellectualistic and rationalistic interpretation."[5] If Christianity is true, it is also something that should be experienced. Many churches have kept the non-rational or experiential element away by focusing more on dogma and doctrine. Both non-intellectual elements (nonrational/experiential) and intellectual elements (dogma and doctrine) are important parts of the Christian faith. We should not neglect the emotional or experiential side of the Christian faith by stressing more on the intellectual side. We need a good balance.

---

[5]   Rudolf Otto, *The Idea of the Holy: An Inquiry into the Non-Rational Factor in the Idea of the Divine and Its Relation to the Rational* (London: Oxford University Press, 1926), 3; Miller and Jensen, *Questions that Matter,* 259.

People of many religions claim to have some kind of religious experience. But it is important to stay away from experiences that are not from the true source (God). It is also possible to have demonic experiences. It is also possible to have drug-induced mystical experiences. Therefore, not all religious experiences are from God. It is important to recognize experiences which are not from the true source. Unbiblical religious experience must be avoided. Such experiences cannot come from God. The Scripture is the point of reference for all spiritual corrections.

Now, let us think about the degrees of knowledge. In his book, *The Degrees of Knowledge*, French philosopher Jacques Maritain presents some valuable insights that can elevate our approach to the knowledge of God.[6] This is also a call to the possibility of experiencing the maximal presence of God during the earthly life– a call to divine adventure.

THE DEGREES OF KNOWLEDGE

Maritain demonstrates that there are different degrees of knowledge under two categories: *the degrees of rational knowledge* and *the degrees of supra-rational knowledge*. I will try to explain the Maritain's category.

The Degrees of Rational Knowledge:

The degrees of *rational knowledge* (or natural knowledge) include experimental science and philosophy. Under experimental science and philosophy, there are three degrees (Degree 1= Lowest; Degree 2: Highest):

---

6   I owe credit to Dr. Bridges, who shared insights from Jacques Maritain's *The Degrees of Knowledge* (Notre Dame, Indiana: Notre Dame Press, 1995).

1.   Degree 1: Physica (Physics)

2.   Degree 2: Mathematica (Mathematics)

3.   Degree 3: Metaphysica (Metaphysics)[7]

Degree 1: Physics involves the apprehension of a sensible being, that is, physical reality. Empirical science comes under this category. This is the lowest form of rational knowledge.

Degree 2: This second degree is unique to the mathematical realm. We can have mathematical knowledge with certainty. This form of rational knowledge is above the degree 1.

Degree 3: Metaphysics deals with the nature of being as being. Metaphysics comes under the domain of philosophy. The reasoning for the existence of God comes under metaphysics. By analyzing the effects in nature, we can reason back to a causal agent (God), which is metaphysical reasoning. As I have argued earlier, God is a metaphysically necessary being. Metaphysics is the highest form of rational knowledge.

All these three degrees give the knowledge of reality using our rationality by experiencing the world. Among these three, metaphysical knowledge is at the top. These are indeed reliable sources of knowledge. Now, we can switch to the second category, *supra-rational knowledge*, which is above the degrees of *rational knowledge*.

The Degrees of Supra-Rational Knowledge:

Within supra-rational knowledge, there are different realms (Realm 1: Lowest; Realm 3: Highest):

1.   Realm 1: The Realm of Reason.

---

7   Maritain, *The Degrees of Knowledge, 41-50.*

2.   Realm 2: The Realm of Faith.

3.   Realm 3: The Realm of the Beatific Vision.[8]

Realm 1: The realm of reason is at the bottom of supra-rational knowledge. The reasoning is metaphysical wisdom. Metaphysical wisdom is natural theology. As I have demonstrated earlier, Natural theology deals with demonstrating the evidence for the existence of God from nature using reason. The existence of God is the lowest knowledge we can have about God.

Realm 2: The level above the realm of reason is the realm of faith. I have presented earlier that faith is complete trust or confidence in someone or something with credible authority. The Bible is God's written revelation. To have a deeper knowledge of God, we should put our trust in what God says about him. This is a higher knowledge (e.g., God is Triune, experiencing God, gifts of the Holy Spirit, etc.) than simply knowing his existence by metaphysics. Maritain further divides Realm 2 into three different levels (Lowest: Level 1; Highest: Level 3):

   (a) Level 1: Faith and Reason.

   (b) Level 2: Faith Alone.

   (c) Level 3: Faith and the Gifts of the Holy Spirit.

Level 1: Maritain calls "faith and reason" as theological wisdom. At the level of faith and reason, we use the tools of human reason upon a book by considering it as God's revelation. Systematic theology comes under this category because it demonstrates theological wisdom in a systematic manner. Maritain calls theological wisdom "the virtually revealed knowledge." For example, the doctrine of the Trinity. The term Trinity is a word that is not present in the

---

8   Ibid., 263-281.

Bible, but it is virtually contained in the Bible as a whole. We can have theological wisdom that God is triune. One does not need to have a personal relationship with God to conclude the doctrine of the Trinity. Someone who studies theology can formulate it just by considering the Bible as God's written revelation. One can have head knowledge without a deeper relationship with God.

Level 2: Faith in God is a qualitative condition of the soul that trusts God. In other words, there is a personal relationship with God involved at this level. At this point, our life is no longer connected with just reasoning, but it is connected to our spiritual life (devotion, prayer, etc.). We are no longer operating the mere human rational wisdom alone (i.e., metaphysical wisdom). There is personal trust involved toward God, which is formally revealed in the Scriptures.

Level 3: Maritain calls faith and the gifts of the Holy Spirit, as mystical wisdom. It is a supernatural experience. These are the divine moments experienced. Since it is essentially supernatural, it is supra-rational knowledge.[9] By getting more closer to the Lord, there is a possibility of a deeper experience with God. We all should desire to have supernatural experiences. This is the highest level of knowledge we can have and desire from this side of our lives.

Realm 3: Finally, one day, the one who is healed by the grace of God through Christ will see God face to face in the *Beatific Vision*. On that day, we will have the greatest of all knowledge of God when we meet Christ. Some people claim to see the risen Christ through vision. Such experiences are far more desirable than any other wisdom or knowledge we can gain through reason or Scripture.

Maritain's insight helps us to understand the degrees of knowledge we can gain in earthly life. The highest level of supra-rational knowledge is possible through faith. That is the true mystical religious

---

[9]   Ibid., 266.

life. It is the highest degree of supernatural knowledge we can have in this life on Earth. The highest level of faith goes beyond reason. There are many church attendees who have theological knowledge but lack exercising a deeper faith and the work of the Holy Spirit in their lives. Maritain writes,

> ...let the theologian lose theological faith; he still can keep the whole machinery and conceptual organization of his science, but he keeps it as something dead in his mind; he has lost his proper light. He is no longer a theologian except in the way that a corpse is a man.[10]

We should not live our Christian lives without proper light. This often happens among intellectuals and scholars. Once they have good knowledge, they think they know too much. Some try to reason things that go beyond reason. In one sense, it is also a display of pride, whether knowingly or unknowingly. The Christian life is something to be lived with full energy through a personal relationship with God. The exercise of the highest level of faith should not be replaced by all kinds of reasonings with dogmas and doctrine, although they are important. We should desire the highest level of supra-rational knowledge. The most devout Christian would love the presence of God more than anything else in the world. Finally, I have one more thing to say about Scripture.

Scripture! Scripture! Scripture— The Knowledge of Higher Realities

We can gain all kinds of knowledge in the world, and there is nothing wrong with gaining knowledge. However, the Scripture comes from God, who has the bigger picture of the world, life, and destiny. It reveals the knowledge of the higher realities. The Scripture (the Bible) is written for human beings. The more one meditates the Scripture, the wiser one gets because this is perfect wisdom revealed by God.

---

[10]   Ibid., 269.

As the everlasting journey continues, the Holy Spirit unlocks, guides, and reveals the deep mysteries of God and his ways through the Scripture. It is a true, adventurous journey along with Christ. A wise person digs deeper into the word of God more than anything else and exercises a personal relationship with the divine.

The primary resource must always be the Bible. My book is only a secondary resource or supplement to give reasons to believe that the Bible is the written revelation of God. The Bible is the ultimate authority (Ps. 119; 2 Tim. 3:15-17; 2 Pet. 1: 19-21). There are many books written to assist in reading and understanding the Scripture. However, we should always dig deeper into the primary resource than any other supplementary books. Be wise! Now it is time for an everlasting journey in relationship with the triune God by touching the highest reality. Enjoy God forever and glorify him throughout your life.

Scripture says, "Taste and see that the LORD is good" (Ps. 34:8). In my life, I set out to taste and see the goodness of the God I defend. What about you? Tonight, you may go outside and watch the stars and moon in the sky and praise God for his magnificent creation. Tomorrow, when you meet people from the other faiths, you should think that they are also made in the image of God with value and dignity, and they, too, need Christ. We ought to love God and love our neighbors. Let's conclude this book with a quote from Schaeffer's writing,

> My concluding sentence is this: The world is lost, the God of the Bible does exist; the world is *lost*, but truth is truth. Keep on! And for how long? I'll tell you. Keep on, keep on, keep on, keep on, and then KEEP ON![11]

---

[11] Francis Schaeffer, *The Complete Works of Francis A. Schaeffer: A Christian View of the Church* Vol. 4 2nd ed. (IL: Crossway Books, 1994), 256.

Yes, Keep on! And if you find this book helpful, take it out to those who are seeking the truth. Let them read it. You will see God leading you to many people if you are properly equipped with the right tools for evangelism. Take the gospel message to the ends of the world. May the light, glory, and knowledge of the Gospel of Jesus Christ shine in you and through you.